NEVER
WORK
harder
THAN your
students
& OTHER PRINCIPLES OF GREAT TEACHING

ASCD MEMBER BOOK

Many ASCD members received this book as a
member benefit upon its initial release.

Learn more at: **www.ascd.org/memberbooks**

NEVER
WORK
harder
THAN your *
students
& OTHER PRINCIPLES
OF GREAT TEACHING

Robyn R. Jackson

Alexandria, Virginia USA

1703 N. Beauregard St. • Alexandria, VA 22311-1714 USA
Phone: 800-933-2723 or 703-578-9600 • Fax: 703-575-5400
Web site: www.ascd.org • E-mail: member@ascd.org
Author guidelines: www.ascd.org/write

Gene R. Carter, *Executive Director;* Nancy Modrak, *Publisher;* Julie Houtz, *Director of Book Editing & Production;* Deborah Siegel, *Project Manager;* Greer Beeken, *Senior Graphic Designer;* Mike Kalyan, *Production Manager;* Keith Demmons, *Typesetter;*

Printed in the United States of America. Cover art copyright © 2009 by ASCD. ASCD publications present a variety of viewpoints. The views expressed or implied in this book should not be interpreted as official positions of the Association.

All Web links in this book are correct as of the publication date below but may have become inactive or otherwise modified since that time. If you notice a deactivated or changed link, please e-mail books@ascd.org with the words "Link Update" in the subject line. In your message, please specify the Web link, the book title, and the page number on which the link appears.

ASCD Member Book, No. FY09-4 (Jan. 2009, PS). ASCD Member Books mail to Premium (P) and Select (S) members on this schedule: Jan., PS; Feb., P; Apr., PS; May, P; July, PS; Aug., P; Sept., PS; Nov., PS; Dec., P. Select membership was formerly known as Comprehensive membership.

PAPERBACK ISBN: 978-1-4166-0757-1 ASCD product #109001
Also available as an e-book through ebrary, netLibrary, and many online booksellers (see Books in Print for the ISBNs).

Quantity discounts for the paperback edition only: 10–49 copies, 10%; 50+ copies, 15%; for 1,000 or more copies, call 800-933-2723, ext. 5634, or 703-575-5634. For desk copies: member@ascd.org.

Library of Congress Cataloging-in-Publication Data

Jackson, Robyn Renee.
  Never work harder than your students and other principles of great teaching / Robyn R. Jackson.

    p. cm.
  Includes bibliographical references and index.
  ISBN 978-1-4166-0757-1 (pbk. : alk. paper) 1. Effective teaching. 2. Teacher effectiveness. I. Title.

  LB1025.3.J333 2008
  371.102—dc22

                    2008037437

20 19 18 17 16 15   6 7 8 9 10 11 12

To my grandparents, Dorothy L. Colbert-Blake, Robert T. Colbert Sr.,

Grace E. Jackson, and the late John F. Jackson II, who never

had the opportunities I now enjoy.

Thank you all for your sacrifice and your

lavish, unfettered love.

NEVER
WORK
harder
THAN your
students
& OTHER PRINCIPLES OF GREAT TEACHING

PREFACE

The Gift

I loved being in Dr. Benn's English 301 class. Sure, we were learning pretty boring stuff—past participles, nominative predicates, and the like; but, something about the way he parsed a sentence seemed, well, *profound*. It was as if he were unlocking the very secret of language itself. I'm not kidding. We would sit in his class in rapt attention for 90 minutes straight. Sometimes, I think I even forgot to breathe.

It wasn't just the way he explained some obscure phrase in a poem that did it. No. He made us feel *smart*. He had a way of asking questions that led us to the discovery of the answer ourselves. Years later, I realize that he was using Socratic questioning; but, as a college freshman, I just thought he had it. He had the gift.

✳

Five minutes into talking to Sarah and I knew she had "the gift." It was more than just her enthusiasm—I'd seen that plenty of times before. It was that she literally vibrated with a love for teaching. I watched her eyes light up as she shared how she got to know each of her students individually and learned to tailor her instruction to their needs. Her voice quivered with excitement as she talked about the growth her students made by the end of the year. The interview went on for 20 more minutes, but I had already decided to hire Sarah. She had the gift.

*

From the moment I entered Laura's classroom, I was excited. It was contagious. At first, I couldn't understand why. It seemed like a typical history class—she was showing slides of the artwork of the Renaissance—but something was different. I watched as she put the next slide on the screen. As if on cue, students jumped out of their seats to hold an 8.5 x 11 inch white board up to the screen and highlight what they noticed about the picture. They were explaining to the class how what they noticed indicated something about the Renaissance—the society, the social norms, the way of thinking. The students were having excited discussions about the influence of the Renaissance on modern thought and making comparisons between the Italian and English versions of the Renaissance. Laura asked a few probing questions and changed the slides every so often, but she largely remained quiet and let the students drive the discussion. She has it, I thought to myself as I left the classroom. She had the gift.

*

If you asked me to define "the gift" back then, I wouldn't have been able to do it. I just knew it when I saw it. I'd walk into a classroom and see a teacher completely engaging a class full of squirmy 9th graders and I knew that teacher had "the gift." I'd read a book written by one of those master teachers, those legendary ones who make you want to be a teacher yourself, and I wanted to touch the hem of that teacher's garment to see if it rubbed off on me. The gift.

When I first became an educational consultant and worked with districts to improve the quality of teaching in their schools, I began to wonder if the mythology surrounding teaching was true. What if "the gift" really was some innate talent, some rare, mysterious, divine endowment? What if it couldn't be taught? If so, I was in the wrong business.

Clearly there are some people who are born with it. They have a natural propensity to be master teachers. But, is there hope for those of us who weren't so lucky? If "the gift" were something that was bestowed upon the blessed few, what, I wondered, would become of the rest of us?

But, after years of working with teachers and school leaders, I now know that "the gift" is not some mysterious birthright. In fact, it's not really a gift at all. Being a master teacher is the result of a critical understanding of the principles of good teaching. It's a mindset that anyone can learn and by learning this mindset, you too can become a master teacher. True, some people come by this mindset naturally, but the rest of us can develop it too.

This book will show you how.

My Story

When I first started teaching, I applied all the theories I had learned in my methods classes to my students. I didn't smile at them for the first month. I wrote lesson plans every day. I faithfully followed the book. I used proximity when they were talking out of turn and followed that up with a rigid set of consequences. I posted and enforced my classroom rules—all 10 of them. I created elaborate differentiated lessons designed to tap into each student's learning style and multiple intelligences. I used technology. I used collaborative learning, cooperative instruction, inquiry-based learning, multiculturalism, you name it. But, it wasn't working. They, and I, were simply going through the motions.

The problem, I thought, was that I needed new strategies. So, I expanded my repertoire. Sometimes the strategies worked, sometimes they didn't. Either way, I was working awfully hard. In fact, not only was I working much harder than my students, I was starting to see diminishing returns.

The assignment I was so excited about, the one that took me two weeks to plan and prepare for, didn't excite my students as much as I had hoped. That really cool strategy I picked up at a conference didn't work as well as the presenter had promised. Although I was acquiring a large repertoire of skills according to the textbooks and my evaluators, I wasn't seeing the payoff in the classroom. My students still struggled, they were still bored, and to be honest, I wasn't sure that they were learning anything.

Finally, I decided that perhaps I just needed more time, smarter students, more supportive families, stronger leadership, and more money. But, after beating my head against *that* brick wall for a while, I realized that I had better chances of winning the lottery—and I don't play the lottery.

Still, I knew that there was a fundamental difference between much of what I was taught to believe about teaching and what I was experiencing in the classroom. So, I spent the next year reading everything I could get my hands on. I pored through books about teaching. When I heard of school districts or teachers somewhere making a difference, I called them and grilled them on what they were doing that worked. If I read a really good research article about teaching, I hunted down the author and asked follow-up questions. I attended conferences. I observed successful teachers and tried to uncover their secrets.

Then, I tried out what I was learning on my students. I raised my expectations. I started an online community to help build my students' capacity and independence. I created tiered assignments. I looked at the data. I took them on trips to expand their experience. I even baked them cookies if they registered to take the AP exam in the spring. Sometimes, these things worked really well. Other times, at least I did no harm.

What I eventually learned was that there was no magic in the strategy. It wasn't so much what I did that made a difference, it was how I thought. I started to ask myself why certain techniques worked and others didn't. I soon noticed that when a strategy was wildly successful, it had more to do with the fact that I honored a principle than the strategy itself. When a strategy was less successful, that too could be directly related to a principle I violated. Almost without realizing it, I was slowly incorporating principles of effective instruction into my practice.

As I began to pay attention to the principles rather than the strategies, I noticed a powerful shift in the way that I thought about teaching. Before, teaching for me had been a matter of applying the right strategy in the right way at the right time. As I studied effective teaching, however, I began to focus less on what strategy or technique I would use, and more on why I was doing what I was doing. Instead of trying to acquire more or better strategies, I worked on understanding the principles that undergird good teaching.

Paying attention to the principles also forced me to look at my disposition toward teaching and my students. I realized that much of what I was doing in the classroom was designed to serve my own ego needs rather than help my students learn. I wanted my students to do well because their doing well meant that I was a good teacher. I wanted my students to grow up to be famous and give Oscar acceptance speeches that ended with, "And it was all because of Dr. Jackson. She turned my life around." I wanted to be the teacher they made a movie about. This is why I was so frustrated because a lesson didn't work or my students didn't achieve as much as I wanted them to. It was about my needs.

Once I understood that the problem wasn't my students—that it had more to do with the way I thought about teaching rather than their inadequacies—I was free to look at my students differently. I shifted my focus from trying to manipulate my students to learn to showing them how to learn and helping them see the value in learning. I moved from trying to find just the right strategy to making sure that I faithfully applied the principles of effective instruction. Concentrating on the principles rather than the strategies and my own ego needs freed me up to actually teach.

As the school year passed, I began to notice radical changes happening in my classroom. Because I no longer used my teaching to meet my own ego needs, I was free to enjoy my students. When they faltered, I didn't take it personally. Instead, I focused on helping them understand why they failed and how to correct their mistakes. My process was messier, but much more successful.

I noticed that my students began to relax. They asked questions and tried to understand not just what we were doing but why it was important. They came to class prepared to do the work and when they were in class, they worked hard. I believe that they could see the shift in me—that now, I was focused on their success. I saw them as fundamentally capable and therefore stopped trying to protect them from the messiness of learning. Learning is frustrating. Mistakes will be made. When they saw me take risks in my teaching they learned that they too were safe to take risks. They learned that learning was the hardest, most demanding, and ultimately, most rewarding thing they could ever do.

It wasn't magic. You wouldn't be able to make a two-hour Hollywood movie about the changes that happened in my classroom. There were days when the messiness of learning was, well, too messy for us. We didn't always arrive at closure by the time the bell rang. There were days that my students and I left the class frustrated. On those days, I would remind myself and them that the frustration was a natural part of learning. I kept coming back to the principles, and held onto them even when it looked like they weren't working.

It made all the difference in my teaching. Suddenly, I too had the gift.

The Master Teacher Mindset

There are many books out there that break teaching down into discrete behaviors or offer a laundry list of strategies that, if you just try them, will make you a good teacher. This is not one of them. Instead, I believe you don't become a master teacher by simply doing what a master teacher does. You become a master teacher by thinking like a master teacher thinks.

All of us know the facts of teaching. What separates master teachers from the rest of us is that they know how to think about teaching. They have integrated the facts of teaching into their thinking and as a result, they do things automatically. From the outside, it looks like they have the gift. But on the inside, it is simply a matter of rigorously applying a few simple principles to their teaching.

When it comes to good teaching, I think we pay too much attention to the strategies, without fully understanding why those strategies work in the first place. What would happen if we didn't focus on the facts and behaviors of teaching? How much better might our teaching be if we focused on developing a mindset toward teaching instead?

I think that if we did focus on developing our teaching mindset, teaching would become fun again. Rather than worry about the next state-mandated test or the next round of evaluations, we would focus on helping our students understand the magic of a cell or the possibility of the written word, fully confident that no matter what test they faced, they would pass it. If we were to master this mindset, we would stop being batted around by the latest trend and focus instead on what makes the best sense for our students. If we shift our emphasis from what we do to how we think about what we do, it would dramatically alter the way that we diagnose student difficulty, assign homework, design tests, plan lessons, grade work, and see ourselves as teachers. In short, this mindset would take our emphasis off the minutiae of teaching and put it back where it belongs—on our students.

That is my hope for you as you read this book. I believe—and I hope you will come to believe it too—that the gift is not the exclusive domain of a blessed few. In fact, it isn't really a gift at all. It is instead, a mindset, a disciplined way of thinking about teaching. And, with this mindsct, the gift is ours, all of ours, for the taking.

ACKNOWLEDGMENTS

Although I would like to think of myself as a painter, creating a master-piece from nothing more than a blank canvas, some paint, and the vision in my artist's mind, the time has come to admit that I am more of a collage art-ist. I take scraps of things other people have created and put them together, hoping that the total sum will be greater than its parts. And so, this book is a collage of all the gifts given to me by the very brilliant people in my life.

The master teachers in my life—Cynthia Gill, Tom Gillard, Helen Marshall, Esther Mattox, and Marjorie Richardson—gave me wisdom. Experiencing their classrooms and working alongside them has made me a better teacher.

Any understanding I have of the way schools work and the best way to reach teachers I took from Traci Townsend and Dannette Lartique-Menaker, who started this consulting journey with me many moons ago; Nicole Brown, Dr. Donna Redmond-Jones, and Valda Valbrun who, by being my own per-sonal cohort of experts, keep me grounded professionally; Michael "The Turtle" Zarchin and Erika Huck who taught me how to lead a school; Dr. Frank Stetson and Steve Bedford who trusted me enough to allow me to find my own path as an administrator and teacher; Dr. Genevieve Floyd and John Q. Porter who supported me along the way; and Rasheed Meadows, Sherwin Collete, Linda Ferrell, and Lawrence Pendergast, who remind me all the time what truly visionary leadership is all about.

From Shauna Leung, I took the beginning of an idea. Her question two years ago about what good teachers do became in many ways the gen-esis for this book. And by playing Spock to my Kirk, Mohamed Ali inspired me to develop the framework of this book around principles rather than strategies.

To even believe that I could write a book, I took courage from Dr. Sara Kajder, who showed me that it could be done; Doug Schiffman, who continues to give me brilliant advice all for the price of a plate of pancakes; my attorney Shawn Wright (who has enough faith in Mindsteps for both of us); and Melissa and Allessandra Bradley-Burns, who convinced me I could do it when I wasn't so sure.

I could not have written this book without taking the advice of Kenyatta D. Graves (a fantastic writer in his own right), who read multiple drafts of these chapters; Claire Lambert, whose insightful questions helped me reflect and refine my thinking; and the remarkable women of Calliope—Diane MacEachern, Susan Orlins, Sue Katz Miller, Colleen Cordes, Mandy Katz, and Chris Intagliata—who showed me how to write my first book proposal, and who suffered through multiple unpolished drafts of this book so that my readers wouldn't have to.

I borrowed liberally from the wisdom of Scott Willis, Genny Ostertag, and Deborah Siegel, my editors at ASCD whose insightful comments helped shape this manuscript. They gently guided me through the process and were absolutely wonderful to work with!

From my parents Frank and Gail Jackson, my sister Sheri Jackson (who is, by the way, my absolute favorite person in the entire universe), my uncles Daryl Colbert, Bobby Colbert, and Gregory Jackson, and my dear friends Melissa Preddie, Dr. Dawn Nelson, Jonathan Morgan, Charles and Katina Taylor, Dolores and Bill Miller, Shaun Robinson, and my Dupont Park Church family, I continually take my anchor. Their love and unfailing support make it possible for me to do what I do.

And finally from the teachers who have trusted me to help and support them over the years, I took my purpose. By opening their classrooms and sharing their stories with me they remind me again and again that this work of providing every student with a quality education is the hardest, most important, most rewarding work there is.

Together, these marvelous people have given freely to me and, as a result, they are co-creators of the collage of ideas you hold in your hands. In return, I give them all my deepest gratitude.

INTRODUCTION

As to methods, there may be a million and then some, but principles are few. The man who grasps principles can successfully select his own methods. The man who tries methods, ignoring principles, is sure to have trouble.

Ralph Waldo Emerson

I am going to say something scandalous: Just because we went to school for teaching doesn't mean that we come out of school as master teachers. Even if you were a good student in school, it does not mean that you will be a good teacher. The tasks you were asked to do in school are fundamentally different from the day-to-day tasks you are asked to do as a teacher. In fact, most teachers will tell you that although their education courses and their student teaching gave them a good theoretical background, what they really learned about teaching, they learned on the job.

But teaching for many years is not enough to make you a master teacher either. There are some teachers who have been teaching for more than 20 years and still think and behave like novices; other teachers have become master teachers after only a few years of experience. And, the sad truth is that some of us never become master teachers no matter how many years we've been teaching.

Experience alone does not make you a master teacher any more than practicing scales twice a day makes you a concert pianist. Mastery teaching is not about the time you put in. It's what you do with your time that counts.

You see, mastery teaching requires specific, intentional practice.

That's good news because it means—and this book is built on this very premise—that *anyone can become a master teacher with the right kind of practice.*

This book will help you get that kind of practice. And the more you practice the principles of this book, the more you will begin to think and act like a master teacher. I call this process developing a *master teacher mindset.*

What Is the Master Teacher Mindset?

The master teacher mindset is really a disposition toward teaching. It is a way of thinking about instruction, about students, about learning, and about teaching in general that makes teaching fluid, efficient, and effective.

Many of us think that in order to be a good teacher, we need to have all the answers. We focus our time and energy accumulating strategies and skills, hoping that if we have a big enough bag of tricks, we will be prepared to face whatever happens in the classroom. The master teacher mindset means knowing that having all the answers isn't nearly as important as knowing what questions to ask. It means knowing that if you ask the right question the question itself will lead you to the information that you need to examine in order to find the answer. Good questions reveal what information is relevant, when information is sufficient, and how that information should be used appropriately.

The master teacher mindset also means knowing how to ask students the right questions, the kind of questions that lead to deeper thinking, increased motivation, and more student ownership over their own work. Master teachers spend more time refining their inquiry skills and their own curiosity than they do collecting strategies and skills.

Most of us experience a problem and quickly rush to find a solution. Developing a master teacher mindset means knowing that defining the problem correctly makes it more likely that you will find the appropriate solution. Master teachers spend more time thinking about why the problem is occurring than they do trying to find solutions. They examine the problem from all sides. The master teacher mindset means being willing to own your own contribution to the problem but at the same time, being reluctant to cast blame on others because you know that casting blame is not nearly as useful as looking for causes. Master teachers are willing to confront the brutal facts of their reality and account for those facts when developing a solution.

The master teacher mindset means not trying to teach like anyone else. Instead, you teach in ways that fit your own style. At the same time, you look for ways to make your teaching style relevant to your students' needs. Master teachers understand that there isn't just one way to teach and that effective teaching can be accomplished in a myriad of ways. They find ways that work for them *and* their students.

At the end of the day, most of us are so exhausted, we just want to go home, wade through the stack of papers we need to grade, plan for the next day, and go to bed. We rarely take the time to meaningfully reflect on our teaching. But with a master teacher mindset, you understand that meaningful reflection is critical to honing and refining your teaching craft. Master teachers take the time to reflect on their teaching in order to expose unwarranted or harmful assumptions they may hold, reveal fallacies in their thinking, illuminate problems, and determine directions for new growth. They see reflection as a necessary part of their day.

Ultimately, master teachers don't just magically develop the master teacher mindset. Teaching requires a vast body of knowledge. We have to know pedagogy, but also must be experts in our subject area or areas. This huge body of knowledge can be an overwhelming hodgepodge of largely disconnected facts, unless we have a system for organizing the information. Master teachers learn how to organize their teaching knowledge into meaningful patterns and from these patterns develop a set of key instructional principles. Their entire instructional practice is governed by this small set of core principles and they rigorously select strategies and teaching approaches based on these principles rather than become enamored with every new strategy or technique that becomes in vogue.

I call these principles the mastery principles and the rest of this book is devoted to helping you learn to apply them to your own teaching practice.

The mastery principles are

1. **Master teachers start where their students are.**
2. **Master teachers know where their students are going.**
3. **Master teachers expect to get their students to their goal.**
4. **Master teachers support their students along the way.**
5. **Master teachers use feedback to help them and their students get better.**
6. **Master teachers focus on quality rather than quantity.**
7. **Master teachers never work harder than their students.**

Master teachers often have a difficult time explaining the decision-making process that makes them masterful in the classroom. They have practiced these principles for so long that much of what they do has become automatic and seems almost natural. In the same way that learning to drive initially requires a lot of conscious effort and attention but eventually becomes so automatic that we rarely think about it, the disciplined practice of the master teacher principles will at first seem very awkward but will soon become automatic. Once you have practiced these principles to the point where they become automatic, it will take very little effort to maintain them.

You may be surprised that none of these principles seems especially earth shattering. They almost seem to be common teaching sense. Most of us know already that we need to set goals or to assess student progress. We learn it the first day in college. It's Teaching 101.

I would venture that most of us will claim we are already abiding by these principles in our daily practice. We already set high expectations for our students. We already try to get our students to do their own work. After all, what teacher will admit "I don't have high expectations for my students," or "I don't provide my students with the supports they will need to be successful"?

So why is it that so many of us still find teaching so challenging? Why is it that we are still not successful with *all* of our students? If the principles are so effective, and if we are already using the principles in our daily practice, why are we still struggling to reach every student, every day?

Here is the crux of *Never Work Harder Than Your Students and Other Principles of Great Teaching*. We all learned these principles in school, but what separates master teachers from the rest of us is that master teachers learned how to use the principles effectively, and rigorously apply these principles to their teaching. In fact, these principles have become such an integral part of their teaching that master teachers no longer have to consciously think about them. Applying these principles has become a natural response to students' needs.

Wouldn't it be marvelous if good teaching became that natural to all of us? Wouldn't it be wonderful if we no longer had to struggle through every teaching challenge? Wouldn't it be fantastic if we got to the point where we were faced with a teaching challenge and could quickly and automatically figure out how to address it effectively? Wouldn't it be great in short, if we all thought like master teachers?

Many of us for years have been looking for a way to do just that. So, we go back to school and get more degrees, or attend professional development workshops to gain new strategies, or spend our summers taking classes in the latest instructional approach, or read books that promise us "the secret" to improving our teaching.

But the master teacher mindset is not simply a response to good training. We don't go through school and come out automatically thinking like a master teacher. The master teacher mindset develops as a result of systematically taking all that we know about teaching, organizing it into a few governing principles, and rigorously applying these principles to our teaching until they become our spontaneous response to students in the classroom. The more we practice these principles, the more we begin to think like master teachers.

How to Use This Book

If you are a teacher, this book will help you figure out where you are on your journey to becoming a master teacher and how to move from one stage to the next. For staff developers and instructional leaders, this book will help you learn how to support teachers on their journey to becoming master teachers by helping you diagnose where they are on that journey and showing you how to help them reach that next step.

At the end of this introduction is a self-assessment to help you diagnose where you are on your journey toward becoming a master teacher. Take the assessment and give yourself two scores: an overall score to assess where you are on the master teacher trajectory, and an individual score for each principle. You can use your overall score to focus your reading of the chapters and figure out how you can move to the next level. You can use your score in the individual principle to help you choose which chapters to read first and on which principles you need to spend the majority of your energy.

Chapters 1 through 7 outline each of the principles in more detail and explain how you can begin to practice the principle in your own classroom. Each chapter begins with a vignette that illustrates what most of us were taught about teaching and the challenge that such thinking often presents for teachers. Then, you will be introduced to a principle and the research that explains why the principle is important. The next section, *Practicing the Principle,* gives you concrete advice about how you can integrate the principle into your own practice and provides practical examples of how the principle plays out in the classroom. These strategies are grouped under the heading *Try This.*

Throughout each chapter are sections that address any hesitation you may be feeling by providing you with suggestions for overcoming your resistance. These sections, titled *Yes, but. . .,* provide responses to common objections you may be having as you are reading the chapter. They will help you resolve some of the practical challenges that would otherwise get in the way of your being able to implement the principle.

Each chapter ends with a section entitled *Getting Started,* which summarizes the main steps to applying the principle. You can use these steps to help you focus your thinking on the most important points of the chapter and as a reminder of the ways you can begin to apply the principle in your own classroom. This section also provides concrete steps you can take to move from where you are (as determined by your overall score on the self-assessment) to the next level in the mastery trajectory.

Chapter 8 will take you step-by-step through the process of moving toward becoming a master teacher by systematically applying the master teacher principles to your practice. It helps you develop a viable action plan that you can immediately put into place, discusses the challenges you may face, and provides resources for getting support as you improve your teaching. It can also serve as a great reminder three to six months down the road to help you analyze your progress, tweak your plan, and stay the course. To keep you up to date on the latest resources and to help you extend your thinking once you have finished this book, I have also created a companion website at www.mindstepsinc.com where you can download additional resources.

The pathway to becoming a master teacher is by no means linear; there is more than one pathway to expertise. You may develop expertise in one area and still be at the novice level in another area. Thus, although I think it's best to read each chapter in order, you can figure out in what principle you received the lowest score, flip right to the chapter where that principle is covered, and discover ideas and strategies that will help address your immediate needs. Later, you can move through the rest of the book at a more leisurely pace and see how all of the principles connect.

However you choose to use this book, I hope it will inspire you to take a close look at your teaching, to challenge some of your assumptions about both teaching and the way that students learn, and to adjust your instruction or your instructional leadership so that your students can learn more effectively. Developing a master teacher mindset will change the way you feel about students, about learning, and about teaching in general. Your values will evolve. Your interest in your subject and in teaching will be revived. Your identity as a teacher will expand. In the process, you will rekindle your sense that what you do truly makes a difference in the lives of your students. And most of all, I hope that by reading this book you too will discover for yourself the gift that good teaching really is.

The Mastery Self-Assessment

Mastery cannot be measured in the number of years you've been teaching. It is measured by how well you apply the mastery principles to your teaching. Thus, the first step to moving toward mastery is to assess how well you are currently applying the mastery principles to your own practice by taking the quiz on the following pages. Answer each question as honestly as you can; think not about what you would like to do, but about what you are currently doing in your own practice. There are no right or wrong answers.

Use the scoring sheet on page 22 to keep track of your answers. Next to each number, write your answer to that question in the box provided. When you are finished answering the questions, use the scoring sheet to give yourself two scores. First, calculate an overall score. Then, give yourself an average score for each mastery principle. Your overall score will be between 49 and 196. Your average score for each principle will be between 1 and 4.

1. Which of the following statements is most true for you?
    a. I tend to look at my class as a whole and think of my students in terms of their group characteristics.
    b. I see my class as a group of groups and cluster certain students together.
    c. I see each of my students as individuals.
    d. I pay attention to the individual needs of my students but also notice how those needs and individual characteristics interact in the entire group.

2. Which of the following best represents what you do when you are faced with a new curriculum?
    a. I use the lesson plans included in the curriculum guide.
    b. I figure out how I will cover all of the material in each unit and start creating lesson plans.
    c. I look at the assessment at the end of each unit and back map my plans from there.
    d. I use the assessment to figure out what the need-to-knows are and determine how well students need to know each objective. Then I plan the assessments and learning activities based on each objective.

3. When a student does poorly on a test you think
    a. The student did not study hard enough.
    b. It was a poorly designed test and I will need to make a better one next time.
    c. The student did not understand the material. I will need to remediate so that he or she will do better on the next test.
    d. I need to work with the student more carefully to ensure that he or she does better on the reassessment.

4. When you examine data, you
    a. Consider all available data before making an instructional decision.
    b. Examine only the whole class data before making an instructional decision.

    c.   Examine both whole class data and individual student data when making an instructional decision.

    d.   Examine only the data that gives me the best feedback that will help me reach my goals and deliberately ignore the rest when making an instructional decision.

5.   Which of the following statements is most true for you?

    a.   I am still learning my discipline and I try to stay at least one step ahead of my students.

    b.   I understand my discipline well enough to teach it although there are times when I get stumped as to how to explain something to a student.

    c.   For the most part I understand my discipline and have more than one way of explaining the major concepts to students.

    d.   I understand my discipline and take time not only to explain the concepts and skills to my students but also to show them how to learn my subject on their own.

6.   Which of the following statements is most true for you?

    a.   I follow the curriculum guide step by step and try to cover everything.

    b.   I follow the curriculum guide as well as I can but I realize that I cannot get to everything.

    c.   I pick and choose what I want to teach from the curriculum guide and try to cover those things that I think are most important.

    d.   I assess the curriculum guide and divide it into those things students absolutely need to know in order to master the learning objectives and those that are nice to know.

7.   Which of the following statements is most true for you?

    a.   I am working much harder than my students.

    b.   I am working somewhat harder than my students.

    c.   I am working about as hard as my students.

    d.   I am doing my work as the students do their work.

8. When faced with a discipline problem in the classroom, what do you do?
   a. Look for a solution.
   b. Try a variety of solutions to see which one works best.
   c. Think about what may be causing the problem and select a solution that fits the situation.
   d. Look for patterns and develop a solution that will address not only the surface problem, but the underlying causes revealed by the pattern.

9. When you look at the curriculum standards, what is the first thing you do?
   a. Try to figure out how I am going to teach them all in the time I have.
   b. Try to figure out which assignments and activities will best help my students achieve the standards.
   c. Try to figure out what assessments I will use so that I will know when my students have mastered the standards.
   d. Try to figure out whether the standard is asking students to master content or a process.

10. What causes your success or failure in the classroom?
   a. It depends. Some days things go well. Other days, they just don't. You really can never tell how things will go.
   b. It depends on how difficult the teaching task was. If it is an easy teaching task, I am likely to be successful. But, the harder the teaching task, the less likely I am to be successful.
   c. It depends on how good of a teacher I am. When things go well, it is because I am good at that part of teaching. If things go poorly, then it means that I do not have that teaching skill.
   d. It depends on my effort. If things go well, it is because I worked really hard at making sure that things went well. If things go poorly, then it means that I have to work harder to make sure things go better the next time.

11. When you grade students' papers, you
    a. Write a great deal of comments on their papers to point out where they went wrong.
    b. Mark student errors but write few if any comments. The final grade is what matters to students.
    c. Make a few marks and write summary comments at the end to give students an overall assessment of their performance.
    d. Mark student errors and write only comments that will coach students towards better performance next time.

12. When a student seems to misunderstand a concept, you
    a. Press ahead and hope that the student will understand later.
    b. Try to meet with the student after school or during lunch to clear up his confusion.
    c. Give the student an alternate reading or supplementary materials to help clear up his confusion.
    d. Try to understand why the student is getting confused and then work to clear up his confusion.

13. When it comes to homework, you
    a. Assign homework just about every night. I think it is important that students have homework.
    b. Use homework as a way to cover those things I just can't cover in class.
    c. Use homework to help students develop good study habits.
    d. Use homework to provide students with independent practice for those things we have learned in class.

14. Which of the following statements is most true for you?
    a. I keep track of my students' grades. If students wants to know how they are doing in my class, they can ask me or wait for the progress report or the report card.
    b. I keep track of my students' grades but I regularly post their grades online so that they can also keep track of how they are doing.

   c.   I keep track of my students' grades but I post them regularly and also show students how they can track their own grades and figure out their course average.

   d.   I keep track of my students' grades but I also require that they track their own data. In fact, analyzing their own achievement data is a part of how we regularly run class.

15. When it comes to "soft" skills such as how to study or organize their notebooks, you

   a.   Expect my students to know how to do those things already. It is not my job to teach them how to study or organize their notebooks.

   b.   Require that my students use specific skills in my classroom. I give them a quiz on the chapters I assign for homework to make sure that they study and conduct notebook checks to make sure that they keep their notebooks organized.

   c.   Show my students how to gain these skills. For instance, I give students a study guide and I have a system for how notebooks should be organized.

   d.   First look at how students are studying and organizing their notebooks, and then show them how to improve what they are already doing.

16. When you write objectives, you usually

   a.   Try to state them using the wording favored by the district.

   b.   Figure out what activities I want my students to complete and list them.

   c.   Figure out what concepts or skills I want my students to master.

   d.   Figure out what I want students to learn and then how I can communicate that in a way that students will understand.

17. You believe that

   a.   All students can achieve at high levels if they have supportive parents, a strong educational foundation, and have the innate intellectual skills they need.

   b.   All students can achieve at high levels if they are motivated to do so.

    c.   All students can achieve at high levels if they are given the proper support in school.

    d.   All students can achieve at high levels and can actually get even smarter if they are taught how to exert effective effort.

18. After you have graded a set of papers, you
    a.   Record the grades in my grade book.
    b.   Record the grades and look to see which students passed and which students failed.
    c.   Record the grades and get a general sense of how the class is doing as a whole.
    d.   Record the grades and, based on student performance, figure out how I need to adjust my instruction going forward.

19. When a student has demonstrated that he or she has mastered the objectives of my unit already, you
    a.   Give the student an A.
    b.   Ask the student to help some of the other students in the class who haven't gotten it yet.
    c.   Try to find an enrichment activity for the student that can be done while the rest of the class works through the unit.
    d.   Take what I am already teaching and introduce more complexity and ambiguity into the concepts and skills to keep the student challenged.

20. Which of the following statements is most true for you?
    a.   I stick to the curriculum guide.
    b.   I stick mostly to the curriculum guide but I do include a few assignments that are just for fun.
    c.   I use the curriculum as a guide but I add in assignments that cover material that I think is important or enjoyable.
    d.   I choose what I teach based on what assignments will best help my students master the objectives stated in the curriculum guide.

21. Which of the following statements is most true for you?
    a.   I try to give my students as much help as I can but sometimes I
         wonder if I am really doing the work for them.
    b.   I try to limit the amount of help I give my students because they are
         going to have to learn how to learn on their own. They won't have
         the same supports once they get to the next level.
    c.   I try to balance helping my students with teaching them to be inde-
         pendent, but there are some times when my students seem unable
         to figure things out on their own.
    d.   I only give my students just enough help so that they can figure out
         how to do things on their own.

22. When your students come to class without the "soft" skills that they need
to be successful, you
    a.   Talk to their counselors to make sure that they are properly placed
         in my class.
    b.   Try to teach students the skills the students need even if it means
         that I don't always get through my entire curriculum.
    c.   Look for ways to help students acquire those skills that are most
         necessary while trying to get through as much of my curriculum as
         I can.
    d.   Look for ways I can show students how to capitalize on the skills
         that they do have in order to acquire the skills that they don't
         have.

23. When it comes to assessments, you
    a.   Use the ones included in the curriculum guide.
    b.   Write my own usually after I have taught the unit.
    c.   Write the assessment after I have planned the unit once I have a
         sense of what material I will be able to cover.
    d.   Write the assessment prior to planning the unit.

24. When you look at data, you
    a.   Select which data I will pay attention to. I tend to focus on the data
         I know and understand and disregard the rest.

    b.   Look at all of the data but sometimes make excuses for the information that is unfavorable.

    c.   Average the data. As long as most of the students are doing OK or my averages are high enough, then I am fine.

    d.   Consider all of the data important and consistently analyze the information in terms of individual student progress rather than averages.

25. During class discussions, your typical response to students' answers can best be described as

    a.   Praise: I want to encourage them to participate so I praise them even if the answer is not exactly right.

    b.   Evaluative: I want to encourage them to participate, but I also want them to know when they have given the wrong answer.

    c.   Corrective: If they give the wrong answer, I want to show them where they went wrong so that they will know how to give a better answer next time.

    d.   Coaching: If students give the wrong answer, I want them to figure out how to arrive at the right answer.

26. You decide how to help a struggling student

    a.   Once the student has failed the marking period.

    b.   Once the student has shown that he or she is failing at the interim report.

    c.   At the first sign the student is struggling (usually a failed quiz or test).

    d.   Before the student begins to struggle.

27. When teaching a new skill or concept, you

    a.   Try to cover it as best I can given the time I have.

    b.   Make sure that my students know it well enough to pass the test.

    c.   Make sure that students know it in their sleep.

    d.   Decide whether students need to know it to the level of automaticity or controlled processing.

28. Which of the following statements is most true for you?
   a.   Sometimes I am so busy trying to deal with my students' outside problems that I have a hard time getting to the curriculum I am supposed to teach.
   b.   I cannot solve all of my students' problems, so I just ignore them and focus on what I can do in the classroom to help them learn.
   c.   I recognize that my students' outside problems do influence what they do in my classroom, so I try to find a balance between helping them solve their problems and mastering the curriculum.
   d.   I recognize that it is not my job to solve all of my students' problems, so I focus on finding ways to help them develop the skills they need to solve their own problems.

29. When students do not meet your idea of what makes a good student, you
   a.   Question whether the student is motivated.
   b.   Question whether the student is academically capable.
   c.   Question what I can do to get the student to meet my expectations.
   d.   Question whether my expectations fail to consider alternate ways of demonstrating mastery or motivation.

30. You communicate the learning objectives to students by
   a.   Posting them on the board each day.
   b.   Posting them on the board and reading them to students at the beginning of class.
   c.   Posting them on the board, announcing them to students at the beginning of class, and listing them in my syllabus or in letters home to parents.
   d.   Posting them in class, explaining them to students either verbally or in writing, and listing them in my syllabus and in parent communications.

31. How would you characterize yourself?
   a.   I am an optimist. I believe that all my students will learn.
   b.   I am a realist. I know that some students will not learn because of the various constraints they face.

    c.   I am a pragmatist. I believe that all students can learn, but they may not all be able to learn from me.

    d.   I am a visionary. I believe that all students can learn and that it is my job to figure out how to best make sure they learn in my class.

32. When you notice that a lesson is not working, you
    a.   Press on anyway and hope that things will get better.
    b.   Switch tactics and try something else.
    c.   Use more explanatory devices or other instructional strategies to help students become engaged and to facilitate more student understanding.
    d.   Pay attention to the feedback I am getting from students and make adjustments to the lesson to better meet students' learning needs.

33. When planning your lessons, you can predict where students may become confused based on
    a.   What material seems to have the most explanation in the curriculum guide.
    b.   What material was confusing to my students in the past.
    c.   What I know about my subject and the common misconceptions that exist.
    d.   What I know about my subject and where students are in their conceptual development.

34. In order for students to learn a new skill, you believe that
    a.   They need to study hard and memorize it.
    b.   They need to practice it from start to finish so that they can learn the entire process well.
    c.   They need to build on their emerging skills until they have learned to practice the entire process.
    d.   They need multiple opportunities to practice parts of the skill over time and master them, as well as opportunities to practice the full-length performance.

35. Which of the following statements is most true for you?
    a.   I haven't had a chance to establish routines for everything yet.

   b.   I use routines to keep students in line. I find that if we have routines, students are better behaved.

   c.   I use routines to help our class go more smoothly and maximize students' time on task. When there are routines, students can spend more time on learning and less time on logistics.

   d.   I use routines to help students take on more of the work in the classroom.

36. When you reward students, you

   a.   Decide on a list of rewards and give them to students when they meet some criteria.

   b.   Don't typically reward students. Learning is reward enough.

   c.   Try to find rewards that I think will motivate students to keep up the good work.

   d.   Pay attention to what students value and find a way to connect what they value to what they should be doing in the classroom.

37. How do you differentiate instruction?

   a.   I group my students into high, medium, and low ability groups and plan three different lessons based on students' abilities.

   b.   I group my students in high, medium, and low ability groups and plan three different versions of the same lesson.

   c.   I focus on planning lessons that accommodate students' multiple intelligences.

   d.   I plan one lesson that starts at the standard and make adjustments to that lesson designed to help all students meet or exceed the standard.

38. Which of the following statements is most true for you?

   a.   Although I hold very strong beliefs about the value of what I do in the classroom, I am often so overwhelmed or pressed for time that my teaching practice often does not reflect those things that I really believe are important.

   b.   I used to hold strong beliefs about the value of what I do in the classroom, but over time and after so many challenges, I am not so sure I believe the same way any more.

    c.   I still believe in the value of what I do in the classroom although my beliefs are tempered by the reality I face each day.

    d.   I believe that what I do is important and that belief only grows stronger the more I interact with my students.

39. In your class, an "A" grade means that a student
    a. Is passing my class.
    b. Is smart or potentially gifted.
    c. Has worked hard.
    d. Has mastered the objectives of the course.

40. If a student fails a test, you
    a. Record the grade.
    b. Offer the student extra credit opportunities to make up for the low grade.
    c. Figure out why the student failed and offer remediation.
    d. Institute some corrective action and allow the student the opportunity to retake the test.

41. When you evaluate your lesson plans each year, you
    a. Figure out how I can cover the material better next time.
    b. Figure out how I can combine activities or shorten the amount of time I spend on activities so that I can make better use of my time next time.
    c. Figure out how I can teach the assignments differently and more effectively so that my students can better master the objectives.
    d. Figure out what things I can stop doing so that I have more time to help my students master what is really important.

42. When students do not fulfill their classroom responsibilities, you
    a. Create new rules or responsibilities.
    b. Punish students.
    c. Find a system of rewards to motivate them.
    d. Hold students accountable by applying logical consequences.

43. Which of the following statements is most true for you?
    a.   I feel that culture has no place in my curriculum.
    b.   I don't change my basic curriculum, but I do try to include material such as stories or interesting facts and acknowledge the contributions from other cultures.
    c.   I adjust my curriculum so that it includes multiple cultural perspectives.
    d.   I alter my curriculum so that it can capitalize on my students' backgrounds, experiences, and preferences.

44. When creating learning objectives, how do you make them concrete?
    a.   I state them in kid-friendly language so that my students can understand them.
    b.   I try to figure out what the goal really means and what activities or assignments will best fit each goal.
    c.   I try to figure out how the goal will be assessed and make sure that all the assignments and activities I chose are a good match for the objective.
    d.   I try to figure out what mastery of the goal will look like and what steps students will have to take in order to achieve mastery.

45. Which of the following statements is most true for you?
    a.   I believe that if I have the right strategies and resources, I can handle any teaching task I face.
    b.   I believe that there are just some teaching tasks that I am not prepared to handle.
    c.   I believe that most teaching tasks can be handled, but some are so difficult that I do not have the time or the resources to handle them effectively.
    d.   I believe that there are some teaching tasks that are more difficult than others but that I can handle any teaching task if I realistically assess the situation and maintain unwavering faith that I will prevail.

46. You judge students' progress based on
    a.   Their overall average in my class.

b. Their individual grades on tests, quizzes, and assignments.

c. Formative and summative assessment grades.

d. Various data sources such as formative and summative assessments, assignments, class discussions, and performance tasks.

47. What do you do when a student begins to struggle in your class?

a. I tutor the student one-on-one after school or during lunch.

b. I tell the student to come see me after school or during lunch. If the student chooses to come in, I will provide remediation. If not, then the student has chosen to fail.

c. I try to figure out why the student is having difficulty and provide him or her with help both in class and outside of class.

d. I implement a pre-determined intervention designed to quickly get the student back on track.

48. When selecting what assignments you will give to students, the most important factor for you is

a. What I can reasonably accomplish in the time I have.

b. What I enjoy doing and will be enjoyable for my students.

c. What makes the most sense given my students, my own teaching preferences, and the amount of time and resources I have.

d. What will most efficiently and effectively help my students master my learning objectives.

49. If a student is working on an in-class assignment and comes to me for help on a particular question, you

a. Give the student the right answer. I don't want the student to struggle.

b. Tell the student to ask another student or look up the answer.

c. Give the student progressive minimal cues.

d. Show the student how to find the answer himself.

Scoring Sheet

Give yourself one point for every A answer, two points for every B, three points for every C, and four points for every D.

Principle 1	Principle 2	Principle 3	Principle 4	Principle 5	Principle 6	Principle 7	Row Totals
1	2	3	4	5	6	7	
8	9	10	11	12	13	14	
15	16	17	18	19	20	21	
22	23	24	25	26	27	28	
29	30	31	32	33	34	35	
36	37	38	39	40	41	42	
43	44	45	46	47	48	49	
Principle Total	Principle Total	Principle Total	Principle Total	Principle Total	Principle Total	Principle Total	Overall Total
Principle Average	Principle Average	Principle Average	Principle Average	Principle Average	Principle Average	Principle Average	

Give Yourself an Overall Score

177–196 Points: Master Teacher

Good teaching for master teachers is fluid and automatic. They invest most of their time up front on planning and thinking through their teaching situation. Master teachers unpack the standards and set learning goals for students that represent minimum rather than maximum performance. Not only do they make conscious decisions about what students need to know and how well they need to know it, they decide early on what evidence of student mastery they will collect and use this feedback to inform their instructional decisions while helping students move toward reaching their learning targets. They incorporate supports into their instructional practice to catch students before they fail and appropriately balance the work of learning between themselves and their students. They recognize the currencies students bring with them to the classroom and help students use these currencies to acquire classroom capital. At the same time, master teachers base their expectations not on what their students can do, but on what *they* can do to help their students.

138–176 Points: Practitioner

Most veteran teachers score in the practitioner range. They have been teaching for a few years and make conscious choices about what they do in the classroom based on experience. They unpack the standards of their curriculum and have a pretty clear understanding of their learning goals, but they do not always break down these learning goals into concrete steps toward mastery. Practitioners align their assessments and learning activities to their learning goals most of the time and use this feedback to adjust their own instructional practice. However, they may not always provide students with the growth-oriented feedback they need to improve their own performance. Practitioners intervene with struggling students but may not always intervene *before* students begin to fail. And, although they confront the brutal facts of their reality, their faith is based on outside factors rather than on what they can do to change things. While practitioners recognize and appreciate the currencies students bring with them to the classroom, their focus is on helping students acquire new currencies rather than on showing them how to use the currencies they have already. As a result, in their attempts to balance the work between themselves and the students, they still rescue students when things become too uncomfortable.

98–137 Points: Apprentice

Good teaching for apprentices is based on having the right strategy. They take time to understand curriculum objectives and how they can cover those objectives in the limited time they have. Because apprentices realize that some rules can be broken, they often pick and choose what activities they will use for each unit and decide early on what assessments they will use. However, they do not always use assessment results to inform future instructional decisions. Apprentice teachers make some attempts at differentiating instruction but base their instructional strategies on "high," "on-level," and "low" students rather than on individual student needs. They recognize that students have different abilities and values but attempt to get students to exchange their values for those that are accepted in the classroom. When students do not adopt these values or otherwise do not meet their expectations, apprentices may lose faith and in many cases become disillusioned.

97–49 Points: Novice

There are two types of novices. Some teachers are novices because they have just started teaching and are still learning the ropes. Other novices have actually been teaching for some time, but still approach teaching with a novice mindset. Good teaching for both types of novices requires careful thought and planning. They look for rules or recipes to guide their practice. Many times they are so overwhelmed that they rely on the objectives and activities provided by the curriculum guide without really understanding what they mean. Novices work very hard to get through the curriculum by focusing on coverage and task completion. They have a limited number of explanatory devices and depend on remediation to help students who are very far behind. Novices use assessments to evaluate student performance and often use the tests that come with the curriculum guide. If they do create a test, they typically do so after they have taught the unit. Their understanding of who their students are is based on generalizations and stereotypes and their expectations for students are based on their perceptions of what they believe students can do.

Because of these expectations, novices typically work very hard, doing the lion's share of the work in the classroom.

Give Yourself a Score for Each Principle

Now that you have given yourself an overall score, give yourself a score for each principle. To calculate your score, begin by totaling the number of points in each column of the scoring sheet. Then, divide that number by 7 for your average score. Record your average score for each principle. (For an example of a completed scoring sheet, see p. 217.)

1

Start Where Your Students Are

All learners construct knowledge from an inner scaffolding of their individual and social experiences, emotions, will, aptitudes, beliefs, values, self-awareness, purpose, and more. In other words, if you are learning in a classroom, what you understand is determined by how you understand things, who you are, and what you already know as much as by what is covered, and how and by whom it is delivered.

Peter Senge

I was teaching an on-level class of 11th grade students. The students who were quiet, polite, obedient, and respectful were my favorites, regardless of how they performed in the class. They were what I considered "good students."

Keisha, on the other hand, was not what I considered a good student. She was loud. Her work, when she turned it in, was sloppy. She came to class late and rarely had anything to contribute to the discussion. At first, I tried to believe in her. I encouraged her and told her "you can do it." I gave her extensions on her assignments and invited her to come in at lunch for extra help. I worked hard to believe in her and did my best to treat her as if she had great potential.

But, to be honest, I didn't see any potential in her and I was getting tired of trying. Every day in class was a battle. I'd ask her to take out her pencil and get to work and she'd cross her arms and stare out the window. Some days, I would push it, cajole or order her to do her work and the exchange would erupt into a battle. Many days things got so bad that I would end up sending her to the office. Other days, I have to admit, I just didn't feel like fighting. If she wanted to fail, I wasn't going to get in her way.

One day, in the midst of one of our battles, she yelled, "I hate you!" And, to be honest, I couldn't stand her either.

It had come to that.

I realize now that because I had difficulty handling Keisha, I looked at her in terms of her deficits rather than her strengths. She did not fit my image of a good student so I expected her to fail. More importantly, because I had difficulty reaching her, I blamed her. If I were really honest, I didn't like Keisha because she didn't swoon over my lessons. I had worked hard on those lessons and was working very hard to teach her what I thought was a valuable skill. After all the work I'd done, she sat there with her head on her desk. Surely there must be something wrong with her.

One day, I was complaining about Keisha to Cynthia, one of her other teachers. We both commiserated about her terrible attitude and how hard it was to get her to work. As we talked, I slowly began to realize that although we both had the same view of Keisha and the same challenges with Keisha, we had different results. Keisha did work in Cynthia's class. In fact, Keisha was currently earning a B.

"You know that child is brilliant don't you?" Cynthia commented.

"Yeah," I snorted. "She's so brilliant that she's failing my class."

Cynthia got serious. "I mean it Robyn. That girl is brilliant."

I looked at Cynthia incredulously. "Brilliant? Are you kidding me? She doesn't do work in class. She just sits there during discussions. And the papers she turns in are full of grammatical errors." I was starting to get upset.

"None of that has anything to do with how smart she is," Cynthia replied calmly.

"Of course it does," I began. Then I stopped. Cynthia's words suddenly began to sink in.

"Have you ever had a conversation with her?" Cynthia asked.

I shook my head. "How can I have a conversation with her? She is completely unreasonable. She fights me at every turn."

"Yes. That child can be pretty stubborn and ornery," Cynthia said, smiling warmly. "But you really should try to get to know her."

"Cynthia, I have 130 students. I don't have weeks to spend trying to get to know each one personally. Besides, how does learning her favorite TV show or her favorite band help me get her to do her work?"

"You don't have to take her out to lunch or invite her home for the weekend, you know." Cynthia looked at me, amused. "I am just saying that you need to look beyond how mean or inappropriate or stubborn she is being and pay attention to who she is and what she wants. Keisha acts out because she doesn't have a more appropriate way of getting what she wants. But if you can get beyond that, you will find that she writes really good poetry, and she can out-argue anyone. She has a really good mind. You just have to show her how to use her powers for good instead of evil." Cynthia winked at me.

I thought about what Cynthia said. We had the same student but we saw her in entirely different ways. How was Cynthia able to see beyond Keisha's attitude and uncover her other abilities? And, more important, if Keisha really was as brilliant as Cynthia said she was, why wasn't I seeing it in my classroom?

Common Practice

We all at some time or another have come across a student or two whom we felt we just couldn't reach. In some cases, we've even come up against an entire classroom of students who seemed unmotivated and incapable of learning no matter how hard we tried. We struggled all year to find a way in.

Many textbooks and teacher preparation programs argue that the way in is to get to know your students. They suggest that you do a battery of pre-assessments and getting-to-know-you exercises. While these can be useful, they are not sufficient. Students have their own experiences and therefore present their attributes and abilities in different ways. If you only pre-assess and play getting-to-know-you games, you may be ignoring other powerful components of who they are.

Some teachers recognize that getting-to-know you exercises are not enough to really understand who students are. They realize that students' cultural backgrounds are also powerful influences on how they learn. Many school systems understand at least superficially the power of culture and therefore require their teachers to take a class on cultural competence. But these classes often amount to little more than heroes, holidays, and "foods of the world" classes where teachers spend six weeks eating their way to an understanding of culture.

The problem with this approach is that it treats culture as if it were a monolithic thing that can be reduced to a list of characteristics and prefer-ences. And, it assumes that our students have only one culture when, in fact, our students—all of us for that matter—are members of several cultures. There is their racial or ethnic culture (e.g. Latino, African-American, Asian), their regional culture (e.g. Southerner, urban, Californian, Midwesterner), their religious culture (e.g. Muslim, Christian, Hindu, Jewish), their social culture (e.g. athlete, Goth, egghead, theater kid), and their generational culture. If we spent time trying to understand all the cultural influences that make our students who they are, we would never have time to teach. And, even if we went through the trouble of learning all of the preferences and characteristics of our students' various cultures, how do we use that knowledge to motivate our students or help them learn?

It is undeniable that students' choices and learning preferences are influ-enced by their various cultures. But, rather than focus on learning superficial information about students or even learning the common attributes of their cultures, it is more important to understand the concept of intellectual and cultural currency, how it is acquired, negotiated, and traded in the classroom, and how you can marshal its power to help students learn.

The Principle

Knowing your students means more than knowing their demographics or test scores. It means recognizing what currency they have and value and then using that currency to help them acquire the capital of the classroom.

The capital of our classrooms is the knowledge and skills that lead to high achievement. It includes both *content knowledge*, like the concept of whole numbers and the effect of the Magna Carta on modern government, and *procedural knowledge*, like how to add and divide whole numbers or how to write a five-paragraph essay. When students acquire classroom capital, they do well on achievement tests and make good grades. Classroom capital is what we typically associate with intelligence.

However, simply knowing the facts does not ensure success for most students. Several researchers (Polanyi, 1958/1974; Sternberg et al., 2000) suggest that academic success is not based solely on knowing the right answers: it is also based on an entire subset of "tacit knowledge" or "soft skills" that make acquiring the right answers easier. In order to do well on a test, for instance, you need to know more than just the information being tested. You also need to know how to take notes, how to read the textbook, how to study effectively, how to distinguish what information is important, how to answer multiple choice questions, how to eliminate incorrect answers and make educated guesses when you do not know the answer, and how to pace yourself so that you can complete the test in the time allotted. You might need to know how to ask the teacher for help on the information you did not understand, how to identify what it is that you do not know, how to get the notes from another student if you are absent, or how to allot enough time to study.

These soft skills operate as a form of *currency* in the classroom. In fact, any behavior that students use to acquire the knowledge and skills important to your grade level or subject area functions as currency, and this currency is actively negotiated and traded in every classroom interaction. While these soft skills and behaviors are not often made explicit to students, they are crucial in acquiring the capital of the classroom.

We all have preferences for styles of behavior, communication, and relationships. We all have notions of what is worth knowing. These preferences are what we use to impart value to the currencies we use and accept in the classroom. If students behave in a way that we value—if they head their papers properly, for example, or come in for extra help, if they raise their hands before speaking and refrain from talking during the lecture—they are more likely to receive favorable treatment, extra help, high expectations, and access to opportunities. As a result, they are more likely to learn. If students do not have these currencies, they have a much more difficult time acquiring the capital of the classroom.

We all have preferred forms of currency. Suppose you advertise that your house is for sale and I come take a look. I like what I see and declare that I want to buy your house. "Great," you say as you take out the paperwork and prepare to draw up a contract. Meanwhile, I dig into my pocket, pull out a few shiny beads, some seashells, and a couple of wood carvings, place them on the table, and ask for the keys. How would you react?

What if I told you that in my culture, shiny beads were of tremendous value, the wood carvings were of a sacred nature, and the seashells were our accepted currency? Would you then accept them as a form of payment for your house?

The same type of exchange happens in classrooms each day. We have a capital (knowledge and skills) that we are trying to help our students acquire. Our students have various currencies (knowledge and behaviors) that they bring with them and attempt to use in order to acquire the capital of the classroom. Often however, there is a disconnection between the currency we value and the currency they are spending. Or our students do carry the currency recognized in the classroom but refuse to spend it because they do not find the classroom capital particularly valuable.

This disconnect is to be expected. Just by virtue of being adults, we have preferences for behavior and notions of what is valuable that differ from our students' sense of what is valuable. The trouble comes when we see this disconnect as a sign that our students are somehow deficient because they have currencies and values that are different than our own.

Just because students come to us with alternate forms of intellectual and cultural currency does not mean that they are less capable. It means that they have skills that may be unrecognized in the classroom context and potential that has yet to be developed. Or it might mean that they do not yet see enough value in classroom capital to expend the effort it takes to acquire it. Rather than see them as deficient, we should reshape our approach to instruction so that we capitalize on students' currencies rather than overriding or negating them.

Practicing the Principle

Ultimately, if we want students to be successful in our courses, we have to help them use their currencies to acquire classroom capital. In order to do so, we must first figure out what currencies we are accepting and what currencies our students are spending. Next, we have to determine whether there is a disconnection between the two. If there is, we need to figure out why that disconnection is occurring. There are two possible explanations. One, the disconnection is occurring because students do not have the currencies we are accepting in the classroom. If that is the case, we need to help students acquire this currency. The other explanation is that students have the currency but refuse to spend it. In this case, we have to help them value the capital of the classroom.

Understand What Currencies You Are Accepting in the Classroom

Most classroom problems have at their root a disconnection between the teacher's preferred form of currency and the students'. Thus, while it is important to understand and respect the students' currencies, you must also understand and respect your own.

As much as we may try, we cannot escape who we are. We have values we bring into the classroom. These values will come across in subtle, and not-so subtle ways, so it is important that you are observant of your students and of yourself. Ask yourself how your values affect the way that you see your students and your role in their lives. Examine how the way you teach is affected by the way you were taught, and develop an awareness of how all of this plays out in the way that you understand your students and the lens through which you see every interaction that takes place in the classroom.

Beliefs and values drive behavior. They have a direct consequence on what we teach, how we teach, and why we teach. Yet, how often do we take time to examine our own beliefs and values? If we are going to help students use their currencies to acquire the capital of the classroom, we must first examine our own beliefs about what is acceptable in the classroom, about what makes a "good student," and about what constitutes learning.

Try This

- Divide a piece of paper into two columns. On one side, list the behaviors and characteristics of your ideal student. What would that student look like? What would that student know? What would that student do? (For example your ideal student might be one who is neatly dressed, comes to class on time, raises his or her hand before speaking, completes the homework nightly, participates actively during classroom discussions, and knows how to read critically.) This list will help you see what currencies you value.

Next, place an asterisk next to each characteristic that is necessary in order to master the objectives of your course or grade level. On the other side, list the characteristics, behaviors, and values of the students in your class. What do your students look like? How do they behave? What do they value? Compare your lists to see what currencies your students are spending and what currencies you value. Where are the similarities? Where is the disconnection? How many of the starred characteristics do your students have already? What can you do to help your students acquire the starred characteristics they don't have already?

• Pay attention to the metaphors you use about teaching. Do you see teaching as gardening, or coaching, or shaping students, or leading students on a journey? These metaphors provide powerful clues about your beliefs about students. If you see teaching as gardening, you see your students as plants to be tended. If you see teaching as coaching, you see your students as players on a team. In one scenario, students are passive and must be coaxed and nurtured in order to grow. In the other scenario, students are more active and need to be guided in order to reach peak performance. By paying attention to our metaphors about teaching, we will be more aware of our own beliefs and values and how they influence the way we see our role as teachers, and the way that we currently approach instruction.

• Now ask your students to create similes for learning by having them complete the following sentence: "Learning is like. . . ." Examine your students' metaphors and see how they are similar to and different from your own.

Understand What Currencies Your Students Are Currently Spending

Not only do we need to understand what currencies we value, we need to pay attention to what currencies our students bring with them. Their academic performance will help paint part of the picture, but in order to discover what soft skills students possess and whether or not they are using them effectively, we need to look beyond test scores and grades.

William Sedlacek's (2004) research offers us a useful lens through which we can start to recognize and capitalize on the various currencies students bring to the classroom. In his book *Beyond the Big Test,* he argues that students have noncognitive characteristics and skills that are more predictive of academic success than the traditional measures of intelligence. Standardized tests and prior grades offer only a limited view of a student's potential.

Yes, but... can't I just use what I know about students' backgrounds and cultures already?

The danger in this approach is that it may result in subtle forms of stereotyping. Although there are cultural guidelines that exist that might help you develop an entry point into students' lives, you cannot rely on these stereotypes in order to see your students. Instead, observe your students. Listen, really listen, to them and try to understand what they bring to the table. We tend to think that we must immediately have the answers. When our students exhibit certain behaviors in the classroom, we immediately jump to an explanation of the behaviors. This principle asks that you take a step back and not jump to a conclusion. Rather, take your time to look for ways to help students capitalize on their abilities and potential in order to acquire the capital of the classroom.

Dr. Sedlacek found eight noncognitive characteristics that are predictive of academic success in college.

- *Positive self-concept*: The confidence that leads to the determination to succeed.
- *Realistic self-appraisal*: The ability to accurately assess your own strengths and weaknesses and to use this assessment to further your own development.
- *Successful navigation of the system*: Knowing how to access resources and how to use the system to help you achieve your goals.
- *Preference for long-term goals*: Knowing how to set and achieve long-term goals, delay gratification, and persevere in spite of obstacles.
- *Availability of a strong support person:* Finding someone to confer advice, particularly in times of crisis.
- *Leadership experience:* Having the ability to organize and influence others.
- *Community involvement*: Being involved in a community.

• *Knowledge acquired in and about a field*: Having the explicit and implicit knowledge of a particular field of study.

These eight variables offer us a way to see and value students' currencies that may otherwise go unrecognized in the classroom.

Recognizing the array of strengths students bring with them to the classroom gives you a starting point from which you can help students acquire classroom capital. If you see a student with a positive self-concept, for example, you can help her use her confidence to persevere on more difficult tasks. If you have a student who demonstrates a realistic appraisal of his strengths and weaknesses, you can show him how to use this appraisal to set attainable learning goals and be more strategic about how he studies. If a student has leadership experience, you can show that student how to use it to form study groups or to take on more responsibility during classroom routines.

When you actively look for evidence of alternate currencies, you can show students how to use the currencies they have to acquire the capital of the classroom. And, by showing them that you recognize their strengths, you can challenge them to reach beyond their natural limits.

Try This

• Use the eight noncognitive characteristics to discover what currencies your students already bring with them. Discuss these characteristics with students and help them see what characteristics they have already and how these characteristics will help them do well in your class. Look for ways to help students develop the characteristics in which they are not strong. For instance, if students need help in leadership, find informal leadership opportunities for them within the classroom, such as facilitating a class discussion, being in charge of caring for the class pet, or being the group leader during a small group project.

• Use parent conferences to learn more about your students. Ask parents to talk about their students' strengths, talents, likes, and dislikes and use this information to provide students with opportunities to use their talents and preferences to acquire the capital of the classroom. If you cannot accomplish this during parent conferences, send home a questionnaire for parents to complete.

• Create opportunities for students to share their own stories as a way of not only learning more about students but also making the curriculum more relevant. When giving an example in class, ask students if they have ever had a similar experience. When teaching a new concept, ask students to explain how that concept might play out in their own communities or might be relevant to their own lives. Have informal conversations with students in and outside of the classroom where you ask students to share their stories.

• Use the "artifact bag" exercise suggested by Jonathan Saphier and Robert Gower (1997) as a way of learning more about your students and creating a classroom culture that welcomes and values students' various currencies. Have students bring in an unlabeled shopping bag containing five items that represent something about their lives or their interests. At various intervals during the first month of the year, have a student select a bag at random and display the items one at a time. After the fifth item is shown, ask the class to make a collective guess as to its owner. Then, ask the bag's owner to explain the significance of each item.

• Use information, illustrations, and examples from students' cultures when teaching the principles, theories, and concepts of your course or discipline.

Help Students Acquire Additional Currencies

In addition to recognizing the different forms of currencies students bring to the classroom, we also need to identify what currencies students don't have. From there, we can help students acquire additional currencies that will help them be more successful in the classroom.

When I first was introduced to Dr. Sedlacek's (2004) research, I lamented that my students didn't have many of the noncognitive skills they needed to be successful. Many of them didn't have strong support systems available to them. Most of them had no preference for long-term goals and would easily give up. Few if any of my students had a realistic understanding of their strengths or where they needed to grow. If these eight skills were necessary for student success, I thought, then my kids were in trouble.

So, I decided that if these skills were crucial, and if my students didn't come to me with them already, it was my job to help them develop these skills during the semester they were with me. I looked at how my classroom was currently structured and decided to radically overhaul what I was doing so that my students could not only master the objectives of my course but also develop the skills they needed to be successful in my class and in school in general.

I began by forming student study groups as a way of giving students a strong support system inside the classroom. These study groups met once a week outside of class (either in person during the school day or after school, or virtually in online chat rooms I set up for just that purpose). If a student was absent from class, he didn't check with me to see what work they missed, he checked with his study groups. If a student struggled with a concept, she went to her study group for help.

I also restructured my assignments to make many of them long-term assignments as a way of helping students learn to successfully set and work toward long-term goals. At first, I broke the assignments into smaller parts and set up several checkpoints along the way to help students stick with the project to the end. As the year progressed, I had students break the long-term assignments down and set up checkpoints for themselves so that by the end of the year, I gave the assignment and the students did the work of breaking it down into manageable parts. In that way, I helped students learn how to set and achieve long-term goals.

To help students develop a more realistic understanding of their own strengths and areas for growth, I adjusted the way that I provided them with feedback (for more on this, see Chapter 5) and gave them grade tracking sheets so that they could track their progress toward mastery of the objectives. I met with students regularly to discuss their progress toward the learning targets and to help them figure out what adjustments they needed to make in order to reach those learning targets.

It took some work but by the end of the semester, my students had developed many of the noncognitive skills they needed. And, because these skills were not bound by my subject matter, they could transfer these skills to other courses and subjects.

Try This

- Find out what necessary currencies your students are missing (use the list of eight noncognitive skills as a starting point). Then look for ways that you can help students acquire these currencies while doing the normal work of your classroom.

- Explicitly teach the academic vocabulary of your discipline or grade level as a way of helping students better access the curriculum.

- Set up student study groups as a way of helping students learn from each other and develop strong support systems within your class. For more information on how to set up study groups, visit my Web site at www.mindstepsinc.com.

- Project students into examples as a way of helping them relate to things with which they have had no direct experience. Use phrases like "Suppose you were…" "Imagine yourself…" or "What would you do if…?"

- Help students personalize learning goals by asking them to take the learning objective and identify what specific knowledge implied in the learning goal is of particular interest to them.

- When introducing new material with which students are completely unfamiliar, spend some time early on giving background information and creating context so that students can acquire some of the unstated or implied understandings of the topic.

Show Students How to Carry and Spend Multiple Currencies

It is important however, to be careful that in the process of helping students acquire other currencies you don't cheapen the currencies they already have. How do you avoid imposing your idea of what is valuable on the students and thus devaluing the currency that they bring to the classroom?

You teach students to carry more than one type of currency. Students naturally do this anyway. As Judith Rich Harris (1998) points out in her book *The Nurture Assumption*, children often act differently at school than they do at home. In fact, they are experts at adapting their behavior to their contexts.

When I first became an English teacher, I was told that one of my biggest challenges would be to help my students abandon their slang and learn to use "proper English." I went about my task with almost religious zeal, correcting every "ain't" and "don't got" with a holy conviction. I insisted that my students use "the King's English."

Of course, when I wasn't teaching, I occasionally slipped in an "ain't" or two. In fact, when I talked with my friends, I rarely spoke the "proper" English I was imposing on my students.

One day I was in my office during a lunch period working with a student. The phone on my desk rang and I excused myself for a moment to answer the call. It was my sister and we were trying to make arrangements for getting together later that day. I chatted with her for a few moments and hung up the phone. "I'm sorry about that," I apologized as I returned to my student. He just sat there and grinned at me.

"What?" I asked, as I eyed him suspiciously.

"I knew it!" he exclaimed and began to laugh. "I knew you didn't talk like that when you weren't in the classroom."

And he was right. I didn't. Among my friends and in my neighborhood, I used a very different dialect than when I was in front of my students, or on a job interview, or interacting with my supervisors, or conducting a workshop. If I didn't use the same dialect all the time, why was I demanding that my kids did?

Yes, but... doesn't this just make it OK for students to use nonstandard grammar? And, doesn't that just handicap them from doing well on the tests?

Am I excusing nonstandard English and saying that students should be allowed to only trade in their preferred form of currency? Of course not. Doing so would handicap students by limiting their opportunities in education and their mobility in society. But just because standard English is the language of the tests does not mean it is the language of students' lives. It is not an either/or situation. Rather, it is a matter of giving students more options by giving them multiple currencies and showing students how to use the most appropriate currency in each situation they face.

It was then that I began to introduce to my students the concept of bidialectalism. We talked about how English had several different dialects. I asked my students how they spoke at home. Some used a patois of English and their country's language. Others used a variation of slang. Still others didn't speak English at home at all. I asked them what would happen if they went into their neighborhoods and spoke "proper." They laughed.

"I might get robbed," shouted one.

"Man, no one would know what I was talking about," offered another.

We laughed at the idea of walking up to a group of guys hanging out on the corner and saying, "Pardon me, but do you have any Grey Poupon?"

"What about clothes?" I asked. "Can I go into your neighborhood dressed like this?" I indicated my pants suit and heels.

"Heck no!" laughed one of my students. "Not unless you want to be mugged."

"They would think you were a social worker or a probation officer," another one exclaimed.

"You'd be fine in my neighborhood," a third offered. "Everyone dresses like that."

"Not in my neighborhood," a fourth explained. "Women don't wear pants."

"It's the same way in the business world," I explained to my students. "If you don't dress the part and talk the part, you lose your street cred, regardless of the neighborhood you are in, whether that is Southeast or Wall Street."

"How many of you want to go to college and be a business person?" I asked. They all raised their hands. "How many of you want to be rich?" Again, all hands were raised. "Then you are going to have to learn the language of the dominant culture."

Now they were interested. They weren't being told that the way they spoke was "wrong" or to abandon their own culture; they were being given the secrets to a different culture, a culture to which they previously had been denied entry. The message wasn't that by acquiring the capital of the dominant culture, they would somehow become "better" or "smarter." It just meant that they would become more mobile. They would now be able to move freely between cultures.

How empowering is it for students to now be able to spend several types of currency and to know how to determine which currency works in which economy? How much more empowering is it for kids if they feel comfortable moving between and among cultures? And how many more options will they have as a result?

As teachers, we act as navigators of the unfamiliar social and cultural terrains. Our job is to help students acquire multiple forms of currency so that no matter what culture they enter, they have the knowledge and skills they need to move freely in that culture. Rather than try to erase your students' cultures and get them to conform to the dominate culture, look for ways to help them use their culture as an entry point into the dominant culture. Look for ways to help them become bicultural and to "code switch." Look for ways to value what they bring to the table and yet show them how they can use different currencies to acquire other forms of capital.

Additionally, we need to learn how to code switch ourselves by looking for ways to adjust or even reshape the curriculum to capitalize on students' tacit knowledge, skills, and experiences rather than overriding or negating them. By connecting what we are teaching to students' lives, we not only help students access the curriculum more easily, we honor students' ways of knowing, understanding, and representing information and thus make it more likely that students will learn and retain what we are teaching and interact with the material at a more rigorous level.

Try This

• Early in the school year, ask students to identify at least three areas in which they consider themselves to be "experts." These areas do not have to have anything to do with your subject area or course. Compile a list of classroom experts. Use this list throughout the year to look for opportunities to use students' areas of expertise as a way of explaining a new concept, as an opportunity to invite students to use their expertise to add to whatever it is you are teaching, and as a way to use their knowledge as a launching point for new concepts or skills.

• Model for students the various thinking processes involved in completing a complex task. Explain to students how a task is completed and then ask students to come up with alternative ways to complete the same task. Encourage students to adapt the process to fit their individual learning styles, modalities, and needs.

• Structure your lessons so that students can view issues, events, and concepts through multiple perspectives. For instance, use resources outside the text and de-emphasize the notion that there is one right answer. Have students come up with several answers to a problem or read several perspectives on an issue or event. Or require students to present both the pro and the con arguments on a controversial issue.

Help Students Choose to Spend the Currency They Have

Sometimes students do not have the currencies they need to be successful in the classroom. Other times, students have these currencies but refuse to use them.

There are four factors that influence students' choices to spend their currency in your classroom. The first is whether they think it is important to do well on a particular task. The second is how enjoyable they think doing a particular task will be. The third is how well they think a particular task will help them achieve their goals. And the fourth is what they think doing a particular task might cost them. If students have the currencies you are looking for and refuse to spend them, you will need to address one or more of these factors.

At the root of all of these factors is a question of value. Students will not spend their own currencies if they do not believe that what they will get in exchange is valuable. They'll need to believe that what you are teaching is relevant or worth their effort. There are two ways that you can help students value classroom capital. The first way is to create a classroom community where students can have some ownership over the routines and protocols of the classroom. In this way they will become active participants in the classroom economy and will come to value its capital. The second way is to help students connect what they value to classroom capital. Both ways will be discussed in more detail in the next two sections.

Try This

• Have students come up with their own ways of demonstrating mastery. For instance, after a lesson on scatter plots, have students develop their own scatter plots using something that interests them. One student could create a scatter plot of the batting averages of her favorite baseball players, while another student could make a scatter plot of the various characteristics of his favorite bands.

• Allow students frequent opportunities to discuss among themselves what ideas mean and how they can be applied. This helps students express ideas in their own words and relate what they are learning to what they have learned already.

- Ask students to explain to the class how they arrived at a solution to a problem. Show students that there are multiple ways to solve a problem and help them find a way that works best for them.
- Help students understand how they learn best. Give them an assessment that helps them discover their multiple intelligences or preferred learning modality. Then show them how to use this information to predict the difficulty of assignments that do not match their learning style or preferred modality, how to seek help, and how to adapt their studying, note taking, and even the learning task itself to better meet their learning needs.
- Actively listen to students and demonstrate interest in their lives beyond school. Point out the connection or ask students to connect what they are learning in class to their experiences outside of class.
- In order to find the "hook" for students, look for ways to demonstrate how what students are learning is similar to what they have already learned in the course or to their own experiences. You can also encourage students to create their own hooks by having them create analogies using new concepts and familiar concepts outside of your subject area (e.g. how is the cell like a factory? How is the nuclear arms race like a game of poker?). To make this process a little more concrete, bring a box of common random objects such as an old shoe, a broken toy, a roll of duct tape, an empty soda can, and so forth. Have students randomly select an item from the box and then work in groups to figure out how the new concept you are teaching is like that item (e.g. foreshadowing is like a map because it tells you where you are headed before you get there).

Help Students Value Classroom Capital by Creating a Classroom Community

Walk into Dannette's classroom and it is like walking into another world. The bulletin boards are covered with quotes from everyone from Led Zeppelin to Socrates. There is a picture of John Belushi during his *Animal House* days hanging next to a picture of Audrey Hepburn. Students' artwork and posters from home hang on the walls. There is even a corner of cubbies where students keep their class notes and study materials. In the front of the classroom there is a gong and students walk up to it at seemingly random times and give it a good whack. The class looks up, smiles, and then gets back to work.

During class discussions, students push the desks aside to a back corner and plop down onto bean bag chairs in the center of the room.

One day I walked by her classroom and could hear the students chanting "Eat it! Eat it!" Curious, I stepped in. There, in the middle of the classroom, five students were dangling chocolate covered crickets above their mouths. Surrounding them were other students wearing buttons that declared "I ate a bug." As each student swallowed, the rest of the class erupted in wild cheers and Dannette pinned a button on their shirts.

Why were students in an AP World History class eating bugs? It certainly wasn't part of the curriculum and it seemed almost disruptive to the rest of the class. In fact, it was the kind of thing more appropriate in a frat house than in a high school classroom. Why was she wasting valuable instructional time on something that had no relation to the curriculum and did nothing to prepare students for the test at the end of the year?

"We had just finished studying world cultures and I told my students that in some cultures, they eat bugs. They were so grossed out that I got the idea to bring in some chocolate covered ants and crickets," Dannette explained. "I wanted my students to do something that they didn't think they could do. I wanted them to know that if they could eat a bug, then they could take and pass an AP test."

Dannette created a classroom community. They were not 32 different students any more; they were all a part of the "I Ate a Bug Club."

"We bonded," Dannette said. "I looked at the Marine Corps and I looked at summer camp and I looked at sports teams and I saw how they would take a group of people from different backgrounds with different abilities and make them into a team. Together, that team would do things that seemed impossible to the individual person. These kids have never taken an AP test before and it seems impossible to them at the beginning. But, when they become a team, they encourage each other, they pull for each other. Suddenly, the test doesn't seem as impossible for these kids."

Dannette's classroom is not all fun and games. She doesn't eat bugs one day and play capture the flag the next, nor does she believe that eating a bug alone will help her students pass the AP World History exam at the end of the year. She isn't arguing that eating a bug will somehow magically transform her students into history scholars.

But she is making a powerful argument for using what was important to students to help them acquire what was important to her and to her course. She recognized the huge influence peers had on students at that age, so she used it to help motivate students to meet the rigor of her course. She also changed the context of the classroom. Traditionally, classrooms are set up for individualization. Each student is responsible for his own behavior and learning. They are, in a sense, on their own. But, what would happen, she asked, if collectivism trumped individualism? Challenges that once seemed daunting or even uninteresting when faced alone, suddenly seem possible and desirable when faced as a part of a team.

Dannette used those currencies to help her students meet the challenge of a very rigorous course. She didn't waste time trying to motivate her students to do well. Instead, she created a classroom culture around trying hard and working together to accomplish goals. She then let the students see for themselves that they were capable of doing far more than they thought they were. By starting with currencies that her students valued, she successfully helped students learn to value the classroom capital and work hard to obtain it. As a result, they didn't need her to motivate them; they were motivated themselves because they valued what they were learning.

> **Yes, but... I don't have time for these kinds of fluffy activities. I have to get through my curriculum.**
>
> We often ignore team-building activities because we feel that they detract from our curriculum. But, when used judiciously, these activities can help our students find an entry point to what we are trying to teach them. The key is to make sure that you select these activities with an end in mind, rather than doing them for doing's sake. Use these activities to help you reach a particular curricular goal and they will go a long way toward helping your students buy into what you are trying to teach them and into your class in general.

Try This

• What are the implicit rules of engagement currently in your classroom? I am not talking here of the rules for how students behave that are typically posted on the wall at the beginning of the school year. I am referring to those tacit rules for how discourse takes place in the classroom or those unstated protocols for how things get done. Ask students to identify these "rules of engagement" and discuss ways to make these rules more useful for them. Give students the opportunity to suggest more efficient protocols and procedures and, together, decide how classroom business will be conducted.

• Create interdependence in your classroom by teaching students to use each other as resources. This can be accomplished by reciprocal teaching, jigsaws, study groups, online discussion boards, subject-specific chat rooms, cooperative learning activities, and seeding (teaching some students a skill and then having that small group of students teach the rest of the class).

• Include team-building activities in your curriculum. While these activities are often seen as "fluffy" and unrelated to the curriculum, they actually help create a classroom community that makes students more efficient and interdependent. Team building can also motivate students and help them persevere in the face of difficulty because it creates a sense of "we're all in this together."

• Build in opportunities for students to have some influence or control in what goes on in the classroom. Give students choices about how to complete assignments that best fit their own learning styles, interests, and needs.

• To find ways to help students make connections between the curriculum and their lives, use the following questions suggested by Stephen L. Yelon (1996, pp. 16–17):

  ○ How will students use the topic in their worlds?

  ○ How will the topic help students explain their own experiences?

  ○ How will the topic contribute to or deepen students' current interests?

  ○ How can the topic help students fulfill their aspirations?

  ○ How can the topic help alleviate students' fears and concerns?

  ○ What will students gain if they learn this topic or lose if they do not?

  ○ What will happen if students use this new skill or knowledge well and what will happen if they do not?

Reward Students in Their Own Currency to Help Them Value Classroom Capital

One of the biggest mistakes we make as teachers is that we assume that our students value classroom capital. As a result, we try to motivate students by rewarding them with things they don't value. Many of us think that the good grade should be enough of a motivation for doing the work. But, for many of our students who have not bought into the economy of our classrooms, good grades mean very little. If we want to motivate students, we have to reward them with currencies they value. Take my friend Cynthia, for example.

One day, I dropped by her classroom to work on a presentation we were giving together at an upcoming conference. Although it was also Cynthia's planning period, she had a handful of students in her classroom making up a test. Her teaching assistant, Ms. Bledsoe, monitored the students while we worked at a table in the back of the classroom.

It wasn't long before our work was interrupted by Ms. Bledsoe's exasperated sigh. "Jesse, I have told you three times already to get to work. Take out your pencil and finish this test."

"I'm finished." Jesse slumped in his seat and put his pencil on the desk.

"You are not finished, Jesse. You still have two pages to go. Now get to work," Ms. Bledsoe admonished.

Jesse threw the test on the floor and got up.

"Excuse me," Cynthia whispered, never taking her eyes off of Jesse. "I'll be right back."

She put a smile on her face and went over to Jesse. "Boy, sit your little self down," she drawled playfully.

Jesse didn't smile, but he did reluctantly sit back in his seat. "Miss Gill, I don't want to do this test. It's boring." He crossed his arms.

Cynthia leaned over Jesse's desk and whispered something to him. He looked up at her quizzically, and she looked him directly in the eye and smiled.

Jesse reached for the test. "I don't have a pencil."

"I've got one right here." Cynthia reached in her pocket and handed Jesse a pencil. "Now hurry up. You only have about 20 minutes."

Jesse got to work.

When Cynthia returned to the table, I whispered, "You're amazing. What on earth did you say to him?"

"Who, Jesse? Chile, I just told him that if he finished his test, I'd make him a peanut butter and jelly sandwich."

I laughed aloud and Cynthia smiled enigmatically. "Don't knock it, honey. It works."

We didn't hear a peep from Jesse for the next 20 minutes. He hunched over his desk and completed his test. When time was up, Jesse brought his test over to Cynthia.

"Did you do your best?" she asked him sternly.

"Yes, Ms. Gill. I even went back over it to check my work."

Cynthia flipped through the test and checked each page. Then, she went to her desk and took out a loaf of bread, a vat of generic peanut butter, a jar of store-brand jelly, and a plastic knife. She made what was perhaps the ugliest peanut butter and jelly sandwich I had ever seen, but to Jesse, it was a work of art. When she finished the sandwich, she handed it to Jesse who cradled it lovingly in the palms of his hands, grinning.

"Thank you, Ms. Gill," he said reverently and carefully made his way to the door. As he left the classroom, we could hear him yell, "Hey Tito, DeMarco. Look what Ms. Gill made me!"

I asked Cynthia once about those peanut butter and jelly sandwiches. Why were these kids willing to work so hard for something that seemed so trivial? She used cheap bread and cheaper peanut butter and jelly. The sandwiches she made were positively ugly. What was it about these sandwiches that could get kids motivated when nothing else would? After all, wasn't it just a bribe—the high school equivalent of giving students candy if they finished their work?

"You're focusing on the wrong thing. It's not the sandwich itself that matters. It's the fact that *I* make it for them. Cooking for someone else is one of the most nurturing acts a person can do. These kids don't get enough nurturing at home. Jesse's mother works two jobs. She doesn't have time to make him a sandwich. So, when I make him a sandwich, he feels nurtured and loved. Jesse has to know that I care about him before he will do anything else. When he feels like I care about him, he will do the work."

Cynthia understood the idea of paying kids in their currency. Rather than impose her value system on Jesse, she recognized what currency he was taking and used what worked in his economy.

Yes, but... surely you don't expect me to start making my kids sandwiches!

I am no Cynthia. Although I love to tell the peanut butter sandwich story, I did not go out and immediately buy a loaf of bread and start making sandwiches myself. I am just not that way. But, I got her point. We did, after all, have the same students. My students too needed a certain amount of nurturing in order to be motivated. Most students do.

But, I am not the same kind of nurturer as Cynthia is. If I had gone out and started making sandwiches, I would have been little more than a poor imitation of Cynthia and my students would have seen right through me. I would have come off as false and insincere. No. I had to find a way to nurture my kids that was authentic and that fit with who I was.

Often when we read inspiring stories of great teachers or see a feel-good teacher movie, we want to rush out and do what they do. We grab a bullhorn like Joe Clark, or take them to an amusement park like Michelle Pfeifer did in *Dangerous Minds*. We keep them after class for hours like Jaime Escalante. But we fail to consider whether our students are like those in the movies, or whether we are like those teachers. We want to be like them, sure, but we have to take into account our own personalities. What made Joe Clark or Jaime Escalante so successful was that they found a way to reach their students by being who they were.

Kids are smart. They can see through us. They know when we are being sincere and when we are being "fake." While they may cut us a little slack in the beginning, they will soon begin to rebel against our teacher act if we are not sincere. If we don't believe it, why should they?

So, if making sandwiches is not your thing, figure out what is and do that.

Sure, Jesse should have been motivated by the intrinsic reward of doing well. But, in Jesse's economy, the intrinsic rewards were not nearly as important as that peanut butter and jelly sandwich.

When you start where your students are, you don't think in terms of "should." If you want to motivate students to learn, first find out what currency they are spending (or the currency they value) and pay them in that currency. From there, you can teach them how to find the reward in other things. For many of our students, intrinsic motivation has to be developed. It comes only after they have experienced the pleasure of doing well and know the rewards of success. At the beginning, many of our students haven't experienced consistent academic success and are not convinced that it will bring any pleasure. In fact, academic success has been a source of pain for them because it has been heretofore an unachievable goal. This is why it is so important to start with what motivates them and then as they experience more success, help them transfer or become motivated by that success.

For some students, it will take grades or points or extra credit. For other students, it will take the promise of some more tangible reward like extra time on the playground or a fieldtrip.

For Jesse, it took a peanut butter and jelly sandwich.

Try This

Think about the rewards you currently have in place in your classroom. Are they consistent with what your students value? If not, think about how you can make them more consistent with your students' values. Pay attention to what your students value (or even ask them!). Then, think of how you can reward them in ways that they value.

The Principle in Action

One day, I was doing a formal observation in Chris's 7th grade math class as she was teaching students how to solve quadratic equations.

"How do we solve for x in this equation?" she asked, as she wrote an equation on the overhead projector.

Several students raised their hands. Chris waited a few beats and then called on one student. As the student talked, Chris wrote on the overhead. When the student finished, Chris asked, "Why did you choose to solve the equation the way that you did?"

The student paused for a second and considered his answer. Then he began to explain his reasoning to the class. When he finished, Chris asked the class, "Did anyone use a different way to solve this equation?"

A few students raised their hands. Chris called on a student who explained another way to solve the equation. When the student finished, Chris asked her, "Why did you choose to solve the equation that way?" Again, the student explained her reasoning. Then Chris asked the class, "Is there another way that you could solve this equation?"

This time, the students were less quick to raise their hands. Chris waited and let them think about her question for a moment. When after several moments no one raised a hand, Chris prompted, "Let's see, you've added, subtracted, multiplied...." Again, Chris waited. Suddenly one student raised his hand. Chris called on him. "You could divide the two sides by six," he offered.

Chris smiled. "Okay, tell me how that would help me solve this equation." The student talked her through the equation as the other students took copious notes. Chris put down the overhead marker for a moment. "We have at least three ways of solving a quadratic equation here," she announced as she pointed to the overhead. She summarized each of the three methods. Then she asked, "Why would I use method one?" The students offered a few answers. Chris nodded her head, and then paused. "Well, are there situations where method two might work better?" The students thought for a moment and then offered a few scenarios. Chris listened and probed with more questions until the students had suggested several different situations where method two might work better than method one. "What about method three?" Again, the students explored the different scenarios.

When the students finished, Chris began to hand out a worksheet. "Now that we have learned how to solve quadratic equations, I want you to practice. This worksheet contains 12 problems. I want you to experiment with the three different methods that we just examined and find which method works best for you."

Chris didn't just teach her students one way to do things. She acknowledged that there were several different ways to solve the problem and allowed students to select the method that worked best for them. She helped them examine each method so that they understood the advantages and disadvantages that each offered and then let them decide based on their own preferences. As a result, Chris honored the currencies and preferences of her students and at the same time, helped them acquire new currencies that they could use to be successful in her classroom.

Getting Started

Help your students use the currencies they bring with them to help them acquire the capital of the classroom.

1. Examine your own currencies. Look to see which currencies you value in the classroom.

2. Pay attention to your students to discover which currencies they value and what currencies they are spending.

3. Look for any disconnect between the currencies you are accepting in the classroom and those the students are spending. Also look for ways that you may be spending currencies that the students do not value.

4. If the disconnection is because the students do not have classroom currency, help students use the currency they have to acquire classroom currency by showing them how their currencies are valuable, helping them acquire additional currencies, and learning how to code switch.

5. If students have classroom currency but refuse to spend it, create a shared classroom community and reward them in currency they value.

2

Know Where Your Students Are Going

"Would you tell me, please, which way I ought to go from here?"

"That depends a good deal on where you want to get to," said the Cat.

"I don't much care where—" said Alice.

"Then it doesn't matter which way you go," said the Cat.

Lewis Carroll, *Alice's Adventures in Wonderland*

I stopped by Kristine's class one day to conduct a formal observation. I arrived a few minutes early, chose a seat near the back of the classroom, and watched the students file in. When the bell rang, Kristine walked to the front of the room and pointed to the objectives on the board. "Good morning class," she began. "Our objectives for today are SWBAT: One, complete the warm-up problem on the board. Next, you and your lab partner will go to your microscopes where you will find instructions for today's amoeba lab. You will complete the lab according to the instructions and then write up your findings in your lab notebooks. Make sure that when you are finished, you clean up your lab area according to the clean-up procedures posted at the back of the classroom. Tonight's homework is to read the chapter on cell respiration. Are there any questions?"

Later, when Kristine and I met for the post observation conference, I asked her, "What were your objectives for the day's lesson?"

"Well," she began nervously, "I wanted students to complete the amoeba lab according to the lab procedures we have been going over in class."

"So the objective was that students use the lab procedures?" I asked.

"Well that and I wanted students to understand that amoebas are unicellular organisms."

"Why?" I asked, genuinely interested as I thought back to my own science classes.

Kristine shifted in her seat uncomfortably. "Because we have just started studying cells and most cells are not visible to the naked eye. I wanted them to see a cell and how it could function as an organism and identify the various parts of the cell. It was all in the lab instructions I gave them."

"That's different from the objectives you posted on the board," I pointed out. Kristine's face fell.

"But I thought I *had* posted the objectives," she protested. "I phrased them the way they taught us in school. I started with "Students will be able to do" and listed all the things that I wanted students to do by the end of the period. What's wrong with that?"

"Kristine, you listed what you wanted students to do but not what you wanted students to learn. I think it's great that you gave students a list of what activities you wanted them to accomplish in the classroom today. But it is also important to help students understand why they are completing those activities and how they, and you for that matter, will know whether they learned what you intended them to learn."

Kristine looked at the lab handout. "Well, I kind of tell them the point in the directions. They have to label these parts of the cell and they have to answer the question about single cell organisms."

I shifted tacks. "Kristine, why are you supposed to post objectives for students?"

"Because it helps students know what they are supposed to be learning?" she said, fidgeting nervously.

"Why is that important?"

Kristine paused for a moment. "I think it is so that students can know why they are completing their assignments and how to reach the objective."

I smiled at Kristine. "So, why don't we look at how you can help students understand your objectives and how they can reach them?"

Common Practice

I have a confession to make. When I first started teaching, I planned my lessons and *then* I wrote behavioral objectives to match whatever activities I had planned. After I wrote them, I never thought about those objectives again.

I am not alone. Many of us do the same thing or something similar. We write objectives, sure. We even post them in our classrooms and review them at the beginning of the period with students. But when we select which text we will use, what worksheets will require, what homework we will assign, and what tests and quizzes we will give, are we really doing so with our learning objectives in mind?

How we communicate these objectives is also of concern. Some school districts go so far as to require that objectives be written on the board. The reasoning behind such mandates makes sense. Teachers should communicate the objectives to students. But, few teachers go beyond posting their objectives each day. In school they teach us how to write objectives, but the emphasis is often more on how the objectives are worded than on the quality of the objective itself.

Another pitfall many of us face is that we really don't distinguish between learning goals and the activities we plan. Many times what we call mastery objectives are really learning activities or agenda items that outline what we plan to teach that day, not what we want students to learn. We think that by placing the ubiquitous phrase "Students will be able to" (or SWBAT) in front each activity, we have created an objective, but "SWBAT create a diorama of an African game reserve," is vastly different from "SWBAT understand the principle of conservation." One objective focuses on an activity—what the teacher will teach that day. The other focuses on what students will be learning.

Much has been written on objectives. Some theorists spend time identifying the different types of objectives that are possible and their various uses. Others point out the distinguishing features of a "good" objective. Given all the information and opinions out there, it's hard to figure out whether you should create behavioral objectives, mastery objectives, essential questions, thinking objectives, understanding goals, performance objectives, criterion-referenced objectives, or some combination of all of the above. The problem is that all of them make some sense and there are compelling reasons for each of them.

So what's a teacher to do? We all know that objectives are important, but how to create objectives and how to determine whether or not our students have achieved these objectives remains for many of us a fuzzy science.

The Principle

Imagine that you needed to drive from California to New York by next Friday. What steps would you take? Perhaps you would start by taking out your map and planning your route. I imagine that you would decide how far you needed to go each day in order to make your deadline. You would probably need to figure out where you would stop each night to rest. And, you would have to decide where to eat, how much money you will need, and what you will pack.

Now, imagine that your students had to reach certain standards and benchmarks by the end of the year. What steps would you take? Perhaps you would start by examining your curriculum and checking to see what would be the best route to help students achieve the standards and benchmarks. You would also decide what would be the checkpoints along the way and when and how you will periodically check student progress. Finally, you would need to decide what resources you will need to make students' achievement of the standards more likely.

It is helpful to think of the standards as your final destination. They represent what students need to know or be able to do by the end of their time with you. They are your learning goals. But, because mastery of the standards does not happen all at once, you will need to break these standards down into smaller objectives that will guide your day-to-day interactions with students. These objectives represent the various steps towards mastery and the criteria and evidence you will collect to ensure that students are indeed making progress.

Thinking about planning this way—learning goals that lead to objectives that lead to assessments that lead to learning activities—helps you make sense out of both your curriculum and your state and district mandates. And it helps you plan lessons, units, and semesters that are more likely to help your students meet the learning standards of your grade level or course.

Practicing the Principle

Master teachers spend more time unpacking standards and objectives than they do planning learning activities because they understand that clear learning goals will drive everything else they do. They begin by determining whether the standard emphasizes learning content or a process. They also look to see what other knowledge and skills are implied by the standard. From there, master teachers try to state the goal as concretely as possible in terms of what students should know or be able to do and the criteria for mastery of the goal. They then break these goals down into steps towards mastery that become their daily learning objectives. While master teachers hold all their students to rigorous standards, they state goals in terms of minimal rather than maximum acceptable performance. In that way, they challenge their students to exceed the standards and provide room for differentiation. Finally, master teachers effectively communicate these goals to students and parents and hold students accountable for achieving them.

Unpack the Standards

In many instances, the state or the school district has determined standards that students must reach by the end of the semester, year, or course. But, simply adopting these standards is not enough. If we are going to use these standards to guide our planning, assessments, and our teaching, we need to understand just what they are asking students to know or do.

The first step in developing appropriate and effective learning goals is to unpack the standards. There are two types of learning goals that are implied in any standard. The first type of goal is a content goal. Content goals emphasize content knowledge. Their main focus is on what students need to know or understand. The second type of goal is a process goal. Process goals focus on students' learning or developing a skill. For example, knowing the meaning of irony is a content goal. Knowing how to explain how an author uses irony to strengthen her argument is a process goal.

How do you determine whether a standard implies a content or procedural goal? The first clue is the verb that introduces the goal. If the goal begins with "students will understand or know," then it is likely the goal's focus is on content knowledge. If the goal outlines something that students will be able to do (i.e. write, compute, use, create, etc.), then the goal is likely a process goal.

> ### Yes, but... I don't have time to unpack the standards. I am too busy trying to get my students ready for the big test.
>
> As important as it is, unpacking the standards does take some time. But once you determine whether a standard is asking for content or procedural mastery, you can actually save yourself time because you will only focus on the skills or knowledge that is required by the standard. You will inevitably find that some of the things that you are doing to get your students ready to pass the big test are not actually moving students towards mastery of the standards on which they will be tested. So taking time to unpack the standards will actually help you be more efficient in your preparation for the test.
>
> You don't have to unpack them all at once. Start by going one unit at a time. Even if you don't significantly alter your lesson planning at first, at least by unpacking the standards you can start to think differently and more strategically about how you teach and the learning activities you use.

Making the distinction between process and content goals is not easy. There is a high degree of overlap. Many processes support content learning, and some content makes learning a process easier. For instance, the standard might be that students know how to analyze the geographic, political, religious, social, and economic structures in Northern China, which is a process goal. But in order to analyze these structures, students need to know what these structures are, which relates to content. Although the goal's emphasis is on process, knowing the content is crucial for students to engage in that process. Thus, there will be times when distinguishing between a content or process goal will feel artificial. But there are three reasons why making this distinction is important even when it seems as if you are splitting hairs.

The first reason is that it helps you think through the learning goal and figure out what is really important. Many standards and objectives are written in a way that obfuscates the distinction between content and process and, if we are not careful, we can become so distracted by the process involved that we fail to see that the main point of the goal is content, or vice versa. One of my favorite examples of this is the common English standard that students will be able to analyze the plot structure of a play. Many teachers think that in order to analyze the plot, students have to read the entire play. But, students can effectively analyze the plot by reading a really good plot summary. Or, they can be given an outline of the plot structure and use that to analyze the plot. Or, they can read key scenes rather than the entire play. But, when I suggest this to many English teachers, they get upset. They believe that the students must read the entire play. Perhaps it is important that students read the entire play in order to absorb the language of the playwright or to gain the experience of reading a play from start to finish, but reading the entire play is not required by the standard.

The second important reason for determining whether a goal is a content or process goal is that making this determination can help you find ways to differentiate your instruction so that more of your students can access the curriculum and achieve the learning goal. If the goal is asking students to master content, then you have quite a bit of flexibility on how students learn that content. If the goal is asking students to master a process, you have flexibility in the content you can use.

Third, determining whether a standard implies a process or content goal will help you determine what knowledge or skills are implied by a standard. Once you know that a standard requires that students master a process, you can also think about what steps students will have to take in order to master that process and what other knowledge or skills that process will require. If the standard emphasizes content knowledge, you can start to think about what processes students will need to use in order to acquire and retain that content knowledge.

Unpacking the standards and using them to develop learning goals will help focus your instructional planning. Not only will it help you determine what exactly students should learn, it will help you select learning activities that are well-matched to the learning goals and to students' individual needs.

Try This

- Examine your state or district standards for an upcoming unit of study. Determine whether each is a process or content goal. One way to help distinguish a content goal from a process goal is to look at the verbs used. Content goals typically use the words "know" and "understand." Process goals typically use action verbs such as "analyze," "conduct," "multiply," and "write."
- For each content goal, look to see what processes are implied. For each process goal, look to see what content is implied. Make sure that students know the implied content or skill before you expect them to master the learning goal.

Make Learning Goals Concrete

Even after we unpack the standards and create learning goals, there are times when our learning goals are much too abstract. We say we want students to become "lifelong learners" or to "think like scientists" or to "write persua-sively." But what is a "lifelong learner"? *How* does a scientist think? How do we know what "persuasively" means? These goals are difficult to understand and, because they are vague, they are almost impossible to assess. Our goals need to be concrete and clear to students. The goals should lay out exactly what students need to know and what you want them to do with that knowledge.

One way to make sure your learning goals are concrete is to think about how you will measure whether or not students have achieved the goal. If you are having trouble determining how you will measure whether a student has achieved a learning goal, that is a good clue that your learning goal is too broad and too abstract. If for example, your goal is that students will "write for a variety of purposes," how will you know when students have achieved this goal? If students write a persuasive letter and a narrative, will they have achieved the goal? If they write a poem and a letter to a pen pal, will that demonstrate that they have reached this goal? What about if they write in any genre they choose? Will that do it? As you can see, this learning goal is too abstract. It can be interpreted in a variety of ways and it isn't clear how you will be able to assess students' mastery. A more concrete learning goal might be that "students will write to persuade, to inform, and to explain." You will need to be careful not to make your learning goals too specific however, because doing so will put you in danger of listing activities or assignments rather than overarching objectives.

It is also important that you build your criteria for mastery into your learning goals. Effective learning goals will articulate the learning target and will also spell out for students what mastery looks like. Rather than tell students to think like scientists, we tell students to apply the scientific method to successfully solve a problem. In that way, we are helping them understand what they are expected to do, and we are making concrete those implied knowledge and skills that lie beneath our goals.

A third way to make your learning goals more concrete is to break them down into smaller learning objectives that map out the steps to mastery. It is often unreasonable to expect students to master a learning goal all at once. Breaking the learning goal down into manageable parts helps students focus on the *next* step rather than get overwhelmed by the amount of work it will take to achieve mastery. They may not be able to envision the final goal at first, but the next step is something concrete towards which they can work. Students need to know what the steps are towards mastery so that they can understand how to master the learning goal and so that they (and you) have clear checkpoints to assess their progress along the way.

By making goals concrete for both you and your students, you make it more likely that students will understand and ultimately achieve the learning goals, and you build in mechanisms that help you track their progress towards mastery.

Try This

• Create a rubric or scale for each learning goal as a way of providing students (and you) with a clear description of what mastery of the goal will look like and the stages of mastery along the way.

• Articulate the specific behaviors you expect students to exhibit when they are completing a task.

• Break your learning goals down into discrete steps students can take towards mastery. Present these steps to students along with a visual way (such as a chart, checklist, or graphic organizer) to track their progress towards the learning goal.

- For each learning goal, decide how you will know when students have achieved that goal and how you will know when students are on the right track. Explain these indicators to students.

Set Goals in Terms of Minimum Performance

A big mistake many of us make is that we set learning targets that represent maximum instead of minimum standards of proficiency. Instead, our learning goals should represent the floor, not the ceiling.

Sounds counterintuitive doesn't it? Shouldn't learning targets be pretty high so that our students have something to shoot for?

Yes, and no. Our learning targets should be rigorous and challenging so that our students can stretch themselves to learn and grow. But, they should not be so rigorous and challenging that few of our students are likely to ever reach them.

> ### Yes, but... this sounds a lot like low expectations to me.
>
> Thinking of the standard as minimum rather than the maximum performance does not mean lowering expectations; it actually ensures that more students will be challenged. If you see the standard as the maximum performance, you set limits on what your students can do. You leave them nowhere else to go. But, if you see the standard as just the beginning, not only does it not seem as daunting, but it also presents a challenge to all of your students by setting the expectation that they will *exceed* the standards.

Thinking about our learning goals this way requires that we re-examine what we mean by mastery. Does mastery mean that students are performing at the level of an expert? Does it mean that students are doing what we would expect for a similar student in that grade level? What exactly do we mean when we say that a student has mastered something, and is that kind of mastery a reasonable expectation?

Often, we will find that our expectations for what students should know and be able to do represent an ideal—an ideal not necessarily required by the standards of our course or grade level. Thus, while we would love for students to write like Pulitzer Prize winners, the standards only require that they write like highly proficient third-graders. While we would love for our students to conduct experiments worthy of a Nobel Prize, the standards only ask that they conduct an experiment according to the scientific method.

Thinking in terms of minimum versus maximum performance also allows you to differentiate your instruction both for students who are struggling and for students who need more challenge and enrichment without teaching two curricula. Imagine that you had a class full of students and they were all required to jump over a string that was two feet high. Some of your students are great jumpers and jump over the string easily. Others cannot jump over the string no matter how hard they try. How do you help everyone meet the standard and remain challenged?

One solution is to keep the string at a maximum height of two feet for every student. Those students who can jump it, do, and those students who can't, fail at the task. For some students the task remains impossible, for some, it is just the right amount of challenge, and for others, it is so easy that they soon become bored.

Another solution is to move the string up and down based on the students' individual jumping abilities. For the students who have difficulty jumping over the string, you can lower the string to a more comfortable jumping height. For the students who can easily jump it at two feet, you raise the string to a more challenging height. While this approach will make sure that every student is successful jumping over the string, not every student will do so according to the two-foot-high standard.

The third choice is to anchor the string at two feet high on one end and slant it upward to a height of eight or even ten feet at the other end. Then, line up all the students along the string at a height that is challenging for them and allow them to jump. As soon as jumping becomes too easy for them, they can move up to a higher part of the string. In the meantime you work with those students who cannot even jump the string at the two-foot-high height to develop their jumping skills. In this way, every student is challenged and the standard is not compromised.

It is the same way in teaching. If you see the standard as the maximum performance for students, then the students who have already mastered the standard have nothing else to shoot for and soon become bored. If you see the standard as contingent upon the abilities of the students in your class, then not only do you wear yourself out moving the standard for each student, but the students who might struggle are never asked to meet the standard.

But, when you think of the standard as the minimum that students are required to master, and see that it does not change regardless of where students are, then you not only challenge those students who have already mastered the standard, you also support those students who struggle meeting the standard on their own. In the end, more of your students are likely to meet the learning goals and to be continually challenged while doing so.

Try This

• Examine each standard and decide the minimum evidence that students have achieved mastery of the standard. Then decide what the maximum evidence is. Use this range as the parameters for your differentiation activities with students so that you are differentiating *up* from the standard rather than down.

• Create a learning contract. List the minimum amount of work students will need to complete in order to demonstrate mastery of the standard. Require this work of all students in order for them to receive credit and a *C* grade. Then add other work that represents enrichment or reinforcement activities. If students complete two extra activities, they can earn a *B*. If students complete four extra activities, then they earn an *A*. For more on how to create learning contracts, visit www.mindstepsinc.com.

Design Appropriate Assessments

Grant Wiggins and Jay McTighe (1998) point out in their book *Understanding by Design* that an integral part of designing effective learning goals is to determine when we will know students have mastered the learning objectives, what evidence we will use, and how we will collect that evidence over time. In other words, once we have determined what students should know, how will we know that they know it?

Again, it sounds easier than it is.

After we have determined the acceptable evidence of mastery, we have to figure out by what criteria we will judge mastery. This distinction is often difficult to grasp because once we have determined what mastery will look like, we think we are done. But, we also have to figure out how we will know when students have mastered a particular concept or skill. How will students show us that they have reached or exceeded the learning goal?

Once we have crafted our learning goals, the best way to determine both evidence of mastery and the criteria by which we will judge mastery is to design a summative assessment. Jonathan Saphier and Robert Gower (1997) argue in *The Skillful Teacher* that "The clearest articulation of the objective appears in the assessment task and its criteria for success." *(p. 509)*. It is not until you define your assessment instrument that you have clearly spelled out what your true objective is.

Yes, but... teaching to the final test misses all the steps in between.

Mastery does not happen all at once. While you will start with designing the summative assessment, you cannot stop there. There are different stages or steps to get to the point of mastery and it is useful for both us and our students to identify the points along the way. You will need to break down complex learning goals into smaller, more manageable learning objectives. One way to do this is to create an analytic rubric to go along with the assessment so that you can describe the steps towards mastery along the way. (An example of an analytic rubric can be found on page 206). Another way is to assign points for each step in the process so that students can both focus on each individual step and see how all of the steps come together to make the final process work. The point is to start with the summative assessment as the final evidence of mastery and then identify the evidence that students are moving towards mastery.

For one, how well does the assessment match what you are teaching? Are you trying to see if students can recall information they have learned? Are you looking to see if students have learned information well enough to apply it in new ways? Are you testing to see if students have learned a procedure to the level of automaticity? Are you looking to see if students have reached certain benchmarks? Determine what it is you really want students to know or be able to do and then look for an assessment that will give you the best information.

> ### Yes, but... I don't have time to create all these assessments.
>
> You don't have time not to. Assessments save you time because they let you know what you need to teach and what you can afford to skip. They tell you when you can move on and when you need to spend more time. They allow you a chance be more creative with the time you do have.

In designing appropriate assessments there are two things to consider. The first is whether the assessment gives you an accurate picture of how close the students are to mastery. The second is how well the assessment will allow you to provide students with the feedback they will need in order to improve. In other words, you have to consider how well the assessment is going to give you feedback and how well it will allow you to give feedback to your students.

I remember giving a test once on the different types of sentences. We drilled the types of sentences and on test day, my students were ready. When I graded those tests, I was so proud of the progress my students had made. They knew those sentence types backward and forward. I had few grades below a *C* and I felt my students had mastered the material.

So why was it, I wondered a few weeks later, that their essays still lacked sentence variety? Sure, my students knew what the different types of sentences were and how to identify those sentences when they saw them. They even knew how to take a sample sentence and transform it into a different kind of sentence. But, they didn't know how to use the different types of sentences in their own writing. I'd taught them how to pass the test but I hadn't taught them how to write.

What good was their knowledge of the different types of sentences if they didn't know how to apply it to their own writing? Because I had failed to align my assessment to my objective, I wasted a week of instruction teaching my students something that was immaterial to what I really wanted them to learn.

So often, we undermine our own goals as teachers because we send students mixed messages about what we want them to learn and why. What we assess and how we assess it is different from what it is we really want students to learn. Do you really want students to learn the important dates leading up to World War II or do you want them to know these dates because the sequence of events tells us about the context that created an environment which created a war? Aligning your assessments to your learning goals helps you clarify your objectives and makes it more likely that your students will meet those learning objectives.

Try This

• Consider the following questions when designing your assessments: Does the test measure what you are trying to measure? In other words, is the test designed to tell you what it is you want to know about students' learning? Does the test ask students to provide information in a way that is compatible with how they learned the information?

• For your next unit, decide in advance what will be acceptable evidence of student mastery of the unit objectives. Then design an analytic rubric that describes the various stages of progress towards mastery. Use this rubric to evaluate your assessment and to help students see exactly where they are in relationship to where they need to be.

• Take a look at your grade book. Does it provide you with an accurate assessment of where students are in relation to the objectives of your course or does it record points for completing tasks or completing them accurately?

Match Activities to Learning Goals

All too often, we become enamored with activities without asking whether those activities actually help our students master the objective.

Recently, I was working with a group of sixth-grade math teachers who were planning a lesson that introduced geometric concepts. I had given them a unit planning template to use (see www.masterteachermindset.com for a copy of this template) and they were brainstorming ideas. They began well enough with the lesson objective but after they wrote the objective, they immediately began flipping though the textbook and the district guide looking for activities.

"Hey, we could do a treasure hunt with the kids," one teacher exclaimed. "I did one with my students last week and they really liked it."

"Great idea," another agreed. "And for the warm up, they could list the different shapes like triangle, square, and circle."

"Oooh, I like that," beamed a third.

"There is a worksheet in the workbook on shapes," someone added. "Wait, I found two worksheets."

I interrupted. "What do any of these activities have to do with your objective?" The teachers paused and thought for a moment.

"Well, the objective is that students will represent and analyze shapes using coordinate geometry," one teacher explained.

"Okay." I nodded. "But how do these activities help students get to the point where they can do that?"

"This worksheet right here is about shapes," another teacher pointed out.

"Does the worksheet help students understand how to represent and analyze shapes using coordinate geometry?" I asked. "And, is this worksheet the best way to help students understand and apply that concept?"

The teachers paused. "Well... not really. This worksheet is more about helping students identify the different types of shapes."

"What about the treasure hunt?" I asked. "How does that help students understand and apply coordinate geometry to shapes?"

"It really doesn't," they conceded.

"So why don't we refocus," I suggested. "In order to reach the objective, what do students have to do?"

"Well, they have to recognize the different shapes," one teacher offered.

"Okay. What else?"

They looked at the objective. "They have to both represent and analyze shapes. And, they have to do all of this using coordinate geometry."

"What do they have to know in order to be able to use coordinate geometry?" I asked.

The teachers began listing the skills. When they were done, I asked, "Which of these skills do your students have already and how will you know that?"

"I am pretty sure that the students have many of these skills already but we could use the warm-up as a way to review the skills and also informally assess which skills the students have and which we will need to review more," one teacher offered.

And they were off. Once the focus shifted from activities to learning experiences, the entire tone of the conversation changed. Now, the teachers were more concerned with helping the students master the objective than they were with what specific activities they would do. And that is the point, really.

> Yes, but... does each activity have to be matched to a learning goal? Aren't some activities inherently good without being directly tied to a standard?
>
> We all have activities that we want to use with students because they are fun or because we see some inherent merit in the activity. But, when these activities do not match your learning goals, you have to consider carefully whether you can afford to spend time on them rather than on those activities that will best help your students meet the standards of your course or your grade level. Although they may be fun or interesting or help students meet universal goals not represented by the standards, if you are in a high stakes environment or if taking time away from the standards will somehow place students behind where they should be and endanger their meeting the benchmarks, then the activity should be considered a nice-to-know rather than a need-to-know.

When students are presented with a series of activities without a clear learning goal, then each activity can appear to be of equal value. Because the activities do not ask students to demonstrate their emerging understanding of some larger concept, the students are more likely to participate in those activities that seem most engaging without making the connection between what they are doing and what they should be learning. They are merely going through the motions. But when activities are clearly connected to the learning goals, when there is indeed an appropriate match between the activity and the learning goal, students can engage in the activity with a clear purpose in mind and can see how the activity is moving them towards the learning goal.

Try This

- Plan your next lesson by first looking at your objective. Then, only select activities that will help you reach your objective.
- Take a look at the activities that you are currently using in your class and determine what the ultimate learning goal is for each. If you cannot articulate the learning goal implied in each activity in one sentence, consider whether or not the activity is best suited to helping you achieve your learning goals.

Communicate Goals Effectively

Designing effective learning goals is the first step. You must also communicate these goals effectively both to students and to their parents. Doing so will help them understand the connection between the daily assignments and the learning targets, and will also shift the accountability for students' reaching those targets from solely your shoulders to every member of the learning community.

Early in my career, I noticed that my students completed work regardless of whether they understood why I assigned it. I would introduce a new activity and they dutifully got to work even when they did not understand how what I was asking them to do connected to the objectives. Finally, one day I stopped them and asked, "Why am I asking you to do this?" They looked at me blankly. Some shrugged. "If you don't understand why you are doing this assignment, why are you doing it?" I asked. They were silent. Finally, one student said, "Because you asked us to?" At that, I laughed and my students looked at me as if I were a crazy woman. What followed was a five minute conversation about the current learning goals of the course and an explanation of how the assignment they were completing would help them reach their learning goals. I will admit, some of my students didn't seem to care. They just wanted me to stop talking so that they could get their work done before the bell rang. I began to wonder if I was indeed wasting my students' time. Did it really matter why they were completing the work?

Then, Damon raised his hand. "Dr. Jackson, if the goal of this assignment is really to help us learn how to identify the tone, this assignment isn't going to help us."

A minute ago, I was all aglow with the satisfaction that I was demystifying the process for my students. I was being a democratic teacher first rate. Now, I began to think that students completing assignments just because I told them to wasn't such a bad idea. The class waited to see how I would handle Damon's impertinent remark.

"Okay, Damon," I said cautiously. "Why not?"

"Well this exercise asks us to think of different words to describe tone and tells us what tone means but it really doesn't help us practice identifying the tone of a passage. If that is the objective, then I need practice trying to figure out tone with real stuff."

The other students began to nod in agreement. I looked at the worksheet and realized that Damon was right. "Class, Damon's right. Let's put this worksheet away and take out your anthologies. We can look at a few passages and practice identifying tone."

That wasn't easy for me. When I reflected on the incident later, I realized that the moment I took time to communicate to my students what the objectives were and explained how the work we were doing at any given moment related to the objectives, two things happened: I gave up some of the control I had in the classroom and I was now accountable to the students to make sure that the work I assigned was meaningful. But the benefit of taking such a risk was that once my students saw the connection between the goal and the work, they shared some of the ownership over their own learning and could be actively involved in reaching the objectives. I wasn't comfortable with Damon's comments—it was downright embarrassing to realize in front of my students that I had given them work that wasn't very useful to their learning—but because I was willing to admit and correct that mistake, my students became partners in their own learning.

In the same way, it is also important to communicate your goals to parents so that they too can become partners by supporting your efforts at home. I began to send home assignment packets with the learning goals written on the front. As students completed the steps towards mastery, I recorded their progress on the front of their packets. Parents began to call me not to discuss grades, but to discuss what they could do to help their student reach the next learning objective. Letting parents know what the overall goal is for each unit allows them to understand the point of the homework you send home and helps them monitor their students' progress toward the learning objectives.

Try This

• Periodically stop students and ask them to explain in their own words why they are completing a particular assignment. Make sure that they can connect the assignment to the objective.

• Do more than just post objectives on the board. Discuss with students what the objectives mean and ask for their opinions about the best way to help them reach the objectives. Adjust your planning to reflect the outcomes of this conversation.

• Explain to students how they will use what they are learning before they learn something new. Make an explicit connection between what they are currently learning and what they have already learned so students can see the relevance of any new activity. If you cannot explain to students how they will use what they are learning, question whether or not they really need to learn it.

• At the beginning of each new unit, send parents an e-mail or a letter home explaining what the learning goals will be for that unit and how they can track their child's progress towards mastering these learning goals.

• Have students chart their own progress towards mastery of the learning goals. Give students a blank graph. After they take the pre-assessment, have them chart their score on the graph. Then ask students to set a goal for where they would like to be by the end of the unit. After each formative assessment, have students chart their progress and set goals for the next learning cycle. Discuss with students their progress and provide them with specific feedback that will help them achieve their goal. In this way, you help students make the learning goals personal to them and take ownership over achieving these goals.

The Principle in Action

Lesson planning had always been fun for me. I loved dreaming up new activities for my students and creating interesting units. But lesson delivery was another story. Those lovely lessons I had planned at home often didn't translate to great lessons in the classroom.

One year, I attended a summer conference and the speaker discussed the idea of unit design. He suggested that we plan units first rather than individual lessons. Now, I realize that this isn't radical stuff here—I had been taught the very same thing in my methods courses—but something about the presentation inspired me to take a different approach to my planning.

That summer, instead of planning my lessons based on what I wanted to teach, I started with the learning standards. Not only did I look at the general standards for the course, I also spent several days analyzing old exams and listing the skills and competencies I thought students would need in order to answer each question. Then I looked at my master list and began grouping similar or related skills. Next, I looked at the groupings and tried to determine a logical sequence for those skills. Should they learn to write a clear thesis before they learn to write well-ordered paragraphs? Could they analyze a text for rhetorical strategies before they had learned to use those strategies in their writing?

Once I had a logical sequence, I began to plan my units. For each unit, I listed the skills or knowledge I wanted my students to know by the end of the unit. Then, I created an end-of-the-unit assessment that would tell me whether students had mastered the required knowledge and skills. Sometimes this assessment was a paper and pencil test, but often it was an essay or a project or a Socratic discussion. I chose the final assessment based on what I thought would best allow my students to demonstrate that they had mastered a skill or concept.

After I created the assessment, I created an analytic rubric that not only defined mastery, but also delineated the various stages that approached mastery. This was in many ways my hardest step. While I could define mastery pretty easily, it was a lot harder to define what students would look like when they were in need of more work or when they were almost there. Still, this exercise gave me clarity about what I wanted students to know or be able to do. In the end, I had a very clear picture for me and for my students about what was important and the steps that would get them to mastery.

Now it was time to plan my activities. As I selected books to read or assignments to give, I constantly asked myself how this book or that assignment would help my students acquire an understanding of the skills and concepts I was teaching. My goal was more than just rote memorization. I wanted students to interact with what they were learning and integrate it into their repertoire of skills.

I went through a certain amount of grieving at this stage. I had to give up a few of my favorite activities because I realized that while they were fun and engaging, they didn't allow my students the opportunity to move beyond a surface understanding of the topic. So, they had to go.

I didn't just grieve for the loss of some of my favorite assignments, I also grieved for my former students. There were times when I had to admit that I could have done better by them. I began to notice places where I had missed opportunities to really challenge my students and other places where I expected too much from them too soon. I cringed at the times when I hadn't given them the proper foundation to do the work I later required. I vowed to do better this time.

Finally, I inventoried what I had on hand and what I would need to get or create in order to make the units work. I also developed a plan for how I would prepare for the rest of the year.

In the end, I had a pretty comprehensive plan of action. I hadn't planned every unit for the year, but I had a general idea of my scope and sequence and I knew what work I would need to do to get those units properly prepared in time to teach the students. I also saw what resources I would need. I walked into school on day one with the first six weeks planned and the entire year mapped out. What a difference it made!

My students noticed the difference immediately. Instead of spending the first day playing a get-to-know-you game, we started working right away. They could tell that I had a vision for the year already.

We quickly settled into a rhythm, my kids and I. After two weeks of class, I was amazed at how much farther we were along than my classes in previous years had been. It seemed that because we knew where we were going, we had a much easier time getting there.

There were missteps sure. Lessons that I thought would fly never left the ground. There were days when my kids were not as enthusiastic about a lesson as I had hoped or when I would give an assessment only to discover that they were still not getting it. There were times when my students questioned why we were doing a particular assignment and I couldn't give them an answer. I didn't know myself. On those days, we chucked the assignment, switched gears, and moved on.

I had to let go of a lot that first year. I had to let go of my idea that I was supposed to be the smartest person in the room. I had to let go of my control of the classroom. I had to let go of my notions about what a teacher should do and what students should do. I used to run a pretty tight ship and now I had to share the wheel with 28 16-year-olds. There were times when I didn't want to cede control. There were days when my students would question something we were doing and I wanted to snap back, "because I'm the teacher!" There were days when my students were frustrated because I didn't seem to have the answers. It wasn't always comfortable and it wasn't always fun. Some days, it was just a lot of hard work.

But the end result was that my students were learning more and at a deeper level than my classes in previous years. They were mastering more challenging material and they were more engaged.

Because I had invested the time up front to unpack my standards, define mastery and the steps towards mastery, and identify how I would determine whether my students had reached mastery, I had more time during the year to relax and teach. My lessons were much more focused, my activities were more relevant, and my students were much more invested in their own learning because they could see the connection between what they were being asked to do and the learning goals they were trying to reach.

Getting Started

1. Unpack the standards and objectives of your course by first determining whether they require that students learn content or processes.

2. Then look for what other content or processes are implied by the standard or learning goal.

3. Next, break the goal down into smaller learning segments and more manageable chunks. In other words, chart the trajectory to achieving mastery of the goal and identify checkpoints along the way.

4. Match all of your learning activities to the goal.

5. Make the goal the floor rather than the ceiling and differentiate up from the goal.

6. Clearly communicate learning goals to parents and students.

3

Expect to Get Your Students There

Effort-based ability is the belief that all students can do rigorous academic work at high standards, even if they are far behind academically and need a significant amount of time to catch up. Educators who carry this belief into their practice are not unrealistic about the obstacles they and their students face. They simply have not given up.

Jonathan Saphier

A few years ago, I was leading a workshop on rigor. My audience was a group of high school teachers in a large school district and I was helping them to differentiate their instructional practices so that they could help all of their students access more rigorous content. Early into my presentation, I could tell that the teachers were merely counting the minutes until the break. Many of them sat scowling with their arms crossed, others doodled on the workshop materials, surreptitiously completed crossword puzzles, or read the newspaper. A few even muttered under their breath to each other. Things were not going well.

About fifteen minutes into my presentation, I decided to take a different tack. "I'm going to stop here for a moment because I realize that I have committed one of the cardinal sins of presenting," I said as I turned off my PowerPoint presentation. "I assumed that there was basic agreement about the premise of my presentation and clearly there is not. So, let's back up a bit."

That got a few people's attention. They stopped whispering among themselves and eyed me curiously. "How many of you are here because you have to be here?" I asked. The teachers smiled sheepishly and then raised their hands. "Ahh," I smiled. "Well, since you have to be here anyway, we might as well make it worth your while. Why don't you tell me what you want to get out of this workshop today."

The teachers shifted uncomfortably in their seats and shuffled their materials nervously. Some checked the agenda and looked at the clock. Practicing good "wait time," I leaned against the front table and let an uncomfortable silence hang over the room. Finally, one brave soul raised his hand. "Look, you seem like you have worked hard on this presentation but the problem isn't that we need more strategies. I *know* how to teach my biology class. The problem is the kids. They aren't motivated. Some of them don't even have the basic skills they need. How am I going to increase the rigor when they can't or won't do the work I give them now?"

Before I could respond, another teacher piped in. "These kids today have so many other distractions. They have MySpace and they text each other all the time. The last thing they are interested in is *Julius Caesar.*"

"Yeah," said another teacher. "How am I going to increase the rigor of my course when my kids won't even do their homework? I teach world history and I could assign reading but my kids won't do it. We are so far behind in the curriculum that I worry they won't be ready for the semester exam coming up in a month. I can't worry about rigor right now. I am just trying to drag them through the curriculum."

I stood there and listened to their concerns. Finally, I said, "Although we began this conversation talking about rigor, it sounds like we need to spend some time talking about expectations."

As soon as the words were out of my mouth, eyes began to roll. A teacher raised his hand. "I don't need another lecture about how I am supposed to have high expectations of my students. If you saw my syllabus you would see that I have very high expectations for what they need to do in my course. But, no matter how high my expectations are, the students cannot reach them. I would guess that at least 60 percent of my students will never earn higher than a *D* in my course, not because I don't have high expectations, but because they come to me so far behind and they won't do the work." Other teachers nodded in agreement.

I smiled. "Don't worry. I am not going to lecture you on how you must have high expectations of your students. But, I do think we need to take a look at our expectations of ourselves." I walked to my laptop and turned it off. "Why don't you put away your workshop materials for a moment and we will come back to them this afternoon," I said as I picked up a dry erase marker and walked to the whiteboard. "Now tell me. What do we mean when we say 'high expectations?'"

Common Practice

We have all have been taught that teachers are supposed to hold students to high expectations. Unfortunately, no one explains how we go about doing that. Do we repeat to ourselves the mantra "All students can learn" over and over until we can say it with conviction? Do we manufacture a blind belief in our students even when all evidence is to the contrary? Do we teach the students we wish we had and ignore the students we do have?

So many teachers struggle with high expectations because, in many cases, in order to have high expectations of students, you have to ignore or at least tune out the students in front of you. If, for instance, you are teaching a calculus class, and your students cannot multiply or divide whole numbers, it is difficult to expect that they are going to master calculus by the end of the year. The gap between what the students know and what they will need to know seems too wide. If, after 11 or 12 years of school they have not mastered the basic skills, what would make anyone think they are going to master other, much more complex skills by the end of a short semester or year?

And yet, we are told that we must, that indeed the very key to reaching these students is to first have high expectations of them. On what do we base these expectations? Certainly we can't always base them on the evidence in front of us, especially when that evidence directly contradicts what it is we are supposed to believe about students. Do we base our expectations on the belief that students have an innate ability to learn? Do we doggedly hold onto that belief even when we are confronted with students who do not seem to be able or motivated to learn?

Yes, but... I already have high standards.

Interestingly enough, most teachers believe that they have high expectations for their students, but when you examine what they are saying, what they really mean is that they have high standards for their students. It's a subtle but important difference.

The difference between an expectation and a standard is that the standard is the bar and the expectation is our belief about whether students will ever reach the bar. Standards are the external criteria against which a product is evaluated. A standard does not tell us anything about our beliefs. What we believe about the standard, however, determines our expectations.

One common approach to raising teacher expectations is to impose or raise the standards by which students and teachers will be evaluated. Proponents of this approach argue that by adopting a common set of standards, teachers will be very clear about what students are expected to know and be able to do. They assume low expectations result from a poor understanding of what mastery is. This approach, however, is fundamentally flawed.

As Judith Lloyd Yero (2002) argues in her book *Teaching in Mind: How Teacher Thinking Shapes Education* and on her Web site at www.teachersmind.com/standards.htm, "It is possible to have extremely high expectations without any standards whatsoever. Conversely, it is possible to have very low expectations—even when the external standards are extremely high."

Raising standards is not the same thing as raising expectations. Holding students accountable for more and more information does not change what we believe about a particular student's ability to master that information.

There is no cause and effect relationship between raising standards and raising expectations. Just because you raise your standards does not mean that you have also altered your belief about whether your students will be able to meet your standards. In fact, the opposite may happen. If you do not believe that students are able to meet your prior standards, how can you believe that they will be able to meet your new, higher standards? Higher standards then may actually *lower* expectations.

Typically, most staff development models built around expectations have focused on changing teacher beliefs. They argue that the way to change teacher beliefs is for teachers to "fake it before they make it." In other words, teachers are to pretend that they have high expectations for students even when they don't. They are advised to behave as if they believe in students by doing such things as nodding encouragingly when students are answering questions, praising students liberally, and providing more wait time. The argument goes that students will be convinced by this act and rise to the level of our feigned expectations.

But this is one of the most harmful pieces of advice out there. The problem with this approach is that if you only adjust your behavior without first changing your perspective, sooner or later, your true expectations will leak through. Because an expectation is a belief that something will happen, your behavior will reveal what you truly believe. If I believe that it will rain today, I will take an umbrella with me to work. If I don't believe that it will rain today, I leave the umbrella at home. If you truly believe that students will not meet your objectives, then that belief will play out in your interactions with students.

The Principle

Simply put, an expectation is the confidence that something will happen. When we say that we have high expectations for our students, we typically mean that we are confident that our students will master the material that we are teaching.

Expectation is also a mathematical term. In math, an expectation is what you get when you multiply the probability of an occurrence and the value of that occurrence. I like that definition because it has a lot to say about the way we teach. According to this definition, our expectations are the result of our beliefs about how likely something will happen combined with how much we value what we hope will happen.

Expectations, then, are based on both our beliefs and our values. If you want to raise your expectations of students, you must first understand how values and beliefs interact.

Beliefs are what we think is true. We use beliefs to make judgments about ourselves, others, and the world around us. Because a belief is a generalization based on our experience, what we believe about our students is based on what we see and how we see them. The same goes for our belief in our own abilities. If we have experienced success with a certain type of student in the past, we are more likely to believe that we will be successful with that same type of student in the future. The opposite is also true. If we have not been successful with a certain type of student in the past, we are more likely to believe that we will fail with that type of student when we meet her again.

Values are what we think something is worth. They are based on the principles and qualities that we think have intrinsic worth. Values are at the heart of what motivates us because they help us decide what is important. Your values tell you to do something because it is important regardless of whether you always think it is possible.

Our expectations are the intersection between what we believe about our teaching situation and our own abilities to handle it and what we believe is important. We can only have high expectations of our students if we believe that it is possible that we can help our students and if we believe that it is important to do so.

In George Bernard Shaw's play *Pygmalion*, Professor Henry Higgins brags that he can take a poor girl with a heavy Cockney accent, who sells flowers on the street, and turn her into a lady. He enters into a bet with his friend Colonel Pickering to pass off Eliza Doolittle as a refined lady at the Embassy ball, and then sets out to train her in the speech and etiquette of the upper class. He is so successful that Eliza exceeds his expectations. Not only is she able to pass as a member of the upper class, she is able to enter the middle class and marry into one of its most pretentious families.

The play is based on the ancient Greek myth recorded by Ovid. In this myth, a sculptor creates a work of art so beautiful that he falls in love with his own creation. He loves the sculpture as if it was a real woman—even to the point of kissing it and buying it presents—until one day, the goddess Aphrodite changes the sculpture into a real woman.

We educators use the term "The Pygmalion Effect" to describe what happens when teachers hold students to high expectations. The idea is that if teachers have high expectations for students, the students will rise to the level of the teacher's expectations. We are taught that if we just believe that our students can achieve, our students will meet our expectations, despite their background, their skill level, even their own motivation. In fact, an entire branch of the movie industry has been devoted to depicting the great teacher, the one who walks into a chaotic inner city classroom and just believes in the students. The students give the super teacher a hard time at first but are soon won over by the teacher's determination and belief in them. Forty-five minutes and a few wrenching scenes later, the students have become scholars.

🖅 Yes, but... no matter how talented I am, I can't make a silk purse out of a sow's ear.

It's hard sometimes to have high expectations of ourselves when our students come to us with so many learning needs. Juxtaposing where they are to where the curriculum says they need to be by the end of the year can seem overwhelming. It's almost as if we are being asked to perform a miracle.

But it is at times like these that we need to hold ourselves to high expectations even more. We look at the reality of our circumstances—our students are reading three grades below grade level, they have such poor skills that they cannot complete even the simplest of tasks, they are rarely in school—and we figure out how we can best mitigate these circumstances. Remember the metaphor of Pygmalion the sculptor. When the sculptor first meets the hunk of rock, it is difficult to imagine that rock as a beautiful work of art. But, the sculptor works at it a little at a time, a chip here, an adjustment there, until slowly, things begin to take shape. The same goes with teaching.

It may help to divide your goals into smaller goals and focus on these. Instead of trying to tackle everything at once, focus on those skills that will make the biggest difference for students and start there. Chapter 2 discusses this process in more detail.

This explanation of the Pygmalion effect, however, is not consistent with the Pygmalion myths. *Pygmalion* is not about a professor's or a sculptor's blind belief in his subject; *Pygmalion* is about the professor's and the sculptor's blind belief in their own talent. Professor Higgins does not care about Eliza's background, or her parents, or her own innate ability. The bet is about *his* ability to take anyone and turn her into something better. The Pygmalion of Ovid's story does not fall in love with just any statue. He falls in love with a statue of his own making.

What makes the Pygmalion effect so powerful in the classroom is not the dogged belief in our students' abilities, as we have been taught in our education courses. What makes the Pygmalion effect powerful is our belief in our own ability to take anyone (such as a poor Cockney flower girl) or anything (such as a cold lump of marble) and turn it into something so magnificent that we fall in love with it ourselves.

Notice the pattern here. First, the professor and the artist begin with a piece of raw material and a vision of what they can do with that raw material. They then set out to work. Once they have finished, they fall in love with their creation because it exceeds even what they believed they could do. We want to fall in love *before* we have created anything. We are waiting to believe in our students *before* we get to work. That's not the way the Pygmalion effect works. The professor and the artist begin by having a vision of what it is they will create. They go to work believing that they will end up with a masterpiece, not because the raw material they are working with has some innate potential, but because of the power of their own ability to create a masterpiece.

Practicing the Principle

Mastery teaching means understanding that expectations say more about your own sense of efficacy than they do about your students' abilities. Therefore, master teachers start by examining their expectations of themselves and shift their focus from what the *students* can do to what *they* can do. They apply the Stockdale paradox, simultaneously confronting the brutal facts of their reality while maintaining unwavering faith that they will find a way to prevail with all of their students.

Remember That It's Ultimately About You, Not the Students

Students pick up on our expectations fairly quickly. They then formulate judgments about the kind of teacher we are and decide how hard they will work in our classroom. I have seen students work their tails off for teachers who expected it and the same students barely register a pulse for other teachers—who expected that. It's true. Students rise to the level of our expectations.

But what we rarely consider is that we also rise to the level of our own expectations. If we believe that we can reach a student, we pull out all the stops and do everything within our power to make sure that student is successful. If we are confident in our ability to teach our subject, we share ownership of a student's failure or success. If however, we tell ourselves that there is no way to help these students, we stop trying. If we are not confident in our ability to help students, we lower our expectations to goals that we feel we can comfortably achieve.

Thus, low expectations say more about what you think of your own abilities than they do about what you think of your students' abilities. When you say that you don't think the students can achieve a goal, what you are really saying is that you don't think that you have the skills to help them achieve it.

Some of us err by either not having a rigorous enough program to begin with or having a rigorous program but spending the year not expecting students to reach the goals we've set. Both approaches assume that students can't do the work, one by setting the bar too low and the other by setting the bar high but accepting that students will never jump over it.

Others of us mask our low expectations under the guise of "accepting reality." We argue that rather than blindly—and futilely—believing that students will master the course content, we have accepted a more realistic view and will simply work with students where they are without burdening the students, or ourselves, with false hope.

Both approaches grow out of frustration from years of disappointed expectations, and yet many people vilify these teachers for having low expectations. They argue that these teachers are elitists, or racists, or have simply given up.

I believe that the problem is much more complex than that. The more I work with teachers, the more I understand that lowered expectations are really a self-protective measure. They are designed to reduce the gap between our own understanding about what good teaching should be and our perceptions about our ability to teach effectively given our current teaching situation. Regardless of the reason we give for low expectations, low expectations always say more about our confidence in our own abilities than they do about our confidence in the students. If you want to raise your expectations of your students, you first have to raise your expectations of yourself.

I was working with a group of middle school teachers on how to effectively support struggling students. We were discussing developing intervention plans for students so that we could help them before they needed extensive remediation when I noticed Katherine, an algebra teacher, roll her eyes.

"What is it Katherine?" I asked.

> ### Yes, but... shouldn't we hold the students accountable for something?
>
> It often seems as if students are being held less and less accountable for their own learning and teachers are being held more and more accountable. But holding yourself to high expectations does not take any of the responsibility away from the students. Holding yourself to high expectations is about a disposition toward students and toward teaching. It is not about taking on the students' responsibility to do the work; it is about developing and believing in your own ability to move students to where they need to be in spite of where they are.
>
> Developing this belief requires you to insist that students complete their work, and that they complete it in a way that meets the standards. *If we want students to be more accountable, then we have to insist that they do what accountable people do.* In this way, holding yourself to high expectations actually allows you to hold students *more* accountable. We'll talk about this more in chapter 7, "Never Work Harder Than Your Students."

"What good is an intervention plan when some of these kids are so far behind that they will never catch up?"

"What makes you think they will never catch up?" I wanted to know.

"Because," she sighed. "They are just too far behind. I've got state tests coming up and I have no time to help them catch up on the things they didn't learn before they got to me. Besides, I have a curriculum to get through by the end of the year and there just isn't enough time to do it all. I am killing myself as it is."

I listened to Katherine's explanation and asked, "Do you think that the students are capable of doing any better?"

Katherine thought for a moment. "I know I am supposed to say that I believe that they can, but to be honest, I just don't. I have done my best with them and yet they still don't get it. I even offer to stay after with them and they just don't show up. I am starting to think that they just can't handle the work. Maybe they don't belong in an algebra class."

Katherine's comments are typical of a lot of teachers. She faced external constraints and pressures, and she felt she was working as hard as she could with her students. And yet, she was still not able to move the students forward to where the curriculum guides and the state tests said they should be. She had done her best, so the problem must be with the students.

But, when you dig a little more deeply, you see that Katherine's frustrations had more to do with her own constraints than it did with her students' abilities. *She* was pressured. *She* didn't have enough time. *She* had done all she could and had not seen any results. So, *they* must be the problem. Katherine's assessment of what the students could do came only after she had been unsuccessful with all she knew how to do.

I asked Katherine to take a look at her expectations, not of the students, but of herself. "Do you believe that you could help the students master the material by the end of the year?"

"No," she shook her head. "They are just too far behind."

"How far behind are they really? I mean, what is it that they don't know that they need to know in order to pass the test at the end of the year?"

Katherine was beginning to get annoyed. "They don't know the basics. They have trouble adding and subtracting, multiplying, and dividing. They don't study. They don't know how to take notes."

"Katherine," I asked gently. "Could you teach them those things?"

Katherine looked at me and I could tell that she was trying to figure out where I was headed. "Sure, I could teach them those things," she began slowly, "but I shouldn't have to."

"I know you shouldn't have to Katherine, but do you believe that those things are important?"

"Yes."

"Could your students learn algebra if they had those skills?"

"Yes."

"How long will it take you to review those skills with your students?"

"I don't know," she hedged. "Not long, I suppose."

"Are there ways that you could teach those skills and still move through your curriculum? Mini-lessons, perhaps, or an intensive review?"

"I guess I could do something like that," she conceded grudgingly.

Now the conversation had shifted from what the students couldn't do to what Katherine could do. Rather than focus on the problem, we were now focused on how Katherine could solve the problem. That's the difference between looking at expectations in terms of your expectations for yourself versus your expectations for your students. The question shifts from "can I teach these students?" to "HOW can I teach these students?" Rather than be disheartened by constraints outside of your control, suddenly, you see what you can do to make a difference.

Try This

• Find another teacher in your building who has been successful with your students. Brainstorm strategies with that teacher, collaboratively plan, and participate in peer observation so that you can both learn from and support each other in developing strategies to help you be successful with your students.

• Use the following questions suggested by Rick DuFour (Dufour, Eaker, & Dufour, 2005) to develop a plan you can use to be successful with your students. 1. What is it I want students to learn? 2. How will I know when they have learned it? 3. How will I respond when a student experiences difficulty learning? These three questions will keep the focus on you and what you can do to help students be successful.

• Rather than trying to solve every challenge at once, go for a "quick win." Find one student with whom you can succeed, or one lesson that you know you can make effective. Try one new thing you learned at a conference or a workshop or in this book that you feel the most confident of being successful. Starting small will not only build your confidence, it will help you learn from your small victories and apply the new skills toward achieving larger victories. From here, you can continue to add to your list of wins by tackling more and more difficult challenges.

Understand the Anatomy of an Expectation

In his best selling book *Good to Great,* Jim Collins (1991), talks about what he calls the Stockdale Paradox. The idea of the Stockdale Paradox grew out of a conversation Collins had with Admiral Jim Stockdale who was a prisoner of war for eight years during the Vietnam War. Stockdale was able to not only survive unspeakable torture but also organize the other prisoners so that they could survive as well. During the conversation with Stockdale, Collins asked Stockdale what kind of prisoner didn't make it out of the prison camps. "Oh that's easy," replied Stockdale. "The optimists."

The optimists? Why the optimists? It would seem that the optimists would be the ones who held onto hope in spite of the bleak circumstances. Wouldn't it pay to maintain optimism?

Not necessarily. In fact, as Stockdale explained, optimism could actually create despair. The optimists in prison would focus on a specific outcome, such as getting out by Christmas. When Christmas came and went, and they were still in prison, the optimists would lose hope. Many died not from the torture, but from the broken hearts that came with repeated disappointment. As Stockdale warned, "You must never confuse faith that you will prevail in the end—which you can never afford to lose—with the discipline to confront the most brutal facts of your current reality, whatever they might be" (Collins, 2001, p. 85).

Many teachers suffer from the same misplaced optimism, the same false hope that comes from believing that they and their students will be successful without also confronting the brutal facts of their current reality. We cannot hold onto high expectations for students without also considering the reality of who they are and what they are able to do.

The Stockdale Paradox is the idea that in order to make it "you must maintain unwavering faith that you can and will prevail in the end, regardless of the difficulties," AND at the same time have the discipline to "confront the most brutal facts of your current reality, whatever they might be" (Collins, 2001, p. 86).

Yes, but... I have lost my faith.

Sometimes the brutal facts of your reality are so overwhelming that it is difficult to tap into your values and bolster your faith. Sometimes, things are so rough that it is hard to remember why it is you went into teaching in the first place. You need inspiration, but you are hard pressed to find it.

In times like these, several things may help. You can spend some time reflecting on your successes. Are there times when you have prevailed with a student and seen the results? Can you remember how it felt? Focus on that feeling and ask yourself what you did in that situation to produce that feeling.

You can also read something inspiring. I recommend Parker J. Palmer's *The Courage to Teach* which takes you through a stage-by-stage process that helps you recover your passion for teaching.

Although Collins uses this principle to explain why some companies are able to make the move from good to great and others are not, I think this principle also holds the key to adjusting our expectations. In order to raise our expectations, we must develop an unwavering faith that we will prevail with our students (values) and at the same time have the discipline to confront the reality of the students in front of us (beliefs). The next two sections will go into more detail about how we can do just that.

Try This

- To understand your core values, try this exercise: Make a list of the 10 most important attributes of a teacher (i.e. integrity, love, truthfulness, kindness, wisdom, ability to manage a classroom effectively, intelligence, charisma, sense of humor). Then, go back over your list. Cross out the three characteristics that are least important to you. Next, narrow the list to five by crossing out two more characteristics. Then, narrow the list to three by crossing out two more characteristics. Finally, of that list choose the two that are the most important to you. These represent your core values in teaching for which you are so passionate that you would never give them up. Next, examine whether your current teaching practice reflects your core values.

- To understand what it is you truly believe, pay attention to both your assessment of your teaching situation and your assessment of your own abilities to handle that situation. On one side of a sheet of paper, list your teaching strengths. At what parts of teaching are you really good? On the other side of the paper, list all of the constraints of your current teaching situation. Now compare your two lists. Do you believe that your teaching strengths are enough to overcome your constraints? Are there some constraints that are too overwhelming given your current teaching abilities? What strengths might you need to develop to overcome any constraints you face?

- Based on your assessment of your beliefs and values, determine where you need to work first—values or beliefs—by figuring out which one currently has more sway on your expectations for yourself and your students. If you have trouble identifying your values or if your values are not currently reflected in your teaching practice, work on the values side first. If you find that you have trouble believing that you can help all of your students achieve at high levels, work on the beliefs side of the equation first. The next two sections will show you how.

Adopt an Unwavering Faith in Yourself and in the Importance of Your Work

Unwavering faith is the values side of the equation because our faith can only be as strong as our values. If we believe that what we are doing is important, then we are more likely to believe that there must be a way for us to prevail with our students and that we will find it.

We get into trouble when we base our faith on our external circumstances. We cannot base our faith on what happens outside of us. To do so would be to leave our faith vulnerable to the fluctuations of circumstance, buffeted by every change in the tide. Faith must come from within. It must be based on your ideals, on what you value, on what you believe is important. Only your values can drive your faith.

Values also determine what information we deem important and what information we will ignore. They help us give weight to what beliefs we hold and what beliefs we abandon. The more important you believe something is, the more time, attention, and effort you will put forth to make it happen. Thus, values not only serve as the foundation of our faith, they are what drive our decision to persist "in spite of. . . ."

The problem with values however, is that while they are closely held, they are not always so apparent. In fact, it may take some time to unearth what we truly believe is important. That is why we need to periodically reflect on our practice and consciously remind ourselves of why we went into teaching and what we see as our fundamental role in our students' lives. We need to spend time reflectively thinking about our own values and how they affect our success in the classroom.

Of course, while it is easy to say that we hold certain values, our behavior will reveal what we actually believe. Therefore, it's not enough to simply reflect on your core values, you also must be alert for times when your practice contradicts your values. Do you say one thing and do another? Are you modeling the behavior you want to see from your students? Do you plan lessons that you know won't challenge your students enough because challenging them more will take more work? Do you give a test that you know

Yes, but... I don't have time to reflect. I've got real work to do.

Reflection is one of the greatest contributors to our ability to positively alter our own thinking and behavior. If we don't spend time reflectively thinking about our practice and re-examining our values, we are in danger of mindlessly accepting certain assumptions about teaching, about our role in the classroom, about our students, without ever being aware of how these assumptions impact the way that we interact with students. Without reflection, we ultimately lose effectiveness in the classroom.

There will always be too much work to do. And yet, by taking time to reflect on your practice, you can actually figure out a better, more effective, and therefore more efficient way to manage all of that work.

Yes, but... surely you don't expect me to believe that all my problems in the classroom will magically go away if I just have a little faith?

I am not preaching that faith will magically solve all of your problems, but it is a crucial first step. Because teaching is dynamic, you will not always discover the solution to the challenges you are facing in the classroom right away. What will help you persist with students until you do find the right solution is your faith in your values. You have to believe that what you are doing is important in order to go through all that you may have to go through to make sure that it happens in the classroom. So, while faith is not the only step, it is a vital first step toward resolving your classroom challenges.

students aren't prepared to pass simply so that you can move on to the next part of your unit? Pay attention to what you have identified as your core values and see if those core values actually play out in your interactions with students. If not, then you will need to re-examine whether you truly value what you say you do.

I first understood the importance of values on my own behavior one fall when I was faced with a particularly unruly group of students. I had a class of 23 boys and 5 girls that met right after lunch. Every day, it took 20 minutes or so to get the class settled down and focused on the work. Even then, I had to keep a constant eye on my students. They took twice as long as my other classes to get through their work, and they seemed completely unmotivated. Their writing was abysmal, and they rarely did their homework. If they weren't fooling around during class, they were asleep. I did my best at first. I tried to motivate them. I tried to engage them in class discussions. I tried to point out the interesting parts of Shakespeare—the sword fights, the clever insults. They couldn't care less. I cajoled and pleaded and bribed and begged them to turn in their homework. I called their parents, I kept them in at lunch, I got their counselors involved, I sent them to the office, I gave them zeros. Nothing seemed to work. I knew I had reached a low point the day I was working with a student at his desk. Suddenly, I smelled smoke. I turned around to see that one of my students had started a fire in the trashcan. These students, I determined, were not interested in learning.

I'd always thought of myself as a dynamic and inspiring teacher, but these boys didn't seem to see me that way. They weren't inspired by my lessons. They would much rather be anywhere else but in my classroom and they made sure that I knew it. So, I started spending the majority of my time controlling the classroom rather than teaching. I instituted a host of rules and executed every part of the lesson with military precision. I even cut out all class discussions because I was afraid that they would quickly dissolve into examinations of bodily functions and crude references to drugs, guns, and sex. Soon, my classroom looked nothing like the kind of classroom I'd envisioned.

One day, in the midst of a particularly boring worksheet I looked at their glazed over faces and realized that while they were now compliant, they were not learning a thing. At that point, I came face to face with my values. Was it more important that my students be quiet and cooperative, or was it more important that they actively engage with the material and learn to be critical thinkers and effective communicators? Was it more important that I feel in control of the classroom or was it more important that my students learn?

I wish I could tell you that somehow my classroom magically transformed that very moment, but it didn't. It took me another week of grappling with my values before I even decided to make a change. And, it took another few weeks after that before I could figure out a better system for engaging my students and muster the courage to try. Even then, there were a lot of missteps along the way. The class remained a frisky bunch, but by the end of the semester, they had settled down and were not only doing their work, they were learning. Once I made the decision that it was important that they learn what I was teaching, I also found the will to find a way to help them learn it. Once I decided to let my values rather than my constraints drive my teaching, I found the energy to figure out how to make sure that my classroom reflected my values in spite of my constraints. Reconnecting with my values helped me find the faith to persist with my students despite all of the constraints before me.

Try This

• Revisit why you went into teaching in the first place. What did you hope to accomplish as a teacher? What attracted you to the profession? These ideals, these values drive your faith. That means that if you want to increase your faith, you have to remind yourself of your values and remember why you chose to be an educator and why you still think education is important. If you can come back to that passion, to those ideals that propelled you toward this profession, you can increase your faith.

• Spend time helping students see the value of their education both by explicitly making connections between what they are learning and their lives and by explicitly explaining the implicit value of learning. Once students begin to value their education, they will begin to take more responsibility for their own learning.

• Insist that students complete every assignment. If you really believe that the assignment was worth assigning (see chapter 6 for more on this) then it is worth completing. The consequence for not completing work or completing it well should be that students have to spend more time getting it right. Do not offer students the reprieve of a poor grade. Build time into the school day (during lunch, after school, during recess, etc.) to work with students who do not complete their work and do not let students get away with sloppy or shoddy work. Insist that they give their best effort and provide them with the necessary supports to ensure that they do.

Confront the Brutal Facts of Your Reality

There is a wealth of information available in the classroom. We cannot realistically focus on all of the information that is available to us. The way that we decide on what information to focus is determined by what we believe about our own abilities and what we believe about the teaching task before us. Our beliefs function as a filter through which we sift our reality.

For one, our beliefs influence how we interpret information and formulate perceptions about our teaching situation and our students. Three teachers can see the same information and interpret it in three different ways based on their beliefs. For instance, one teacher may look at a group of students who are reading one or more grades below their current grade level and, because that teacher believes that she is not capable of bringing up their reading level by the time the state tests take place, she will see the teaching task as impossible. Another teacher may look at the teaching task and understand how much work it will entail and decide that it cannot be accomplished in such a short time. That teacher may lower his expectations for what students can, in his mind, realistically accomplish during the school year, and teach accordingly. A third teacher might look at the same teaching situation, decide that he is capable of moving students to where they need to be by the time the state tests are administered, and get to work making sure that the students meet the standards. All three teachers face the same teaching situation, but based on their beliefs about the magnitude of the teaching task and their own abilities to handle it, they each make a different decision.

In each case, the teachers used the same information, but *how* each teacher interpreted that information determined the outcome. In the first case, the teacher looked at the fact that students were below grade level and decided that, based on her beliefs about her own teaching ability, she would not be able to accomplish what needed to be done. In the second case, the teacher looked at the teaching task and, based on his beliefs about the demands of the task, decided that it could not be done. In the third case, the teacher looked at the teaching task and based on his beliefs about his own abilities, decided that the task was doable. Each of these teachers filtered the facts through their own beliefs.

So, if your beliefs determine what you pay attention to and how you interpret that information, how do you change your beliefs so that you can interpret information differently?

The answer lies in asking the right questions. Asking the right questions helps you become more intentional about what facts and experiences you pay attention to and helps you deliberately look for multiple interpretations of that data. When you do so, you can more easily adjust your beliefs and thereby alter your expectations.

Asking the right questions starts from being humble enough to understand that you do not and cannot have all the answers. It means being reflective about your own strengths and limitations as a teacher. It means talking to your students and trying to understand their perspectives. It means examining student data looking for patterns and trends and being open to more than one interpretation. And it means collecting this information without placing blame on your students or on yourself.

There are four important questions you need to ask:

1. What are my current skills and teaching strategies?
2. What are the requirements and the constraints on the teaching task at hand?
3. Are my current skills and strategies sufficient for the teaching task at hand?
4. If not, what can I do about it?

The answers to these four questions enables us to make better instructional decisions. When you take time to confront the brutal facts, the right decisions often become glaringly apparent. Sometimes you will see that you need to do something, or do something differently. Other times, you will see that you need to stop doing something (see Chapter 6 for more on this).

Confronting the brutal facts in this way helps you calibrate your beliefs about what will happen in the classroom to your current reality. Once you have made this adjustment, what you do with the information is also important. Many people are aware of the brutal facts but either ignore them or use them as an opportunity to blame someone else. If for instance, the students are not turning in their homework on a regular basis, teachers may either ignore this fact and plow ahead anyway or explain this lack of homework on students' being unmotivated. This is not confronting the brutal facts. Confronting the brutal facts means seeing that students are not turning in their homework and delving into the reasons why. It means being open to multiple reasons for their not turning in the homework. It means accepting that they may not be motivated but also asking the question "Why aren't they motivated?" It means digging until you get to the bottom of the problem. It means looking beyond the blame and shifting our focus from what the students can and cannot do to what we can do to help them. Then and only then can you begin to figure out how to solve the problem.

> ### Yes, but... the brutal facts are overwhelmingly brutal.
>
> Many teachers are overwhelmed when they face their students and understand their students' deficits. They feel pressure from external demands to teach and the internal pressure to do well. Sometimes, these pressures can make it hard to maintain an unwavering faith. In times like these, it is helpful to determine which brutal facts are actually relevant to your situation and which facts you can, for the moment, ignore. Not all facts carry the same impact on your classroom. For instance, you may be overwhelmed by the fact that the parents in your school community do not seem involved and do not give you the support you need with your students. Rather than trying to change the parents, focus on what support systems you can provide for students in the classroom. Ask yourself why you need parental support and then ask yourself if you could get these benefits some other way. Although it is important that you are aware of all of the brutal facts, don't try to take on everything at once. Spend your energy focusing on those brutal facts that have the greatest impact on your students' success and work to resolve them first.

Try This

• To assess the demands and constraints of your current teaching task, think about how difficult the task will be and what will it take to be successful at the task. Consider such things are what are your students' current abilities and motivation, what are the appropriate instructional strategies and how proficient are you at utilizing them, what managerial issues will the task present, what resources do you need and which ones are available, and how will you need to organize the space to maximize student engagement and success.

• Based on your assessment of the teaching task, which factors do you currently see as excuses for student failure? How can you remove or mitigate these excuses so that students can be successful?

• Rather than another "to do" list, create a "stop doing" list in which you list all the things that you are currently doing that are not getting you the results you desire. Stop doing them.

• Develop a plan for students who don't get it the first time. Use Tool 9 in the Appendix as a guide.

Make Sure to Use the Whole Equation

Both sides of the equation are necessary in order to raise your expectations. Here is where many of us fail. We only focus on one side of the equation. We face the brutal facts and become discouraged. We look at the students in front of us, see their deficits, and give up. We face the systemic restraints and throw our hands up in despair.

But we forget the unwavering faith. We must confront the brutal facts, yes, but once we have confronted the brutal facts, we must return to our faith. Confronting the brutal facts helps us understand our reality, but unwavering faith causes us to ask "What can I do today to move toward my goal *despite* the reality of my circumstances?"

Or, we focus on the other side of the equation and adopt an unwavering faith in our mission as teachers and persevere with our students, but we ignore the facts of our reality. We don't pay attention to the real demands of our teaching task or our own limitations and fail to take action to mitigate both. As a result, we are not consistently successful with students in spite of our faith. Soon, we lose our faith altogether.

You need both sides of the equation if you are going to be successful. Even still, it's really hard work. It is much easier to blame the kids or their parents or the school system or a lack of resources or anything else. But, let's face it. There are teachers out there who are in the same situation as we are and yet they manage to help their students succeed. They face the same type of students, the same institutional barriers, the same bureaucracy, the same lack of resources, the same diversity of student needs, and yet they manage to succeed. What makes the difference between whether a teacher succeeds or fails? It has little to do with the teacher's individual reality. It does however, have everything to do with how these teachers see their individual reality. They recognize the brutal facts, yes. But doing so does not change their unwavering faith in their own ability to reach their kids *no matter what.*

No matter what.

Try This

• Deny yourself the option of failure. If you start to become discouraged, look at both sides of the equation for encouragement. Examine the brutal facts of your reality to look for ways that you can overcome the barriers before you and return to your values to find the unwavering faith you need to believe that you can triumph. Keep looking for ways that you can overcome your obstacles.

• Use both sides of the equation to assess your current reality. Rather than trying to assess everything, use your beliefs to determine what information you focus on, and your values to determine the relative importance you will give to the various information you collect.

• Deny students the option of failure. Structure your course so that students cannot choose to fail. If students do not complete work, give them an incomplete rather than a failing grade and insist that they complete their work. If students earn a failing grade on an assignment or assessment, give them an incomplete and insist that they take some corrective action either with you (come in for extra help during lunch or after school) or on their own (i.e. online tutorials, simulations, read supplementary material, try practice problems, etc.) and then redo the assignment or retake the assessment.

The Principle in Action

When I was an administrator at a middle school, we had team meetings twice a week. At these team meetings, we reviewed the progress of students on our team. We would start with students whom we considered to be in jeopardy, either because of their behavior or because of their grades, before moving on to discuss a predetermined list of students. One day, we started the meeting by discussing Jack.

"I don't care how many times I go over the material, Jack still fails his quizzes," complained Cindy, his English teacher. "It's driving me crazy."

"I have the same problem with him in math class. He just doesn't seem to get it," Richard chimed in.

Laura listened as the teachers expressed their frustration. "I had the same problem with him too, but I think I figured out what's going on with Jack."

"What did you do?" they asked, curious.

"Well, last week, we had a map test and he bombed it as usual. At first, I thought it was because he didn't study so I made him stay after school with me so that we could go over the material and then he could do a retake of the test. Well, we reviewed the material together and I realized that he had studied and knew the material already. So, I gave him the test again and he didn't do any better."

"Do you think he has a learning disability?" Erika, his guidance counselor asked.

"I thought about that," Laura admitted. "But I wasn't sure. He didn't seem to have a problem learning the material. He just had a problem showing me that he knew it. I got curious about how I could get him to show me he knew the material."

"So what did you do?" Richard asked.

"Well, I gave him another map and told him to tell me orally where places were."

"Did that work?" Brenda, his science teacher, asked.

"Well, it worked a little but I still thought we could do better. After the quiz, he told me that he was still having trouble deciding what each of the countries were and that he still got a lot of them confused. He said that he could see the map in his head but that he still had a hard time getting started when he was faced with the actual map. I didn't feel like I had figured out the problem yet."

"Good grief, Laura," Cindy sighed. "You sure did spend a lot of time and effort on this thing with Jack."

"I know," Laura smiled. "But I was curious. I wanted to figure out how I could get through to him."

"Did you figure it out?" Cindy asked.

"I think I did," Laura said slowly. "I gave him the map again. This time, I asked him to look at the whole map and then cover up a third of the map. After he filled out that third of the map, he was to cover it up and work on the next third, and then do the same thing for the last third. When he did that, he got an 80 percent."

The team discussed Laura's technique and how it might work in their own classes. After the meeting, I asked Laura how she was able to figure out what Jack needed and why she spent so much time trying.

She shrugged. "I didn't feel right having a kid in my class fail time and time again. If he was failing, then it meant that I hadn't found the right way to get through to him yet. So, I kept trying until I figured it out."

That's the power of having high expectations of ourselves. When we do, we will keep trying with a student long after we might have otherwise given up, not because we are propelled by some blind belief in that student, but because we are propelled by the very real belief in ourselves.

Getting Started

Remember that expectations have more to do with you than with your students.

1. To raise your expectations of yourself, you must raise both your values and your beliefs.

2. To raise your values, learn to maintain unwavering faith in what is important.

3. To raise your beliefs, first confront the brutal facts.

4. Be sure to tend to both sides of the equation in order to maintain your high expectations and extend them to the students.

4

Support Your Students

True learning is figuring out how to use what you already know in order to go beyond what you already think.

Jerome Bruner

When I first started teaching, I never ate lunch. At least, not during my lunch time. I was too busy working with students (individually and in small groups) reteaching material, tutoring, and otherwise remediating their understanding of something I wished they had understood the first time. Sometimes, I even had a backlog of students waiting for my help and attention. It seemed like a never-ending cycle.

I thought that if I just did a better job explaining things in class, I could cut down on the number of students waiting for me during lunch and after school. So I adjusted how I delivered my lectures, I refined my handouts and worksheets, I even used more wait time when asking questions. But nothing stopped the endless line of students needing my extra help.

I couldn't work any harder than I was already working and there didn't seem to be enough hours in the day to plan my lessons, teach my lessons, grade student work, and individually tutor students on what they didn't get the first time. I was so frustrated that I began to resent my students and begrudged the very help I knew they needed. Especially when, test after test, they did not seem to be improving or improving fast enough. I even began to blame them.

They weren't studying hard enough, I reasoned, or they were too far behind and would never catch up.

Eventually I learned a better way. But not until I had spent years working harder and harder trying to remediate my students and becoming more and more frustrated and disillusioned. If only I had understood then how to uncover confusion and be more proactive in my support. If only I had known how to combat the "Curse of Knowledge."

Common Practice

Typically, in schools, we give an assignment, test students on their mastery of the assignment, give a grade, and then, when students show that they haven't mastered our carefully crafted assignment, teach. It's a pattern that is based in what Chip and Dan Heath (2007) call the "Curse of Knowledge." In their book *Made to Stick*, they relate an experiment conducted by Elizabeth Newton that illustrates perfectly the classroom dance we do each day because of the Curse of Knowledge.

Dr. Newton designed a game where she took a group of people and separated them into two groups. One group was assigned to be the "tappers" and the other group was assigned to be the "listeners." The tappers' job was to pick a song from a list of well known songs such as "Happy Birthday" and "Twinkle, Twinkle Little Star," and tap out the song for the listeners. The listeners' job was to guess the song being tapped.

Dr. Newton asked the tappers to predict how many times their listeners would guess correctly. The tappers predicted that the listeners would guess correctly at least half of the time. The task seemed easy enough. How could you not get "Happy Birthday" or "The Star Spangled Banner?" Everyone knows those songs.

It seemed like an easy task, guessing the song being tapped, but it was not. In fact, out of the 120 songs that were tapped out, the listeners only guessed right 3 times.

Why could the listeners identify the song correctly only 3 times out of 120?

The problem was what the Heath brothers call the Curse of Knowledge. You see, the listeners did not know ahead of time what song was being tapped. So, when the tappers began, the listeners heard what seemed like a disconnected set of taps on the table. The tappers, on the other hand, knew what song they were tapping and were actually singing the song in their heads as they tapped it out on the table. When they were tapping, they could not imagine what it was like for the listeners because while the listeners were hearing isolated taps on the table, the tappers were hearing a song.

That's the curse in the Curse of Knowledge. Once we know something, it is hard to understand what it is like to not know it. Our knowledge makes it almost impossible for us to imagine what it is like to lack that knowledge.

The Curse of Knowledge plays out every day in the classroom. We teachers are diligently tapping out the Pythagorean theorem or the principles of the Magna Carta and, if we are not careful, all our students may hear are a set of disconnected taps on the board.

It gets even worse. Once we realize that students don't understand our taps, we tap harder. We tap at lunch and before and after school. We keep tapping instead of going over to the students and humming the song in their ears.

Although you cannot unlearn what you already know, there is something you can do about the Curse of Knowledge. You can be proactive about supporting students so that you catch them before they fail.

The Principle

If we truly want our students to be successful, then we cannot afford to leave to chance what we will do when a student does not learn. We need to be proactive about developing interventions before students fail.

That is not, when you think about it, a radical notion, but what they typically teach you in school to do is this: Plan a lesson. Teach the lesson. When students do not understand the lesson or fail the test, remediate students.

But waiting for students to fail before you intervene is one of the most passive stances you can take as a teacher. It says that once students fail, you can do things to help them improve—hold remediation sessions, reteach the material, offer alternative assignments or extra credit—but there is very little you can do to prevent them from failing in the first place. This stance focuses our attention on remediation rather than on prevention. So, instead of proactively supporting students before they falter, we prepare extra worksheets, plan to stay after school, hire extra staff to tutor students, set up extra study halls. We plan our lessons and once we find students unsuccessful, *then* we intervene.

In essence then, we plan for students to fail.

But what if we planned differently? What if we put measures in place in our lesson to catch students before they failed? What if we carefully monitored students throughout the lesson so that we could intervene when they first start to flounder?

Once we realize that there is something we can do to prevent students from failing in the first place, our strategies change. We plan differently. We teach differently.

Master teachers know that once a student fails, it is almost too late to begin implementing a solution. The solution, if it is going to work, needs to be in place before students begin to fail.

Proactive support is merely a matter of matching our teaching style to students' learning styles. It is both about providing challenge and meeting the students where they are, and it is rooted in the belief that all of our students can achieve at high levels given the right conditions.

Practicing the Principle

The master teacher mindset sees teaching as a matter of specifying what students must know, subtracting what it is that they already know, and teaching them the rest. It's the "teaching them the rest" part that requires the most planning and skill. Master teachers are proactive in their interventions even to the point of setting up a clear intervention plan before they ever teach the lesson. They think about potential problems students may have before they begin a unit and put supports in place for students to help mitigate these problems and make it more likely that students will be successful. Throughout the unit, they are vigilant about looking for areas of confusion and clearing these up as quickly as possible. They analyze each learning task in order to identify the prerequisite skills or knowledge students need and then break down complex tasks and processes in manageable chunks. Once students have developed some proficiency, master teachers gradually remove these supports so that students eventually master the learning goals on their own. And for those students who have already mastered the learning goals, master teachers provide additional support so that these students remain challenged and can deepen and enrich their learning.

Set Up an Intervention Plan Before Students Need It

One of the best ways to be proactive in supporting students before they begin to fail is to develop an intervention plan that is concrete and specific. It's one thing to say that when students start to slip, they will be required to meet with the teacher, but it is not effective if you do not have a clear understanding of why you are meeting and what you hope to accomplish during the meeting. It is another thing altogether to say that when a student's GPA falls to 76 percent, the student will sit down with the teacher to review his grade tracking sheet and discuss his difficulties. The teacher and the student will then develop a plan with shared accountability for how the student will raise his GPA within the next two weeks as well as consequences if the student does not fulfill his side of the bargain. This type of intervention plan has four components that will ultimately make it more successful.

First, the plan is developed before students begin to fail. It is outlined in the course syllabus, shared with parents during back-to-school night, sent home in the class newsletter the first week of school, or posted on the course Web site. It can even be developed into a contract. Students and their parents know from the beginning the purpose of the intervention plan, which students will receive intervention, when the intervention will take place, what interventions will be put into place, and what responsibilities will be shared by the teacher, the parent, and the student.

Second, the plan has a red flag mechanism that triggers action. A red flag mechanism is when you take information about students' progress and turn it into something that cannot be ignored. In the case of the example above, falling below 76 percent is the red flag. Notice that the red flag is concrete and objective. You don't wait until you think the student is struggling or until the student comes to you with a problem. The moment the student's GPA falls below 76 percent, the intervention plan goes into action. This removes the guesswork and prevents students from slipping through the cracks. Notice too that the red flag is focused on academic concerns rather than behavior. It is designed to signal that a student is not mastering the objectives of your course rather than address behavior problems. (For strategies to address behavior concerns, see Chapter 7).

The third element of an effective intervention plan is that once the red flag is triggered, there is already a concrete procedure for what comes next. Again, it removes the guesswork for both the student and the teacher. You have thought through what types of interventions will be most effective with students ahead of time and automatically begin applying these interventions the moment a student triggers a red flag. Of course, as you work with students you can customize the interventions to better meet their needs, but you have some basic interventions in place so that students can immediately start to get the help and support they need. These interventions are not punitive or busy work; they are designed to get students back on track as early as possible.

The fourth element of an effective intervention plan is shared account-ability. The teacher plays a specific role, but the student also has responsibility for making this plan work. These roles are clearly outlined and students are held accountable for doing their part. Notice too that the intervention is not voluntary. You do not wait for students to ask for help nor do you give them a choice about whether they receive help. Students are required to engage in the intervention and their role is clearly outlined for them.

An effective intervention plan is really a systematic way of supporting students as soon as they begin to falter. It signals to students and parents that you are invested in your students' success and that they have some recourse when they struggle. By putting the plan in place early, you make it less likely that students will fail later on.

> ### Yes, but... I don't have time to meet one-on-one with every student who is failing.
>
> Intervening with students does not require that you meet one on one with each student. That is the beauty of an intervention cycle. If you set up structures ahead of time, you can often automate many of the initial interventions and get students back on track before they require more intensive one-on-one intervention.
>
> Think about how can you automate your interventions. Is there some computer program or online tutorial or simulation you can use? Perhaps there is a workbook or an extra handout. Maybe your school offers tutoring services through a club or through outside volunteers. Look for interventions that will help your students but that do not always require one-on-one sessions with you so that you can intervene with more than one student at a time.

To develop an effective intervention plan, ask yourself five questions:

1. What does mastery look like in your course? Is it a specific GPA? A certain score on a test or series of tests? Successful performance of some learning task? What evidence of mastery have you identified for each unit of study?

2. What would signal that students are not moving successfully toward mastery? In other words, what will be your red flags? How will you systematically look for these red flags? Will you calculate grades once every two weeks, for instance, or identify red flags after each unit test?

3. What interventions will help students get back on the right track?

4. How will you know when students are back on track and no longer need the intervention?

5. How will you communicate this intervention plan to students and parents?

Once you have answered these questions, use Tool 9 in the Appendix to develop your own intervention plan.

Anticipate Confusion

Anticipating confusion means taking steps to clear up confusion before students encounter it. It also means helping students uncover what is not obvious about what we are trying to teach them. This is difficult for us as experts because we have already done the work of making connections and giving meaning to our subject. But for our students, these connections and meaning may not be obvious to them.

A lot of times, we already know where students will be confused. But, rather than clear up this confusion, we play "guess what's on the teacher's mind" with our students. We don't make our expectations clear and we expect them to perform sophisticated academic processes without giving them a model or the proper instruction.

I stopped by Melody's classroom for a few minutes one morning to informally observe her class. When I walked in, she was collecting students' homework assignment from the night before. After she had collected the papers, she said, "Now, here is the right way to do the assignment. I know that many of you last night probably forgot to underline these key words here. And, most of you probably didn't circle these nouns here. And, if experience is correct, you probably didn't see that these two words here were synonyms."

The students looked at the board and groaned. Melody smiled triumphantly and asked, "Am I right?"

Yes, but... I haven't taught this lesson before so I don't know where they will be confused.

Even if you have never taught the lesson before, you can still anticipate where students might be confused. Think about how you first learned that content or that skill and what was initially confusing or difficult for you. Talk to other teachers who have already taught the lesson and ask what parts were difficult or confusing to their students. And think about the common misconceptions or difficulties with your topic. What are some common mistakes almost everyone makes when learning the new skill? What are some common misconceptions many people have about your topic? Finally, give students a pre-assessment to determine what they already know about your topic and what they still need to learn. You can use a traditional paper-and-pencil test or an informal assessment such as a KWL chart or a word splash. Use this information to predict what parts of the lesson or unit will be confusing to students.

She was right alright, but she was also horribly wrong. If she knew what the students were going to get wrong on their homework assignments, why didn't she anticipate their confusion and clear it up before they attempted the assignment? How much more valuable would the assignment have been if she had shown them where they might have tripped up before they attempted the work? Instead, she did the equivalent of a carnival side show where she predicted where students would fail after they had done so. Entertaining? Sure. Useful? Hardly.

How often do we do the same thing? After years of teaching, we know what math problems students are going to miss on the test or which countries on the map they will confuse. We know what mistakes they will make on the essay or during the lab. We know, and yet we don't take measures to help clear up their confusion ahead of time. What if, instead, we anticipated where students would be confused and made sure that we clarified the point before the students made their mistakes? How much more productive might our teaching be?

Anticipating confusion means that we examine each lesson and each learning task to see what parts might give students trouble. Then we take steps to clear up the confusion before students encounter it. That does not mean that we completely sanitize the lesson ahead of time. We want students to grapple with difficult material because doing so will increase and deepen their learning. But we want to make sure that when students do struggle, their struggle is productive. In order to do that, we have to clear up any unnecessary confusion so that students' attention and energy can be focused on their learning.

Try This

• Think about your next assignment. Where might students be confused? If you have taught the assignment before, what mistakes did most of your students make? What trouble spots might exist that will break students' momentum? What material will be hard for students to learn? What common misconceptions might students have that will get in the way? How can you clear up this confusion ahead of time? Will you need to rewrite the directions so that they are less ambiguous? Will you need to teach students a skill before you introduce the assignment? Will you need to break the assignment down into smaller parts so that students can complete one process before moving on to the next? How can you structure the assignment so that students are more successful?

• Provide students with models of what you expect them to do.

• When helping students learn a process, point out the pitfalls and mistakes that are common to the process and show students how to avoid them.

Pinpoint Confusion and Uncover Misconceptions

Although you have anticipated confusion prior to delivering a lesson, there will be times when, in spite of your best efforts, students will still be confused. When this happens, it is not enough to know that students don't understand the material. Before you can effectively intervene, it is also important to know what part of the material they do not understand.

For instance, I was helping out in a math class where the teacher, Paul, was trying to help the students understand how to organize and interpret raw data using mean, median, and mode. He had students enter raw data into an Excel spreadsheet and then use the various functions in Excel to compute the mean, median, and mode. The students struggled with the assignment.

At first we thought that the students were having trouble understanding the concepts, but after taking a closer look, we found out that the students struggled with the assignment not because they did not understand mean, median, and mode, but because they did not understand how to use Microsoft Excel. They could compute mean, median, and mode manually, but struggled with the intricacies of the computer program.

When our students struggle, it may not be for the reasons we think, which is why it is so important to clarify the source of students' confusion. Once you pinpoint exactly where students are confused, you can clarify their confusion and get them back on track by asking probing questions that help you uncover exactly where the student is confused. From there, reexplain only that material which they do not understand and persevere with students until they get it.

There are also times when our students are confused because they come to the learning task with misconceptions that prevent them from understanding the material.

This type of confusion is not as easy to uncover because sometimes students can get the right answer without really understanding the material.

A few years ago, I had some friends over one Saturday night for a game party. About midway through the evening, someone pulled out a collection of brain teasers and suggested we try them. We each took a sheet and got to work. You could feel the tension in the room as everyone attacked the problems. What had been a rowdy group of young adults noisily competing and ribbing each other became a studious group of young scholars earnestly marking their papers. The room was absolutely silent for the entire 10 minutes. When the time was up, we anxiously came together to go over the answers.

This was a highly competitive group so everyone was invested in getting the answers right. The winner of the game would get the bragging rights of being the undisputed smartest person in the room. We all coveted the title.

The competition was close. As we went over each answer, the score shifted only slightly. In fact, we all remained neck and neck and in the end it all came down to the last question. "A hunter left his cabin and hiked two miles south, then turned and hiked two miles west, shot a bear, and then hiked two miles north back to his cabin. What color was the bear?"

What color was the bear? You've got to be kidding me right? Most of us took a guess and said either black or brown. But Justin said, "No, the bear was white."

David, who was functioning as our informal MC, pointed at Justin and said, "You're right! The bear was white."

A collective groan erupted in the room. How on earth, we all wanted to know, did Justin know the bear was white?

"Well," Justin began shyly, "I noticed that all of the numbers in the problem were the number two."

"Go on," we prodded.

"And, on a job application, when they ask you about your race, white is usually the second option. So, I figured the bear must be white."

Of course that wasn't the explanation the brain teaser game provided. The real explanation had something to do with the fact that the only place on earth where you could walk in that pattern and end up back where you started was on the north pole and the only bears on the north pole were polar bears. But, Justin hadn't used any of that reasoning. He got the answer right, but he didn't really understand the problem.

What's so bad about that? After all, he may not have used the so-called "correct" reasoning but he did get the answer right, and in the end, isn't that all that mattered?

Not necessarily. You see, Justin's right answer made it appear that he understood the concept, but his reasoning was not transferable. What if the problem had said the hunter walked four miles in each direction instead of two? The correct answer would have been the same but Justin's reasoning would have led him to an entirely different conclusion. Although he got the answer right in that instance, given a similar problem or situation, there is no guarantee he would have performed the same way.

Students can take guesses and get the answer right sometime or they can arrive at the right answer using the wrong route. While that might help them on that particular test, in a different situation they would not be as successful. If, however, they truly understand, then no matter what the details of the question, they will still be able to arrive at the right answer. That's why it is important to do more than just check to see whether students got the answer right or wrong. Uncovering confusion will help you find out if they truly understood.

Yes, but... once I figure out where they are confused, I have a hard time finding a way to clear up their confusion.

Knowing how to clear up students' confusion so that they understand the concept you are trying to teach requires two things. First, you must have a range of explanatory devices available so that you are more likely to find one that will help your students understand when they become confused. Second, and most importantly, you need a thorough understanding of your subject. Even if you don't have a huge repertoire of explanatory devices at your disposal, if you understand your subject, you can find alternate explanations, examples, demonstrations, and other ways to help students understand it. So, if you are having trouble clearing up your students' confusion, make sure that you understand the subject yourself and work on refining your subject area knowledge. Doing so will reveal other ways you can use to explain the material and help students understand.

Try This

• When students are unsuccessful on an assignment, ask the following error analysis questions to figure out exactly why they were unsuccessful:
    o What is the key error?
    o What is the probable reason the student made the error?
    o How can I help the student avoid this error in the future?
• When planning an assignment, think about the implied skills or competencies students will need in order to complete the assignment successfully (i.e., using a microscope, understanding how to use a word processing program, basic keyboarding skills, knowing how to read a particular type of graph, etc.). Check to see that students have these skills prior to giving them the assignment, and for students who do not have these skills, provide a tutorial or mini-lesson to bring them up to speed or provide other supports to help students access the assignment without having these skills (such as word recognition software for students with poor keyboarding skills).

• In order to uncover students' misconceptions, have students describe their thinking about a concept. Ask questions such as "How did you get that answer? What steps did you use to solve this problem? Why did you choose this approach? What does this word mean to you? As you listen, look for clues to students' assumptions and logic and use these clues to uncover what misconceptions students may have about the subject. Then work to explicitly clear up these misconceptions by reexplaining the material using the students' misconceptions as a starting point.

• Use what Jay McTighe calls the "three-minute pause." Stop every 10 or 15 minutes and ask students to summarize what they have learned so far (For a great list of summarizing activities, check out the book *Summarizers* by Jonathan Saphier). Listen to their summaries and identify where students are still confused. Clear up any confusion before moving on.

• Don't just ask students for the answers; have them explain their thinking, show their work, or otherwise demonstrate how they arrived at their answer. During class discussions, ask follow up questions such as "How did you get that answer?" or "What steps did you use to solve that problem?"

• True-false quizzes are great pre-assessments to check for misunderstanding. List common misunderstandings of your subject and ask students to rate them true or false.

Demystify the Process

Another way to reduce the amount of confusion students experience during the learning process is to make the learning process more transparent.

We are not only obligated to teach our discipline; we are also obligated to teach students strategies that will make them more successful in our discipline.

Often, we don't realize that the things we take for granted after years of being in school are a mystery for our students. We admonish students to study but we don't teach them how to study. We tell them to read a chapter, but we don't teach them how to identify the important information. We give them tests without ever explaining to them the logic of test taking and test design. We tell them to write a lab report and give them a format but we don't tell them why we write lab reports or how to use a lab report to enhance their understanding of a particular topic. Although our students have become very adept at performing academic tasks, do they really understand why they are doing what they are doing or how to use what they are doing to exponentially increase their learning?

The key to demystifying the academic process is to make the process as explicit as possible. This can be accomplished by explaining all of the steps in the process in a clear way that leaves no doubt as to your meaning. First, clearly explain to students the purpose of each assignment or activity. How will this new activity help students reach the objectives of the course? It is also important to show students how each new activity or assignment fits with what they have done in the past so that they can make connections between what they are learning and what they have learned already. Additionally, explain to students how the skills they are learning can be used in other contexts. Finally, provide all of the necessary steps in written directions so that students know exactly how you want an assignment completed. In this way, you avoid making assumptions about what the students know already and you make explicit the necessary steps in the process so that students can then internalize them.

Every year, every student in my grade level was required to write a 10-page research paper, and every year my colleagues and I struggled to drag our students through the process. After one particularly brutal year, I decided that there had to be another way. I was also in graduate school at the time and regularly wrote 20- or 30-page papers. The next time I had a paper due, I paid attention to the process I used. Then I used that process to break down the research paper my students had to write.

The next year, I handed my students a research paper packet. In that packet, I explained, was everything they needed to write their research papers. On the cover of the packet was a breakdown of each part of the research process, a date when it was due, and a line for their grade. That way, students could track their own process toward a final paper with many checkpoints along the way. The packet also contained an explanation and a model of how to create and organize bibliography cards and note cards, a skeleton outline, a model of a first draft and works cited page, and explanations of how to move from one part of the process to the next. I also explained to them that rather than write 10 pages at once, we were going to write five smaller papers that would average about two pages each. The first paper would be the introduction and thesis (one page). The next paper would become our background section (two pages). The third paper would become our body (four pages), the fourth paper would become our refutation (two pages) and the fifth paper would become our conclusion (one page). I developed a system for each part of the process.

Yes, but… isn't this just dumbing down?

Many worries about "dumbing down" are rooted in the belief that students must start acting like experts as soon as they are introduced to the material. This is an unrealistic expectation and flies in the face of what we know about how human beings learn.

When students are first exposed to a new idea or concept, the best way to help them understand it is to make it as concrete as possible. Over time, the ultimate goal is to help them abstract more and more, because experts deal with abstraction. But before a person can move to abstraction, they must first experience the idea or concept as concretely as possible. Concreteness helps us understand. We use a concrete idea and build an abstract concept on top of it. Concreteness is the foundation for abstraction.

When you are introducing students to new concepts or processes, demystifying them by breaking them down into concrete ideas or steps builds better understanding and helps students integrate the concepts or process into their thinking. Once they are integrated, the students can begin to think about them at an even higher level.

Concreteness does not dumb down what you are trying to teach. Instead, it provides a foundation on which you can build more abstract ideas later on.

That spring, not only did all of my students write a 10-page research paper but their papers were very good. Years later, I still have students contact me and tell me how they continue to use that process in college and graduate school. By demystifying the process for students, I was able to help them tackle something they thought was impossible and develop systems not just for the work in my class, but for the work they faced in other courses and other contexts.

In the movie *The Wizard of Oz*, Dorothy and her friends were terrified of the wizard until Toto pulled back the cloth and revealed that the wizard was nothing more than a machine operated by a tiny little man. Suddenly, the wizard didn't seem so scary. In the same way, many students are intimidated by high standards because they haven't a clue how they will ever reach them. It is our job to pull back the veil and show them the steps to reaching the standard. When we do, our high standards suddenly seem achievable.

Try This

- Share with students the learning strategies you use yourself. What steps do you take to solve a problem, or study, or learn a new concept? What strategies do you use to practice? What kinds of tools do you use to help you learn (note-taking methods, graphic organizers, mental imagery, etc.).

- Teach students how to use various organizational, rehearsal, and mnemonic devices to learn and memorize important material. Explain to students why each device works or the type of thinking it supports. Then discuss with students why they might choose a particular strategy. Finally, let each student choose a strategy that works best for them.

- Show students how to take effective notes by a) providing them with an objective for each reading assignment or lecture (to memorize material, to recognize important characteristics, to organize or classify material, to paraphrase important points, etc.); b) showing them an effective way to structure or organize the information (outline form, Cornell notes, main idea, summary, etc.); and c) showing them how to use their notes to study.

- Break complex tasks down into manageable chunks and a logical sequence. Use a flowchart, checklist, or a decision-making heuristic to help students see how all the parts work together.

- It isn't enough to simply model a process or behavior to students. Explain to students beforehand what they will be seeing and to what they should pay attention. As you are demonstrating, explain what you are doing. And, when students try the process or behavior themselves, cue them along the way.

- One of the best ways to make a concept more concrete is to have students create some sort of visual representation of the concept. You can have students make physical models or pictorial representations of the concept, or act out the concept. For instance, once I was trying to teach students the logical fallacies. For years, I had students memorize the definitions of the various fallacies to no avail. One year, I asked students to draw a picture that represented a logical fallacy. After drawing their pictures and sharing them with the class, students understood and could recognize the fallacies.

• Another way to make ideas more concrete is to create, or have students create analogies between the abstract idea and something more concrete. For instance, you can create an "Analogy Box" filled with random objects such as a bar of soap, a spool of thread, a toy train, etc. When you are trying to help students move from concreteness to more abstraction, have students reach into the box and pull out a random object. Then ask students to work in pairs or triads to come up with an analogy between the item and the idea they are trying to understand (e.g., democracy is like a spool of thread because _____).

• Have students organize information using graphic organizers that visually represent how ideas or concepts are connected. You can provide them with the organizers or have them create their own.

• To help students move from concrete thinking to more abstract thinking, begin lessons by making an idea as concrete as possible. Once students understand the idea, gradually shift to more abstract concepts by asking students "what if" questions, having students apply what they have learned to unfamiliar situations, or introducing ambiguity into the lesson.

Gradually Remove Supports as Students Improve

One of the hardest jobs we have as teachers is managing students' frustration. It's like playing a game of Jenga. Pull out the wrong piece and the whole structure comes crashing down. The way to manage frustration is to *gradually* remove supports. That means that when you introduce the support, tell students that it is only a temporary tool and that at some point, they will be expected to do the work without it. In that way, you set realistic expectations and help the students not get too attached to the support. Then, as you are removing the support, help students understand that they no longer need it because they have developed the internal resources to be able to complete the task without support. Coach students through their frustration by pointing out what they can now do on their own.

This is the step that many of us neglect. We may provide students with support but we don't include in our plans a strategy for gradually removing that support once students become more proficient. Removing the support is a crucial step. Otherwise, we make students dependent on our supports and never help them learn to do things on their own.

Many of us also err by changing the learning task, making it easier at the beginning and more difficult as students acquire skills. A better approach is to keep the learning task the same but manage the student's role in the learning task so that at the beginning the students are receiving more help and support, but as the students develop proficiency, their role increases and they become more independent, until the students are working completely on their own. Don't change the task, change the students' role in relationship to the task. Support should only be given for those parts of the tasks that are beyond the learner's current capacity.

The key to gradually removing supports is to provide students with a manageable challenge where the task is just beyond a student's current capacity but not so challenging that a student cannot complete the task with minimal support. This sounds a lot easier than it really is, of course, but there are a few steps you can take to determine when you should begin to remove support. First, identify what each support you have in place is intended to do so that once students demonstrate that they can do it on their own, you know that you no longer need that support. For instance, if you have given students a graphic organizer to help them read their textbooks and take effective notes, after students have used the organizer a few times and learned to think about their text in a particular way, give them a less detailed organizer for the next chapter, and then for the next chapter ask them to create their own. Finally, you can get to the point where you assign the chapter with no organizer at all.

Next, look for ways to gradually wean students off of the supports you have put in place rather than removing them all at once. For example, if you have allowed students to use their notes on their quizzes, announce that for the next quiz, students will not be allowed to use their notes but that you will give them an extra five minutes at the start of the quiz to create a note sheet from memory that they can then use on the quiz. Then, a few quizzes later, you can just give students the quiz without any notes or time to write their notes down.

Finally, allow some room for struggle. When you first remove supports, some students may protest or seem to struggle. Resist the temptation to rush right back in with the support. Instead, allow the student a chance to grapple with the new challenge a bit and coach the student on ways to meet the challenge.

Learning to be comfortable with a little struggle will help students learn to effectively manage challenges.

Try This

- To help students to eventually be able to perform on their own under testing conditions, match practice conditions to those students will eventually face on the test.
- Once students come close to mastering a task, provide them with challenging practice that pushes them beyond the original demands of the task.
- Vary practice activities so that students can learn to apply what they are learning to unfamiliar and new situations.

Support the Learning of Students Who Have Already Mastered the Learning Goals

Support goes both ways. Although much of this chapter has been devoted to helping students who struggle, students who are not struggling with the material also need support structures to help them stay engaged, to offer them appropriate additional challenges, and to enrich and deepen their learning. In the same way that you need to proactively develop an intervention plan for students who fall behind, you need an intervention plan for students who are ahead of the rest of the class.

The same steps apply. You still need to decide what is mastery, but your red flags will signal that a student has *exceeded* mastery. You will also need to decide what interventions you will put into place once a student triggers a red flag. This does not necessarily mean more work for the student, but it may mean different work or adding more ambiguity or complexity to existing assignments. For instance, if a student demonstrates that she has mastered the skill of writing an effective hypothesis, you could make the task more complex for her by requiring her to create a hypothesis with two or more independent variables.

In the same way that you have to work to uncover misconceptions and pinpoint confusion for struggling students, you need to look for opportunities for ambiguity and complexity in the material for students who have already mastered the learning goals. Ambiguity can typically be found as you work to anticipate confusion. Those areas that are potentially confusing are typically ambiguous in nature. Thus, while you will work to mitigate some of this ambiguity for students who are struggling with it, you will intentionally allow other students to grapple with multiple meanings and sort them into significant patterns on their own. The goal is to help all students learn to deal with ambiguity but students become ready to handle ambiguity at different rates. The key is to determine whether unraveling ambiguous content will help advance students' learning or be an impediment to their learning. If it will impede student's progress, clarify any confusion that the ambiguity may create. If it will advance students' progress, support their efforts to deal with ambiguity on their own.

Complexity refers to ideas that are interacting and overlapping. Often we deal with complexity when we are working to pinpoint confusion. Those ideas that are most complex are also the ideas that are most confusing. But while we need to unpack these ideas for some students, other students may benefit from having to unpack these ideas themselves. If students have already mastered the learning goals of your content, you can resist the urge to simplify some of the more complex ideas of the unit and provide supports to help them grapple with the complexity of the ideas themselves.

What do these supports look like? They look a lot like the supports that we put in place for struggling students. We are not talking about additional work for the teacher here. In the same way that you have to demystify the academic process for students who are struggling, you must also demystify the academic process for students who are excelling and in need of more challenge. Show students how to untangle complex or ambiguous ideas. Show students how to organize their notes so that they can notice patterns, elaborate on what they are learning, and marshal evidence to support their own hypotheses or theories. As students get better, gradually withdraw these supports so that they learn to learn on their own. There is really no difference between supporting struggling students and supporting students who have met or exceeded the learning goals. Both groups of students need the same proactive support mechanisms in order to maximize their learning potential.

Try This

- Provide students with opportunities to represent complex or ambiguous concepts or problems visually without using words. This will help them think about the material in a different way and help them work through the complexity or ambiguity.
- Develop an intervention plan for students who master the material early. Decide on your red flags (100 percent on three consecutive quizzes, a 95-100 percent overall class average, etc.) and specify what you will do once a red flag is triggered (for example, introduce more complex material such as primary documents or more ambiguous math problems with multiple ways of arriving at the answer). Publish this intervention plan in the same way that you publish your plan for students who struggle.
- Sometimes student interest will propel them to master one aspect of a subject or unit. Therefore, do not base your assessment of mastery only on students' overall performance. If you notice that a student is particularly motivated to master some aspect of your curriculum, capitalize on this interest by putting supports in place to further the student's study of that topic.
- Continue to demystify the academic process showing students how experts in your particular discipline or field think and behave. Or, ask students to conduct an interview with an expert or research experts to see how they behave and think in a particular field in order to further demystify the process.

Applying the Principle

When I first started teaching, my process looked something like this:

1. Teach the skill.
2. Give students an assignment or test to measure their mastery of the skill.
3. Students complete the assignment or test.
4. Grade the assignment or test.
5. Return papers.
6. Move on.

It was the process I had undergone as a student and it was the process I was taught in my teacher preparation classes. On the surface, it seemed to work.

But, as I gained more experience, I began to dread grading those papers. I already knew what mistakes the students would make and what I was going to have to do to undo the damage.

Every year, I especially dreaded the first essays of the semester. I knew that they would be pretty awful. And, every year, I would grit my teeth as I graded them, lamenting over how much work I would have to do to get my students ready for the end of the year assessments.

One year, I decided to do things differently. I assigned the same paper I always did, but this time, I wrote the paper first and in it, I made all the mistakes I knew my students were going to make. About a week before the assignment was due, I passed out copies of that paper to my students and told them that I had written the paper and that it was an example of what their final drafts should look like.

As we read the paper aloud in class, I could tell that my students were a little confused. After we finished the paper, I asked them, "So, what do you think?" Politely, they said that they thought it was pretty well-written. Some students even sincerely complimented the paper and said that they only wished they could write so well.

"Let's take another look," I coaxed, and we began with the first paragraph. "Is that a compelling opening sentence?"

"Not really," one brave soul offered.

"Well what would you do to fix it?" I asked, and we were off. I took out my laptop and projected the draft onto a screen. I turned on the track changes feature in the word processing program and students were able to see what we struck out and what we changed. As we made changes in the draft, I inserted comments explaining why we were making the changes.

We spent the entire class period revising that draft. After we were done, I posted my first draft, the messy revised draft with the strike outs and the comments, and the clean final draft onto our class website. Then, together we used the rubric and graded the final draft. I posted the graded draft online too. Now students had not only a final draft posted, they had an example of how we got to the final draft.

When I collected their papers the next week, my students were so excited. They told me how their first drafts had looked a lot like mine but that they had used the messy revised draft to compare to their own drafts and had caught a lot of mistakes.

I was excited to grade their papers too. And, when I graded them they were far superior to what I was used to seeing in students' first papers. I was thrilled. Because I had anticipated where they would be confused, and demystified the writing process by explicitly showing them how to revise their papers, my students had written papers far beyond what they might have written otherwise. Because I intervened before they failed, my students were able to successfully master the learning task.

Getting Started

1. To be more proactive about supporting students prior to the lesson, anticipate confusion, set up an intervention plan that includes red flag mechanisms, and look for ways to demystify the academic process.

2. During instruction, help prevent confusion by moving from the concrete to the more abstract and by providing models. When students do become confused, work to unpack their confusion through targeted questioning and error analysis.

3. The moment students trigger a red flag, begin implementing the measures you outlined in your intervention plan.

4. As students become more proficient, gradually remove supports.

5. Look for ways to support students who have already mastered the learning goals in order to deepen and extend their learning.

5

Use Effective Feedback

We use the general term *assessment* to refer to all those activities undertaken by teachers—and by their students in assessing
themselves—that provide information to be used as feedback to
modify teaching and learning activities.

Paul Black and Dylan Wiliam

When I first started teaching, I didn't understand the true purpose of grading. I knew I had to assess students, but I didn't understand how to use the grades or the test results to guide what I should do next.

Typically, I assigned homework and in-class worksheets which I would often have the students grade for each other. When I was about 80 percent finished with a unit, I would start looking around for a test I could use. If I found a test, I would change those test items that didn't quite match what I'd taught and give the test to my students. If I didn't find a test, I would make one up. Many times, as I was preparing the test, I would discover that I hadn't taught something I'd planned to teach or that I hadn't taught something on the test. I would usually excuse students from that item and make a mental note to teach that concept the next time around.

My quizzes were even more haphazard. If I taught something new, I gave a quiz the next day to make sure that they had learned it. Often, I made up the quizzes right before class. I graded the quizzes and returned them to the students all the while admonishing them that they needed to study better or warning them that they had better straighten up before the test. Sometimes, I used quizzes to punish students for misbehavior. "If you keep this up," I'd threaten, "I am going to give a pop quiz." Other times, I used quizzes for classroom management by starting class with a quiz to get my students to settle down. There was a time when I started every class with a five-point quiz to make sure that they had done the reading the night before. It was the only way that I could get them to do their homework, or so I thought.

About once a week, I would hand back assignments to students. Again, I really had no system. I collected work, graded it as fast as I could, recorded the grades, and handed back the papers with little comment. Students quickly glanced at their grades, shoved their papers into their notebooks (or tossed them into the trash can), and went on with their lives. At interim time, I added up my grades, sent progress reports home to the parents, and waited for the phone calls. I was often surprised that a student who I thought was doing fine was actually failing. Or, a student who I thought was failing was not doing nearly as badly as I thought.

Although I was doing what I thought I was supposed to do—assigning work, grading it, and passing it back (with comments no less!)—I was not using my assignments, assessments, or my comments to students in a way that meaningfully altered my instructional practice or my students' likelihood of success. I had failed to see the power of effective feedback.

Common Practice

Traditionally, the purpose of grading was to measure students' progress and mastery of materials. According to Ken O'Conner (2002) in his book *How to Grade for Learning,* grades are typically used to

- communicate to parents how well their children are achieving
- determine promotion, graduation, extra-curricular eligibility, and academic program admission
- provide incentives
- make guidance and placement decisions

While assignments, assessments, and grades are typically used to evaluate learning, rarely are they used to facilitate learning itself.

Many of us are still unclear about why we grade, what our grades really mean, and how we can use assessments to help our students learn. As a result, we develop assessment practices that can actually interfere with students' learning. When we use grades to control students ("If I don't grade it, they won't do it") or to reward students ("He worked so hard so I will give him a B for effort") or to punish students ("She turned her assignment in one day late so she will earn a zero"), we undermine our goals and make the grade, rather than learning, as the end.

We all know that we have to somehow assess students. It's one of the first things they teach you about teaching. We practice creating worksheets and writing effective homework assignments. We experiment with different grading techniques. We even take tests on how well we can write a test. Everyone has to give class work, homework, and tests, we're taught. How, after all, will we assign grades?

But assessing students is not nearly as important as how we use the assessment data. If we just grade assignments and never use that information to help inform our instruction, we have wasted our students' time and we have reinforced to students the false notion that the only reason they are learning the material is to take a test. In addition, we have missed an opportunity to help our students see why what they are learning is meaningful.

The Principle

Assessment—assignments, quizzes, tests, and informal measures of student progress—provide valuable feedback that lets us and our students know whether we have met our learning goals. But, the purpose of assessments and grading is more than to simply measure students' progress. When used correctly, assessments also provide feedback that actually facilitates the learning process and helps students master the material. In fact, Robert Marzano (2003) reports that giving effective feedback is one of the most powerful ways to improve student achievement. Thus, rather than be an evaluation of the learning process, assessment results can become a part of the learning process itself.

The feedback that you provide students about their progress (typically in the form of grades and comments) has a powerful influence on how students learn. Carol Dweck (2006) in her book *Mindset* illustrates the power of feedback in her discussion of the two different kinds of students. The first kind, performance-oriented students, sees intelligence as fixed. These students believe that they are born with certain abilities and there is nothing they can do to change them. The second type of student is learning oriented and sees intelligence as incremental and something that can be changed through effective effort.

What is fascinating about Dweck's work is that there is a huge difference between the way these two orientations affect student achievement. Performance-oriented students avoid new challenges, are more likely to cheat, and are more likely to become crippled by failure because they see failure as a personal indictment of their intelligence and a fatal threat to their self-esteem.

Learning-oriented students, however, see failure as an opportunity to learn. They love new challenges because they see these challenges as a chance to stretch and grow. These children are willing to take risks and to try new things because they don't see failure as a threat to their self-esteem.

The good news about Dweck's research is that you can train children with performance goals to adopt learning goals through the kind of feedback we provide.

For the most part, the feedback we give students is evaluative. We mark answers right or wrong, we give final grades, we divide performance into pass or fail. Such feedback casts us in the role of evaluator rather than that of resource or guide. Rarely do we give feedback showing students where they went wrong and how they can improve.

Even when we write extensive comments on students' papers, those comments are rarely helpful. We put things like "vague," and "sp" (for a misspelled word), or we mark grammatical errors. We cross out unnecessary steps in solving an equation or write in missed ones. Our comments point out student errors but they rarely show students how they can improve their performance next time.

Effective feedback, however, shows where we are in relationship to the objectives *and* what we need to do to get there. It helps our students see the assignments and tasks we give them as opportunities to learn and grow rather than as assaults on their self-concept. And, effective feedback allows us to tap into a powerful means of not only helping students learn, but helping them get better at learning.

Feedback is all around us. But, it is how we collect, interpret, communicate, and use feedback that makes the difference.

Applying the Principle

Master teachers use every assignment, assessment, and grade as feedback, both to themselves and to their students. They gather as much feedback as possible through a variety of assessments, and set up red flag mechanisms that help them objectively interpret the feedback their assignments and assessments render. They analyze this feedback to assess where students are in relationship to the objective and revise their instructional approach in order to better meet students' needs. Master teachers also provide students with feedback designed to coach them toward a better performance. Master teachers help students collect and analyze their own data and understand what their grades really mean. And, by showing students how to use even their failures as feedback and giving them opportunities to reassess, master teachers help students learn from their failures and use more effective effort to succeed in the future.

Collect Feedback from a Variety of Sources

When most people think of assessment, they immediately think of tests. How can you blame them when the emphasis these days seems to be on helping students pass tests and therefore make Adequate Yearly Progress (AYP) under the guidelines of the No Child Left Behind laws?

But assessment, when you use it right, goes beyond testing. Sure, testing is a part of assessment, but there are many other assessment options. You could use performance tasks, for example, or informal measures of students' progress such as oral responses during a discussion or Socratic seminar. You should be using a variety of assessment techniques.

There is an overreliance on paper and pencil tests these days. The reasons many teachers and politicians advocate these kinds of tests is that they are easy to grade and easy to quantify. But frequently these tests are artificial, or contrived, or only test one aspect of knowledge. If you want to see if your students truly understand the material and have mastered your objectives, you should use a range of assessment.

Sometimes the pendulum swings too far in the other direction and teachers rely almost exclusively on performance tasks rather than on traditional tests. Often considered to be a more authentic form of assessment, performance tasks can quickly become inauthentic if they are forced or contrived. I have seen many well-intentioned teachers create performance tasks that are clunky and artificial for the sake of providing students with something more "real," regardless of whether the task was the best or more efficient way of providing the teacher and student with the feedback they needed.

Yes, but... the state tests come in one format.

Okay, but your job is to equip students to be able to master what is on the states test. You can prepare students for the state or AP test and provide them with a variety of meaningful assessment opportunities. The two are not mutually exclusive. When I taught AP, the AP test came in a set format—50-60 multiple choice questions based on reading passages and three essay prompts (one persuasive, one comparison, and one free response.) So, it was my responsibility to help my students become familiar with the AP test format and I did, but my greater responsibility was to make sure that my students mastered the knowledge and skills the test was testing. If I only taught them in the test format, I could not know whether their performance on the test was due to their mastery of the subject or mastery of the test format. If I gave them multiple opportunities to demonstrate their mastery in a variety of settings, formats, and conditions, then I could be assured that their performance on the test represented their mastery of the subject and, regardless of the testing format, that they would be able to demonstrate their mastery of the material.

Neither paper-and-pencil assessments or performance tasks are inherently bad. It is only when we use them ineffectively that they become a problem. Different stages of mastery call for different types of assessment. At the beginning of a unit of study, when students are acquiring basic or foundational knowledge and skills, paper and pencil tests are often appropriate because you are usually testing how well they remember facts or steps of a process at this stage. As their understanding becomes more nuanced, you will need to provide a wider range of assessment options in order to capture their emerging understanding and mastery of a subject. Paper and pencil tests may still be appropriate, but so will performance tasks that call for students to integrate several skills and automate some of the foundational knowledge and skills or use the foundational or basic skills to solve more complex problems. Otherwise, you are teaching students to acquire knowledge for the sake of knowledge.

We often neglect the informal or formative assessment opportunities that take place in the classroom daily, such as student-to-student interactions, your interactions with students, choral responses, discussions, student questions, and other manifestations of student understanding. In fact, anything that you do to check to see that students are understanding the material (verbal questioning, one question quizzes, exit cards, practice exercises, lab notes, teacher observations, some worksheets, homework, etc.) can be used as a formative assessment. Checking for understanding throughout the class period gives you an opportunity to see in real-time how students are progressing toward mastery and adjust your instruction based on their needs.

Formative assessments are one of the most powerful ways to improve student achievement because they provide real-time feedback to you and your students on their progress toward the learning goals and they help students see a direct relationship between how hard they work and what they learn. These assessments are given *during* the learning process and provide students with feedback they can use to improve their process or their product prior to the final assessment.

You should be careful not to overdo it on any one kind of assessment technique. While you want to collect information on students' progress often, you don't want to emphasize assessment so much that the focus moves from *what* students are doing to *how* students are doing.

Using a variety of assessment techniques also helps you give students multiple ways to show what they know. Just because a student does poorly on one type of assessment does not mean that the student hasn't learned. It might mean that the way you are asking students to communicate what they have learned is not a good fit for that student. By using a variety of assessments, you can be sure to get more accurate feedback about what students know and are able to do.

The key is to find a balance between collecting the various types of data available to you in the classroom. Focus on collecting the most robust and accurate feedback you can by using a variety of assessment techniques daily to check whether students are moving toward mastery of the objectives.

Try This

• Pay attention to how you currently collect data in the classroom. Look to see if you are relying too heavily on one form of data collection and ignoring another. Try to balance your use of formal tests, performance tasks, and informal or formative assessments so that you can collect a variety of data.

• Look for other ways to have students demonstrate mastery such as exhibitions, checklists, profiles, and portfolios.

• Use what Madeline Hunter calls "dipsticking" (quick strategies to frequently monitor students' understanding simultaneously on the same topic during instruction). Dipsticking techniques such as one-question quizzes, thumbs up/thumbs down, or unison responses can help you quickly assess students' understanding.

• Give each student a dry erase marker and an individual white board (you can have a large sheet of white board cut into 11 x17 inch squares pretty inexpensively at your local hardware store). At various times during the class period, ask students a question and have them write their answer on the white board and hold it up. Scan student responses to check whether students understand the concept or skill you are teaching and quickly correct any mistakes students may have made before moving on.

Use Feedback to Revise Your Instructional Approach

It is one thing to collect feedback about students' progress, but if you simply collect this feedback and never use it to adjust your instruction, then you are collecting it in vain. The data you receive from grading your assignments and assessments will give you feedback about the effectiveness of the curriculum and your own instruction.

Both formative and summative assessments give you feedback on how well you are teaching the material. If you give a test and none of the students pass the test, then it is either because the test was poorly designed or because you need to teach the material in a different way. Assessments also give you clues about your pacing. If your formative assessment reveals that your students have already mastered the material, you can move on in your unit.

Conversely, your assessments may reveal that students do not understand what you are teaching and that you need to slow down, reteach, or explain the concept in a different way.

Yes, but...the test results are depressingly low.

That can be discouraging, but the test results simply provide you with information. If the test results are low, that means that the kids didn't understand the material. Guess what? They didn't understand the material regardless of whether you test them or not. At least with the test, you know that they don't understand and, if you have assessed them the right way, you will also be able to diagnose why they aren't getting it. Armed with this information, you are now prepared to help them learn the information. Subsequent assessments will be better.

This feedback can also help you decide how you will differentiate your instruction to meet the various learning needs in the classroom. It will help you determine the appropriate level of challenge for each student. From there, you can adjust your level of instruction using the various differentiation techniques such as compacting for students who demonstrate that they have mastered the material already, or offering simplified steps for students who are struggling with complex processes.

Another way to use feedback to inform your instruction is to create early warning devices, red flag mechanisms that signal when a student is struggling and needs more support. If we wait until the summative assessment to find out that a student does not understand the material, it is often too late to intervene. But, if you build formative assessments into your plan for the semester and pay attention to them, they will tell you in real time how students are doing and signal ways you need to adjust your instruction before it is too late. In this way, they become a powerful component in your intervention cycle with students (for more on developing an intervention cycle, see Chapter 4, and Tool 9 in the Appendix).

I remember a conversation I once had with Helena. She was frustrated because she had been working so hard with her students and yet their quarterly reading scores were not improving.

"I worked with them all quarter and when it was time to take the test, I was fairly confident that they would do well. But, when I got the test results back, I found that they were still reading at one or more grade levels below where they should have been. I don't know what else to do," she said as she leaned back in her seat and rubbed her temples.

"Why did you think that they were going to do well on the quarterly reading test?" I asked.

"Because they were so good in class," she sighed. "They did all of the work I gave them. They started out a rowdy bunch, but they soon settled down and worked really hard."

"That's great, Helena, but what does that have to do with reading?" I asked.

"But they were reading," Helena said, straightening up in her seat. "They were doing the work."

"How do you know that the work was helping improve their reading?"

"Because. . . ," Helena started to respond. "You know what? I really don't know. Obviously it wasn't helping because their scores didn't change."

"Maybe," I shrugged. 'Maybe not. The point is that you have no way of knowing unless you check somehow."

Helena and I looked at her curriculum and decided to add formative assessments to her reading class. She decided to assess her students each week to see if they were moving toward their reading goals and to give students reading journals where they could track what they were reading, react, and ask any questions. In this way, she could monitor their reading comprehension and it also gave the students a chance to share any feedback about their learning needs with her. She also decided to have her students do self-assessments and track their own progress. And, she planned to meet with each student every two weeks to discuss the reading targets, the students' progress, and what steps they would need to take next. Helena had been so busy teaching that she didn't take time to check and see whether her teaching was making a difference. But, by developing a feedback loop, she was able to collect the information she needed to adjust her instructional approach and to prevent surprises at the next quarterly test.

One caveat is that in order for you to effectively respond to feedback, you need to make sure too much time does not elapse between the time students take the assessment and the time you grade it and return it. If too much time (more than one week) passes between the time students take the assessment and the time they receive feedback, neither you nor they will learn as much from the feedback and you limit your ability to make adjustments or intervene.

Try This

• Create a red flag mechanism by taking information that you learn from an assessment and making it something you cannot ignore. When you are deciding how you will assess students, decide what will count as acceptable performance. Any student who falls below that level of acceptable performance triggers a red flag. Those are the students with whom you will need to intervene.

• Use pre-assessments to determine how you will differentiate your instructional units to meet the revealed needs of all of the learners in your classroom.

• Look to see what formative assessment opportunities already exist in your classroom. Then, use the feedback these provide to adjust your instruction.

Help Students Collect and Analyze Their Own Data

In addition to providing students with feedback about their progress, we should also create opportunities for students to collect and analyze their own data.

I learned this lesson not out of some noble desire to help my students but out of my own frustration over the fact that my students would constantly bug me about their grades. Every day at least one of my students wanted to know what his or her grade was. "Why don't you keep track of your own grades?" I would ask as I took out my calculator and began adding up the rows in my grade book.

I finally decided to require that students keep track of their own grade. I devised a system where every Friday, during the last 10 minutes of class, I would return papers. While students passed the papers out, I put up an overhead of all the assignments students had had that semester as well as the point value for each. I gave each student a grade tracking sheet to keep in their notebooks and as they received their papers, they would record each grade in their notebooks. Then, I showed them how to add up their points and divide them by the total number of points possible in order to determine their grade. If students did not receive a paper or if a paper was graded incorrectly, it was their responsibility to see me during that class period or to make arrangements to see me during lunch to make the correction. I notified parents of this system so they could review their students' grades with them each Friday. Eventually, I moved to a computerized grade book program that allowed me to post grades online, but the same principle applied.

While I thought that the major benefit of making these changes would be a reduction in the number of requests for grades from both students and parents, I was surprised to see that simply having the information about their grades helped my students take more ownership for their success in the classroom. They began to set goals about their work, ask for help on assignments they didn't understand, and make a greater effort to turn in their assignments on time. They became interested in their grades, not just to see what their final grade would be at the end of the semester, but to gauge how well they were doing in the class throughout the semester so they could adjust their performance and their level of effort accordingly.

Another strategy for helping students collect and analyze their own data is to use a strategy adapted from Malcolm Baldrige called data notebooks. Data notebooks provide a powerful way of getting students involved in collecting their own feedback about their learning and have been used with children as young as kindergarteners all the way up through seniors in high school. To create data notebooks, students list the objectives of the course, determine their own goals in achieving these objectives, and then create action plans that are designed and deployed to meet these goals. Their action plans include a mission statement and time line, and identify what evidence they will use to determine whether they have met their goal and how they will monitor their progress. Using this information, students create data charts to monitor their progress toward each goal and use quality tools to help guide their leaning process. There is also a section of the notebook devoted to parent communication so that parents can monitor student progress and provide input as well.

Helping students collect and analyze feedback helps them keep track of where they are in relationship to the course objectives, set both short- and long-term goals, and make midcourse corrections in their progress toward achieving these goals.

Try This

- Create devices to help students monitor their own progress such as grade tracking sheets.
- Have students create portfolios where they collect artifacts of their own work throughout the year and explain how each artifact demonstrates their progress toward mastery of the course objectives. At the end of each quarter, have students write a reflection on where they have been and where they still need to go in order to master the course or grade-level objectives for the year.
- Give students opportunities to provide peer feedback to each other. Make sure that students clearly understand the performance criteria before they give feedback to each other.
- Have students create action plans for how they will achieve the objectives for your next unit.

Explain to Students What Their Grades Really Mean

The purpose of assessment is to provide you and your students with feedback on how well students are mastering the objectives of your course. That's it.

It is therefore important to redefine what grades mean. Typically, students and parents think an *A* means they are smart. A *B* means they are smart but not superstars. A *C* means average and a *D* or *F* means they are dumb. Notice that this view sees grades as final and unchangeable. The grades serve as an evaluation not of the students' progress toward mastery, but of the students themselves. Further, these grades serve as a sorting mechanism and imply that some students will simply never attain mastery.

But if you want to provide students with useful feedback about their mastery then you will need to help them develop a different understanding of grades. With this in mind, an *A* means the student has mastered or even exceeded the objectives. A *B* means the student has mastered or is very close to mastering the objectives. A *C* means the student still needs to work toward mastering the objectives but is making good progress. A *D* or *F* means the student needs more support and practice before he or she can master the objectives. Jonathan Saphier and Robert Gower (1997), in their book *The Skillful Teacher,* even go so far as to suggest that the only grades that make sense are *A*, *B*, and "not yet."

Notice how looking at grades this way keeps you and your students focused on what is really important—mastering the objectives. This way of looking at grades is based on the belief that all students are on a journey toward mastery and that you fully expect that all students will complete that journey. When you help students understand what their grades truly indicate, you give them accurate information that will indicate what steps they still need to take to achieve mastery. Looking at grades this way also provides students with information that can serve as an incentive to work harder or seek extra help. If students see grades as a checkpoint, as a snapshot of their progress at a single point in time, rather than as a final evaluation of who they are and what they are capable of, they will be more willing to try and more likely to improve.

Our grading policies and verbal comments to students also communicate powerful messages about what our grades really mean. Consider the following comments typical in school:

1. "If you earned below a *C* on this test, you can take it again and I will average your two grades."

2. "You're so smart. You got an *A* without even studying!"

3. "You got a *D* on this worksheet. You are going to have to work harder the next time."

Here are the underlying messages to such comments:

1. Speed is more important than mastery. If you take longer to master a concept, you must not be as smart as those who got it the first time.

2. Studying means you're dumb.

3. Low grades are due to a lack of effort.

In all three cases, these seemingly innocent or encouraging comments actually send very harmful messages about what grades really mean and about the students themselves.

Let's revisit the examples from above. This time however, instead of feedback that is implicitly evaluative, what if we based our comments and practices on the idea that grades are a reflection of students' current level of mastery and can be changed by effective effort? What kind of messages might they get instead?

1. "If you earned below a *B* on this test, you will need to come in for a study session tomorrow at lunch and then retake the test on Thursday. I will record the higher grade."

2. "You got an *A* without even studying. You must have paid careful attention in class and taken really great notes!"

3. "You got a *D* on this worksheet which means that the process you used to figure these problems out didn't work. Let's sit down and figure out why you got these answers wrong so that you can correct your mistakes. That way, you can learn how to do these problems better next time. "

Notice the message of these comments:

1. Just because you did not get it the first time does not mean that you won't ever get it. How long it takes to master the material is not nearly as important as mastering it.

2. Although you did not study, you did have a process that helped you to learn the material. By paying attention in class and taking good notes, you were able to master the objectives.

3. You earned a *D* because you have not yet mastered the objectives. But, with effective effort, you will master the objectives and I am going to help you.

How we communicate about grades determines whether students can use their grades as feedback that can help them improve their performance. By sending students the right message about what their grades truly mean, you can help students use their grades to accurately gauge where they are in relationship to the objectives, set goals, seek help, and ultimately improve their performance.

Try This

• When you return your next assessment to students, take some time to explain what their grades mean in terms of how close they came to mastering the objectives. Have students use these graded assessments to set goals for the next assessment. Focus the subsequent work you do in class on helping students achieve these goals by the next assessment.

• Connect individual test questions with the various objectives and standards the test is designed to measure. When students receive their graded tests, help them break down their performance based on the standard. Then, help them determine which objectives and standards they still need to master.

• If you calculate grades based on percentages, try using the median grade versus the average grade for computing final grades. The median grade will diminish the effect of a few stumbles and missteps students may have made along the way and give a more accurate picture of students' overall performance.

• Give some assignments just for practice and do not grade them. That way, you can help students focus on learning versus earning a grade by giving them the freedom to try without fear of evaluation.

• Give students clear criteria for success and models of successful performance. Explain to students exactly why the model meets the criteria for success.

Use Feedback to Coach Students Toward Better Performance

Feedback not only gives students an accurate picture of where they are in relationship to the objective, it also shows students what they still need to do in order to reach the objective.

In order to use your feedback to coach students toward better performance, there are several caveats you should keep in mind. First, rather than inundate students with feedback about every aspect of the assignment in an attempt to correct every mistake, focus your feedback on the essential elements of the assignment. In multistep assignments for example, focus your feedback only on what students need to know in order to take the next step. Second, coaching feedback should be directly related to the learning goal. It should show students where they are in relationship to the objective and what they need to do next in order to move closer to the objective. Students should know what they have done well and what they can do to improve their performance. Third, make sure that your feedback is specific to the learning task at hand so that students know what to do next, but not so specific that you do the work for them. Fourth, effective feedback should be stated in language your students can understand. Rather than tell students that they need to "be more careful next time" for instance, show students where they have made computational or grammatical errors and how they can check their work before turning it in. Finally, students need opportunities to act on the feedback you give them. If you give them feedback at the end of the process and then move on, they never have the opportunity to apply what you have shared and improve their performance.

As an English teacher, I spent hours marking papers, circling misspelled words, correcting grammar, and writing things like "vague" or "support" in the margins. At the end of the paper, I would write an evaluative comment such as "This paper does not meet the requirements outlined in the rubric. Please review the rubric and the assignment sheet." I genuinely thought these comments were helpful and spent a great deal of time writing them in green ink (to be politically correct) in the margins of my students' papers.

So imagine my disappointment when I handed back these papers and my students eagerly turned to the grade and ignored all of the comments I had carefully scripted. Imagine my even greater disappointment when my students made the exact same mistakes on their next papers.

There had to be another way. I had always been intrigued by the idea of rubrics but I had not seen them used successfully. Although I thought rubrics were a great tool, whenever I had used them in the past, my students barely glanced at them. Sure, they saved me time, but I hadn't figured out a way to get my students to use them throughout the writing process.

Part of the problem was that I created a new rubric for each paper. Students couldn't use the feedback from one paper to help them improve on the next paper because the rubric was different every time. So, I decided to create an analytic rubric that I would use for every paper. I figured good writing was good writing and if the skills I was trying to teach were truly transferable, then one rubric would do.

I created an eight-part analytic rubric[1]. Seven of the categories were standard for every paper but I decided to give myself some wiggle room and make the eighth category flexible. I could use that category to provide feedback on whatever it was I was focusing on for that particular paper.

But I didn't stop at the rubric. I also got a box of felt-tipped markers and assigned one color to each category of the rubric. The next time I assigned

---

[1] For more information on this rubric process and examples of the rubrics I used, visit my Web site at www.mindstepsinc.com.

a paper, I reviewed the rubric with the students at the beginning and again during the revision process. When I graded the papers, I did not write a single comment. Instead, I underlined relevant parts of the paper with the corresponding color on the rubric. For instance, I assigned transitions the color yellow. If a student needed a transition or if the students' transition was not effective, I underlined that portion of the paper in yellow and circled the corresponding description on the rubric in yellow.

When I returned their papers to them, the students were a little baffled. What does it mean if my paper has a lot of yellow marks on it? Why is my paper all red? What does this blue mark mean?

Now all of a sudden, students were less concerned about the grade and more concerned about the feedback. If your paper is all yellow, I explained, it means you will need to work on more effective transitions on your next paper. A lot of red? That means you are going to have to proofread more carefully. Those blue marks? They mean that you will need to work on developing your thesis.

Our conversations about their papers shifted from a discussion of their grade to setting goals for how they would write their next paper.

I explained to them the concept of color-coded grading and then passed out a grade tracking sheet. This sheet was a simple graph divided into eight sections corresponding with the eight sections of the rubric. I asked students to graph their score on the grade tracking sheet. We did this for each assignment so students could track their progress on each of the eight standards of the rubric. This tracking sheet also served as a starting point for our discussions of their writing. In the past, when I would meet with students, I would ask them to bring all of their former papers and then quickly skim their papers before I could provide them with feedback. Now I could simply look at their grade tracking sheets and immediately determine the area we needed to work on for the next paper.

That's the difference between using feedback to coach rather than evaluate. Evaluative feedback keeps students focused on the now. Coaching feedback focuses students on the next time. Evaluative feedback is final so there is really nothing the student can do to improve his or her performance. Coaching feedback gives students information they can use to improve their performance in the future. It helps students understand the criteria for mastery, shows students where they are in relationship to the standard, and shows students how to move from where they are to mastery.

Try This

- When students give incorrect responses to questions in class, give them credit for the parts of their answer that are correct. Then, work together as a class to turn their incorrect response into the correct answer.
- Give students a pre-test prior to teaching the unit. Help students use their pre-test results to identify what they need to learn during the unit and to set goals for their performance.
- After each major test or assignment, spend some time helping students analyze their performance and set goals for the next phase of learning.
- Develop analytic rubrics for major assignments that clearly outline the major components of successful performance and the various stages of mastery. Give these rubrics to students when you give them the assignment, and have students periodically assess their progress toward mastery as they are completing the assignment.

Use Feedback to Show Students *How* to Fail

It is fairly easy to praise students when they are making progress toward the objective, but what about when they fail? Is there room for effort based feedback even when students fail?

You bet there is. In fact, it is in moments of failure that students need our feedback the most.

While we are really good at showing students how to succeed, we often fail to show students how to fail. Learning how to fail is one of the most valuable skills we can teach students. If students learn how to fail effectively, they are more likely to succeed later on.

Many of us are well intentioned. When students fail, we don't want to hurt their feelings. So we tiptoe around their feelings by giving them feedback designed to protect them from the pain of failure rather than teaching them how to overcome failure and learn from their mistakes. We minimize their failures and help them make excuses for their mistakes. Or we provide them with vague comments that don't show them how to improve their performance the next time so they can avoid failure in the future.

The best thing we can do for students who fail is to provide them with an honest assessment of why they failed and show them how to do better the next time.

I have always been frustrated by how many of my students are afraid to answer questions in class for fear of being wrong. Learning is about taking risks, but far too many students are afraid to take risks in the classroom lest they be ridiculed by their friends or feel "dumb." For years I cajoled and encouraged my students to take more risks, but few did. One day, I realized that I may be contributing to the problem.

If, during a class discussion, a student gave an incorrect answer, I would do one of two things. I would either tell the student he was wrong but "nice try," or I would say, "almost" and then move to another student who had the correct answer. Either way, I was sending the message that students had to get it right or wrong. No wonder students were afraid to participate in discussion unless they were relatively sure they had the "right" answer.

But I wanted my students to try and to not be afraid of "wrong" answers. I wanted them to learn how to learn from their mistakes.

One day, I ran across a graphic organizer called a Frayer model[2]. This graphic organizer is typically used to help students understand vocabulary or concepts. It is divided into four sections. In the center of the four sections, students write a concept. In one section, students write the definition. In the second section, students write characteristics of the concept. In a third section, students write examples of the concept. But it was the fourth section that stopped me in my tracks. This section was reserved for non-examples.

I immediately seized upon the idea of a "non-example." During the next class discussion, when a student offered what would typically be considered a wrong answer, I said, "That's a great non-example!" and immediately wrote it on the board. The students looked at each other confused. "Now," I continued, "Let's see how we can make this non-example into an example." We spent the next few minutes rewriting the sentence together as a class. Along the way, I explained why the sentence was not correct and how we could fix it. At the end, the class had a better understanding of what made a sentence work and how they could fix their own mistakes. It took a few more tries for the idea to catch on but shortly, I noticed many more students were volunteering to put their work on the board. In fact, a few students would even raise their

---

[2] For an example of a Frayer Model, visit my Web site at www.mindstepsinc.com.

hands and say, "I have a great non-example." Using the idea of a non-example helped my students learn to ask for help without being embarrassed, learn from their mistakes, and take more risks in the classroom.

Another part of showing students how to fail is helping them understand the right explanation of their failure. Many students believe that failure means that they are not smart. This belief limits their efforts because they feel that they have no control over whether they succeed or fail. But, if you can help them see that success or failure is a direct result of effort, your students will understand that they do have control over whether they succeed or fail.

It is also important to teach students that failure isn't just the result of a lack of effort, it could also be the result of the wrong kind of effort. Some students work very hard at a task and still fail. Thus, if we only tell them that success comes from effort without also showing them how to expend effective effort, then we could be setting them up for failure. Instead, use feedback to show students not just how to work hard, but how to work hard at the right things so that they will not fail in the future.

Try This

- Work to remove the threat of being ridiculed for being wrong in the classroom by demonstrating your respect for students' values, beliefs, and preferences.
- Talk to students about times when you took a risk in your own life. Explain to them how you felt and the benefits you derived from taking such a risk. Ask students to talk about times they took risks and the benefits of doing so. Then relate these experiences to taking risks in the classroom.

Provide Students with Opportunities to Retake Assessments or Resubmit Unsuccessful Assignments

One of the best ways to help students learn how to learn from their mistakes is to give them the opportunity to retake an assessment. This give students the chance to reengage with the material and it helps students use the feedback they have received from their assessment to take some corrective action that will actually improve their performance next time.

Of course, retakes are a touchy subject for many teachers. For instance, I was leading a workshop for GT teachers on differentiation strategies when we got to the subject of retesting. One woman in the back of the room, who had been paying only marginal attention to the workshop so far, perked up and raised her hand. When it was her turn to speak, she said, "Are you kidding me? If you give students the chance to retake a test, they won't study the first time. You are teaching them procrastination." Her statement was met with a smattering of applause.

👈 Yes, but… I don't have time to grade all these assessments!

In order for the feedback from assessments to be useful, it has to occur in "real time." That means that the students and you need the feedback during instruction. If students have to wait two weeks in order to receive feedback on an assignment, it is often already too late for them to apply the feedback to improve their performance. By the time they get their assignments back, the class has moved on to a new topic or a new unit.

Juxtapose this plight with the very real plight we face all the time. When will we find time to grade all these assessments and plan new units and do the 57 million other things that we have to do each day? It's a very real problem.

Here is where some of the other principles in this book can help. For one, if you are emphasizing quality over quantity, you should have less work to grade overall. Also, by using distributed practice versus full-length performance every time, you can get and provide valuable feedback that is targeted to specific learning goals without being mired in grading a much longer sample of student work. Also, in chapter 7, we will discuss ways to give the work back to the students and help them collect and analyze their own data about their performance. In this way, students can cull their own feedback and even provide feedback to you.

I paused for a moment and let the applause and the shouts of "you tell her!" die down. "You are assuming students didn't pass the test the first time because they didn't study," I began. She interrupted.

"That's exactly what I am assuming. I go over the material, I give them study guides, I am in my classroom every morning at 7:30 a.m. if they want help. So, if they don't pass my tests, it's because they didn't do what they needed to do." Again, more applause. This woman was on a roll.

"All those are great to help students who already understood the material," I acknowledged. "But what about the student who hasn't really mastered the material? How will the study guide help that student? What do you do about the student who didn't 'get it' the first time?"

"Like I said, I am in my room every morning at 7:30 a.m. If a student needs extra help, he can come in and get it," she replied.

"What if a student can't drive and his parents can't bring him at 7:30?" I asked. "Or, what if the student doesn't know that he doesn't really understand the material? Or what if the student is afraid to ask for help?"

"Well then that student will fail the test. They have to learn to take some responsibility for their own learning," she said, crossing her arms.

"How do they learn to take responsibility for their own learning?" I asked.

"Their parents should be teaching them responsibility," she replied.

"What if their parents don't teach them responsibility? How will they learn it?" I prodded.

"They will suffer consequences and then they will learn to be more responsible the next time."

"Or, they may learn school isn't worth it and stop trying." The room was silent as I continued. "The problem with retesting is not retesting itself; it's often a matter of the way we give tests. The student who takes the test the first time just to find out what was on the test is simply being efficient. It makes no sense to study the first time when you have no idea what is on the test. But, if students know exactly what will be on the test ahead of time, it becomes more efficient to take the test once instead of twice." A few teachers nodded their heads in agreement as I continued. "The other problem is that often we offer students a chance to retake a test without taking any corrective action. The point of an assessment is to tell us and the students how well they have mastered the material and objectives of our course. Once the test reveals that students have not mastered some of the material or the objectives, then we need to reteach the material before we give students an opportunity to retake the test."

Groans erupted in the room. "I know what you are thinking," I quickly said. "You don't have time to reteach all that material and besides, why should you when the students should have been paying attention the first time." The room grew quiet as the teachers waited for what would come next. "There are times when reteaching may require that you work with students individually or in small groups, but most of the time, it will not. You can have students view online simulations, work through an online tutorial, do an error analysis on the answers they got wrong on the last test, read a supplementary text on the same subject, work with their peers, go to after school tutoring, or complete some other corrective procedure independently. You can give them a set amount of time to complete this corrective action and they must show you evidence of it before they can retake the test." The teachers in the room began to visibly relax.

I continued. "Reteaching and retesting actually teaches students how to be *more* responsible, not less. Letting students fail is like letting them off the hook. We are telling them they don't have to master the material. But, if we require them to take corrective action for the parts of the material the assessment tells us they haven't mastered, require them to master that material, and then have them come in and retake the test to ensure that they have mastered the material, then we are making them responsible for learning the material. We are holding them responsible for mastering the objectives."

I was so passionate in my remarks because I have seen firsthand the difference retakes have made for students. When I was the administrator of a middle school, we moved from one-shot only tests, to offering students retakes. At first, teachers were resistant to having to give what seemed like twice as many tests and doing twice as much grading. But after a few months, the teachers reported that they were seeing huge gains in the students' learning and the number of retakes they had to give was decreasing as students developed better skills and a deeper understanding of the subject. Even those teachers who were most resistant grudgingly admitted that offering retakes was helping their students achieve the objectives of their course without requiring a huge time investment on the teacher's part. They learned what all master teachers know, which is that giving students the opportunity to try again when they didn't learn it the first time helps students learn how to use feedback in a way that will lead to more effective effort in the future.

Try This

- On your next assignment, let students know that the only grades you will be giving are *A*, *B*, and *Not Yet*. Students who earn a *Not Yet* will need to redo and resubmit their work.

- To cut down on the number of retakes, tell students clearly what will be on the test, how they will be tested, and how they will be graded the first time.

- Refuse to allow students to take a failing grade rather than retake a test. Require that students retake tests if they score below a passing grade. In this way, they have to re-engage with the material and will see that your emphasis is on learning rather than on grades.

- Require students to engage in some sort of corrective action before they retake the test. For instance, have students complete a tutorial online or through a CD-ROM, view a simulation online and take notes, complete an error analysis of the answers they got wrong on the test the first time, attend a special review session at lunch time or after school, read some supplementary material and take notes, or provide some other evidence that they have used the feedback from the first assessment in order to improve their performance on the retake.

- Set deadlines for reassessments and communicate these ahead of time. You should not have to spend all of your spare time reassessing students. Establish a set time for students to take reassessments.

- If you are going to allow retakes, then you should make them available to all students.

The Principle in Action

Todd's math classroom was one of the best examples of using ongoing feedback I have ever seen. Students entered the classroom and wrote numbers on the board under a sign that read, "The problems I had the most trouble with last night were:" and then took their seats. At the bell, Todd scanned the list and said, "Let's see. It looks like most of you had trouble with numbers 7 and 10 so let's start with those." Then, Todd worked the problems on the board taking time to carefully explain the process to students. After he completed those problems, he asked "OK, based on what we just did, are there any other homework problems you think you cannot figure out on your own?" A few students raised their hands and asked clarifying questions that Todd answered, in some cases by explaining part or all of an additional problem. Then Todd gave students a few minutes to make corrections on their homework while he took attendance and handed back papers. After a few minutes, Todd instructed his students to hand their homework to the front.

After collecting the homework, Todd posted an overhead transparency with a list of the assignments he returned and what each assignment was worth. Students recorded their grades in their data notebooks and filed their returned papers in their folders. Then Todd announced, "Now I just handed back your quizzes from Monday. Many of you showed me that you understood the material but several of you showed me that you don't quite understand it yet. So, I am going to give you another chance to learn this and will be quizzing you again on this material on Friday during lunch. Although any of you are welcome to retake the quiz on Friday, those of you who received below an 80 percent on your quiz from Monday are required to. Your ticket to retake the test is one of the following: If you missed less than five problems, do the problems on page 242–243 of your text and explain how you arrived at each answer. If you missed more than five problems on the test, you can do an error analysis of the problems you missed and explain how you corrected your errors. Pages 233–241 of your text will help you analyze your problems and review the concepts. I also have a great worksheet here that takes you step-by-step for how to solve these types of equations. If you need a little more help, I am having a study session here after school on Thursday. I will spend the first part of the session reteaching the material. Then, I will stick around to answer any individual questions." The students wrote down the date in their student planners.

Todd then began the day's lesson. Throughout the lesson, Todd would pause and ask, "How are we doing so far?" and students would respond with a thumbs up if they understood, thumbs sideways if they were somewhat unclear, and thumbs down if they were completely lost. Based on the response from the class, Todd would ask a few students to tell him where they needed further clarification and reexplain the material. Then, Todd handed students a worksheet to complete. As students worked, Todd circulated among them checking over their shoulders and providing comments like, "Now question 7 is a little different than the others, but if you solved questions 2 and 6, you can use the same strategy to solve question 7," or "Remember last week when we talked about order of operations? This is an example of how using the correct order of operations makes a difference in the answer you get. Try this problem again but this time, use the correct order of operations."

About five minutes before the end of the period, Todd said, "Alright, the bell is going to ring any minute so let's go over what we learned today." After he reviewed the key concepts, he gave students their homework assignment for the night and then handed out index cards to each student. "Before you leave today, I want to make sure that you understand what we learned. So, I am going to give you a one question quiz." Todd put an overhead transparency on the screen that contained a multiple choice question. Students wrote their names and their answer on the index card and handed it to Todd. Once he collected the cards, Todd said, "The answer to the question is C. If you answered A, it means that you didn't simplify your answer. You will need to remember to simplify when you are doing your homework tonight. If you answered B, it means that you didn't use the correct order of operations. Review order of operations before you start your homework tonight and use the diagram I showed you. If you answered D, it means that you made a computational error. Tonight, when you do your homework, take some time to check your work."

Throughout the period, Todd collected feedback that helped him gauge students' emerging understanding of the material. And, not only did Todd share this feedback with his students, but he showed them how to use this feedback to improve their understanding of the material.

Getting Started

1. Assignments and assessments can provide you with valuable feedback you can use to inform future instruction. By collecting a variety of data, analyzing the data in a way that focuses on more than just the right answers, and setting up red flag mechanisms, you can determine where students are in relationship to the objective and figure out how to adjust your instructional approach to help them meet the objectives of your course.

2. Assessment can also provide your students with valuable feedback. Use assessments to coach your students toward better performance by showing them how to collect their own data and understand exactly what their grades mean, how to learn from failure, and how to use feedback to set goals for future performance.

6

Focus on Quality, Not Quantity

It is the quality of our work which will please God and not the quantity.

Mahatma Gandhi

When I first started teaching, I believed that the best way to teach writing was to have students write. My students, who really struggled with writing, were so far behind that I thought they needed as much practice as possible. I designed a nine-week unit focused on writing essays and decided that we would write one essay each week. Here's the way it worked. I picked eight controversial topics—the death penalty, euthanasia, affirmative action, etc.—and I divided the students into pairs. I assigned two pairs to research each topic. One pair prepared a presentation arguing for the issue and the other pair argued against it. Each Monday, I introduced the issue to the class and then we completed vocabulary exercises the rest of the period. On Tuesday, one group argued for the issue. Wednesday, the other group argued against the issue. On Thursday, we had a class discussion about the issue to allow students to develop their own arguments regarding the issue. We ended the class on Thursday by writing an outline of a five-paragraph essay arguing for or against the issue. On Friday, students would come to class and spend the 45-minute period writing their essays.

I thought it was a brilliant plan. It offered students the chance to do research, honed their presentation skills, provided for class discussion, captured student interest, and gave them plenty of opportunities to write. Because they faced a new topic each week, it would prevent them from thinking that the skills I was teaching them were topic-bound. Instead, they would transfer those skills from one assignment to the next. I was quite proud of myself. Only three months out of graduate school and I had this teaching thing licked.

And then I collected the first set of papers. At the time I had about 140 students. After period one, I flipped through the stack of papers and scanned students' responses. "Not bad," I thought to myself. "I should be able to knock these out in no time." While the students wrote in period 2, I graded the essays. At the end of period 2, I'd graded about 10 essays. I noted that the students weren't developing their arguments with as many supporting details and facts as I would like and made a mental note to cover that the following week. Period 3 was my planning period so I stayed at my desk and graded. At the end of the period, I had just about finished the papers from period 1

My 4th period class came in and I got them started and then returned to my papers. By that time, I was weary of grading and had slowed down considerably. At the end of the period, I had only graded about six papers.

It was lunch time and I had a few students in for detention. I took out my lunch and wearily munched on a sandwich while I chatted with a few students who stopped by. Period 5 began and my students began writing their essays. I looked at the stack of papers on my desk with a growing dread and reached for the next paper. At the end of the period, I'd managed to grade another seven. Period 6 was another free period for me, so I ran a few errands around the building and made some copies. I stopped in on one or two of my colleagues and chatted about upcoming weekend plans. Period 7, I was back to work on those papers while my students wrote. By the end of the day, I had made it through the papers for period two and was just beginning to grade the essays from period 4. So much for my weekend, I thought, as I lugged home a canvas bag full of 79 papers that had to be graded by Monday.

Those papers sat there all Saturday long. Sunday afternoon, I made myself a sandwich and finally got to work. I forced myself to sit there and grade those papers. The phone rang, and I didn't answer it. Time for my favorite show but I kept the television off. I got through about 32 of them before I couldn't stand to look at another one.

When I entered the building on Monday morning, I still had 47 papers to grade. Before school started, I rapidly recorded the grades for period one and passed back their papers. I did a quick lesson about using details to support their arguments and reviewed the vocabulary for the week. In between periods, I recorded the grades for period 2 and handed back their papers. During my planning period, I tried to get through the rest of the papers from period 5 and by the end of the period, I was almost done. "I'll finish up the rest during lunch," I planned. By the end of lunch, I was finished with period 5 and had started the papers from period 7 but I still had 22 more to go. I raced through as many papers as I could during my 6th period planning but by the end of the period, I still had to grade another eight papers. I had no choice. I announced to my period 7 students that I would return their papers the next day, promised to do better next week, and took those 8 papers home to grade before I went to bed.

The next Friday, it just got worse. I couldn't grade those papers fast enough. And, no matter how much I graded during the period, at the end of the class, I had a fresh set of 28 papers waiting for me. I began to resent those papers because they ruined my weekends. Sometimes, I would try to ignore them to go out and have a little fun, but when I came home, there they were, sitting in the bag by the door, silently accusing me. Other times, I would gamely cancel my plans, stay home, and dig in. Four hours later, bleary-eyed, I'd look at the stack I had left and wonder when I would ever get through those papers.

It wasn't just the volume of papers that frustrated me. It was the fact that each week, my students were making the same mistakes. They weren't getting any better in spite of my mini-lessons designed to help correct these mistakes. They still weren't writing topic sentences, they still weren't supporting their arguments with appropriate details, and their conclusions were still formulaic and trite. Why aren't they getting it? I would seethe as I stared at yet another unsupported paragraph.

Those papers never did get much better. In fact, some of my students' papers became even more formulaic and trite as we progressed through the unit. I thought that if I just gave them more practice, they would get better. But I was giving them practice on the wrong thing. By assigning an essay a week, I never gave them time to correct their mistakes between essays. I focused on the complete performance instead of on distributed and targeted practice that would have helped my students hone specific skills. As a result, I was actually reinforcing the very mistakes I was trying to correct.

When I taught writing the next year, I decided that rather than focus on providing students with plenty of practice, I would focus on skills instead. If I was working with students on effective introductions, for instance, I would give the students a writing prompt and ask them to write the introduction only. Then, we would examine how we wrote the introduction, make any corrections, and thereby develop the skill I was after. Why did we need to write the entire essay if we were only focused on the introduction?

If I was focusing on organization, I would have them write the outline for the essay rather than the entire essay. That way, we wouldn't get bogged down in the particulars of their writing and could focus on the skeleton of the essay and focus on the principles of organization.

My students' writing improved exponentially. They made tremendous growth without nearly the same amount of work. That's when I realized that it wasn't so much how much work I assigned them; it was the kind of work that mattered.

Common Practice

I had a friend who used to say, "If less is more, imagine how much more *more* would be!" He was joking of course, but many of us subscribe to this very philosophy. Rather than focus on a few quality learning experiences that would allow our students to master a concept in depth, we go for breadth and try to cover the waterfront. Our intentions are noble. We want to make our students more competitive, so we give them as much information as possible.

But in our attempt to give our students more, are we actually giving them less? Does our emphasis on quantity sacrifice quality in the process?

Robert Marzano (2003) points out in his book *What Works in Schools* that there is simply not enough time to address all the state-mandated standards and benchmarks in the majority of curricula. In fact, he has shown that the current national standards in the 14 subject areas would require 15,465 hours to address adequately, and by "adequately," he means to the point where students know and understand the material. The problem is that there are only about 9,042 hours of instructional time currently available from kindergarten to grade 12. That's a little more than half the time we need to teach students all of the national standards in every subject area. We literally cannot cover all of the material we need to cover in the amount of time we have with students. Not if we want them to learn it and learn it well.

But the bigger problem with an emphasis on quantity is that it makes it difficult for students to decipher what the priorities of the unit are. Without clear goals, each topic in the unit can appear to be of equal importance.

The Principle

Master teachers use their time differently than other teachers. They spend more time planning than teaching, and on asking students questions rather than talking themselves. They give fewer learning activities rather than trying to cover everything. And, they focus more on formative assessments than on the big test at the end. Master teachers invest their time up front.

In spite of this investment up front or perhaps because of it, master teachers get things done more quickly than the rest of us. They move through lessons much more efficiently.

The reason? They spend more time designing quality assignments and assessments than they do creating volumes of work for their students and themselves. Master teachers know that it isn't the amount of work that is important; it's the quality of the work that matters. As a result, they don't waste time on assignments or activities that will not effectively move students toward mastery. Master teachers understand that knowing what to stop doing is just as important as knowing what to do.

Practicing the Principle

Rather than trying to cover as much as possible, master teachers are strategic about what they teach and how they teach it. They understand that it is the quality, not the quantity of learning experiences that matter. Master teachers first determine what students absolutely need to know and how well they need to know it before deciding on what learning activities they will use to help students master the objectives. They use curricular flexibility to find spaces in the curriculum to spend the time they need on the things that they think are important, and they provide students with multiple, targeted opportunities to develop and deepen their understanding of the crucial knowledge and skills of the curriculum.

Use Homework Wisely

Sometimes we judge the rigor of a course by the amount of work it requires. We think that in order for a course to be highly rigorous, it must involve hours of homework per night. Rigor however, has nothing to do with the volume of work. It has to do with the quality of the work students receive.

Interestingly, Robert Marzano (2007) in his book *The Art and Science of Teaching* reports that "the amount of time spent at homework is fairly meaningless in itself" (p.69). Rather, it is the quality of the homework assignments that count. He points to research that shows that "large amounts of poorly structured homework will not be beneficial and may in fact be detrimental. Small amounts of well-structured homework, on the other hand, may produce the desired effect" (p.69).

Early in my career, I assigned homework every night. I took it as a given that homework was a necessary part of a students' experience. I wanted to have a highly rigorous course so I made sure that my students had plenty of homework.

Because I was focused on making sure that my students had homework each night, I often assigned them busy work. I manufactured worksheets and looked for extra reading assignments to give them. On the rare night that I had nothing to assign them for homework, I felt a vague sense of guilt.

Not only did I have to grade all of that homework, but my students rarely completed it. It got progressively worse so that by the end of the semester, the homework completion rate was somewhere around 50 percent for many of my students. It was too much and, they figured out well before I did, it was meaningless.

About that time, I went to training by a consultant named Max Thomson. He argued that learning was a socially constructed act. Therefore, we should never ask students to acquire new information at home, isolated. Homework should be for practice, not for acquiring new information.

The next semester, I explained this concept to my students. I announced that I would only assign homework if it was meaningful. I even made some homework optional. When I collected the homework that semester, almost all of my students had it completed every time. The few who didn't stayed in with me during their lunch period and completed it then.

The less homework I assigned, the more likely my students were to complete it because they understood that the assignment was not just busy work. When I explained to them the purpose of each homework assignment and showed them how it would advance their learning, my students were more likely to not just complete their homework but to become engaged in the work because they saw how it mattered.

Sure, there are times when you will legitimately need to assign homework to students. Just make sure that the homework you do assign directly connects to the learning goal and that you make this connection explicit to students. If you cannot connect homework to your learning goals, then you should not assign it.

Try This

• Think about an upcoming homework assignment. Is the assignment really necessary for students to master the objectives of your unit or lesson? If so, how can you design the homework to ensure that students will be able to complete it on their own? What supports might they need and how can you provide them?

• Provide parents and guardians with guidelines for how they can help with homework. Never ask parents to become experts in your subject matter in order to help their students with homework. Instead, provide ways for them to ask clarifying or summarizing questions that help their students articulate what they have learned and thereby deepen their learning.

• Make sure that the homework you assign has a clear purpose and be sure to communicate the purpose of homework to students as you assign it. That way, you will increase the likelihood that students actually complete their homework.

Avoid Coverage Mode and Adopt Curricular Flexibility

Another danger of focusing on quantity versus quality is falling into coverage mode, where the textbook or the curriculum guide dictates how much material we have to cover and in what proportion. When we are teaching in coverage mode, we merely check off the material that we have covered without checking to see if students have actually learned it.

When we are in coverage mode, we focus students' attention on completion rather than on understanding. The idea seems to be that if we have covered it, the students must understand it. Grant Wiggins and Jay McTighe (1998) call this approach "teaching by mentioning it," and make the important point that if we are really going to help students understand the material, we are going to have to be very strategic about the kinds of learning experiences we provide students.

> ### Yes, but... I have to be on a certain lesson by a certain day or I'll be in trouble.
>
> If you are in a situation where you have to be on the same page of the curriculum guide as everyone else in the district, there is still much you can do to emphasize quality over quantity. Just because you are on the same page as everyone else does not mean that you can't approach the material in a more meaningful way. The key is to focus on the objectives of the day's lesson rather than the activities. Then find ways to more meaningfully meet the objective. Do you need to do every activity suggested in the curriculum guide? Are there some activities that you can truncate in order to spend more time on those activities that will best help your students master the objective?

The solution is to shift our focus to the quality of the learning experiences versus the quantity of the learning experiences. Ask yourself, what learning experiences will most quickly help students achieve the goals of the course?

When I was teaching 11th-grade English, we went through a major curricular revision that required every teacher in the district to complete a set of "common tasks" as a way of making sure that the curriculum was aligned throughout the district's 23 high schools. One of the common tasks was to conduct an interview. Another common task was to take a piece of writing from earlier in the year and transform it to a different genre. We also had to teach the research paper. Many of my students had never written a research paper before and were new to research, so I knew that the research paper was going to take more time than the new curriculum allotted. I talked with some people from the district and they suggested that I shorten the research paper from 10 to 5 pages for my students in order to allow more time to explain the research process. That seemed unfair to me. Why should my students be held to a lower standard? No, I wanted my students to have the same experience of learning to write a long research paper as other students in other parts of the district.

> ### Yes, but... busy work is a part of the curriculum and I am required to give it.
>
> You may be required to use the same worksheets or activities as everyone else, but you do not have to use them in the same way. Find ways to make the worksheet activities more meaningful to students by supplementing the activities with additional elements or enriching the worksheets through discussions. You can also use their "busy work" as a launching pad for other work that will help them delve more deeply into the subject. You can adjust busy work in two ways to make it more meaningful. First, you can adjust the focus of the work and second, you can adjust how students complete the work. Have students complete worksheets in pairs or small groups and ask them to discuss the concepts that the worksheet addresses. Use the worksheet as a launching point for a whole class discussion. Find ways to take the activity from the knowledge level of Bloom's Taxonomy to the evaluation level by asking supplementary questions or having the students apply or adapt the worksheet or activity to a new or real-world context.

I decided to combine some of the common tasks. I had students conduct an interview as part of their research process. Then, after they wrote the research paper, I had them transform it into a brief presentation to the class summarizing their research findings. By combining the common tasks, I was able to buy myself more time to teach the fundamentals of research to my students without compromising the other common tasks that I was required to teach.

Curricular flexibility means taking a good hard look at the curriculum and figuring out where the spaces are. Ongoing assessment will let you know which parts of the curriculum need more of your time and attention and which parts the students have already mastered.

This can be especially hard for new teachers or for those teachers learning a new curriculum. When you are learning the curriculum as you are teaching it, it is difficult to find ways to adapt the curriculum. The key is always to focus on the standards. Rather than trying to digest an entire curricular unit wholesale, focus on the end result of each unit. Once you understand the end goal of the instructional unit, you can decide what learning activities will best help you and your students reach that goal.

It helps to treat curriculum guides like a menu rather than an all-you-can-eat buffet. There are curricular goals that need to be mastered and these are of course nonnegotiable, but how those goals are mastered is in many ways up to you. If your students can master the goals through a more efficient means, then by all means, use that. Look for time wasters in the curriculum and eliminate them. Also, look for overlap and find ways to combine assignments in order to reach your curricular goals.

Try This

• At the beginning of each new unit, give students a pre-assessment that is directly tied to the objectives of the unit (many textbooks have this kind of assessment at the end of each chapter). Based on the results of the pre-assessment, determine if students will need to go through the entire unit of study or if there are places where you can quickly review and move on. Use the results of the pre-assessment to plan how much time you spend on each part of the unit.

• Look for ways to combine assignments or learning activities in order to create spaces in the curriculum to cover additional information or to spend more time on topics with which students are having difficulty. Also look to see if there are assignments that can be moved to other units with similar goals.

• Determine whether some assignments can be truncated or eliminated by looking for repetition or overlap in the curriculum.

Be Economical About Filling in Learning Gaps

Grant Wiggins and Jay McTighe (1998) in their book *Understanding by Design* discuss the concept of "enabling" knowledge and skills. Enabling knowledge and skills are those facts, concepts, and procedures that students will need in order to perform effectively and achieve the desired results.

There are times when our students come to us without the requisite enabling knowledge or skills they need in order to be able to learn what we are trying to teach them. It is important to identify what enabling knowledge or skills students will need first and then ensure that they have these before moving on with the new unit or lesson. It is important, in other words, to backfill.

When we see that students are missing skills, we tend to try to solve the problem in one of two ways. Either we spend the year remediating, starting where the students are and trying to catch the students up. Or we start where the students should be and the students spend the rest of the year struggling to catch up. Both approaches are ultimately futile. You cannot make up for every gap in knowledge or missing skill and still help students acquire the knowledge and skills of your curriculum. A more economical way of helping students make up for missing knowledge and skills is to pinpoint only those enabling knowledge and skills that are absolutely necessary for students to be successful in your subject area and focus on helping students acquire these.

Often our students come to us with real gaps in their learning. We want them to understand chemistry and they can barely solve a simple algebraic equation. We want them to write an essay breaking down the various causes of the Civil War and they cannot write a complete sentence. What do we do when the learning gap is more like an abyss?

The idea that you must backfill skills under these conditions is rather daunting. All you see is a huge hole in the ground and right away, you reach for a shovel. Depending on the size of the hole, you may never fill it. But there are several different ways to deal with a hole. One way is to fill it, but another way is to build a bridge to cross it. Rather than think of it as backfilling skills, think of it as building bridges. You can build bridges over students learning gaps by helping students acquire enabling knowledge. Instead of trying to fill in all of students' learning gaps, fill in those that are most important and build bridges over other ones.

The other approach is to fill in enough knowledge so that students become curious and try to fill in the rest themselves. This can be accomplished through acceleration. (For more on acceleration, visit www.mindstepsinc.com.) After you discover through the pretest that students don't have the particular knowledge they need, preteach the most relevant or compelling parts of the lesson to students or provide students with a relevant context for the learning. Then, when you are ready to teach the lesson, they are more equipped to engage in the learning task.

Try This

Use the following questions to identify which skills need to be addressed and which you can skip.

1. What rules or processes will students need to recall or follow in order to complete the task successfully?

2. What principles will students need to understand in order to explain what they are learning, troubleshoot when they reach a difficult point, or make adjustments when they face new conditions?

3. What facts do students need to know before they can successfully engage in the learning task?

4. What knowledge will students need to bring to mind while they are completing the task?

5. What concepts must students apply in order to complete the task?

Teach the Need-to-Knows Versus Nice-to-Knows

An important step in moving from quantity to quality is to take a look at your curriculum and decide what do students absolutely need to know.

There is some knowledge that is necessary in order for students to understand your subject. For instance, in order for students to be successful in general science class, they have to know what a cell is and how cells function in organisms. However, they may not need to know the intricacies of protein biosynthesis. It would be nice if they did know this, but it isn't absolutely necessary. I call this distinction "need-to-knows" versus "nice-to-knows."

One way to determine what students absolutely need to know is to take a look at the unit tests or the state-mandated tests. Another way to identify a need-to-know is to look at what knowledge students will need in order to be successful at the next level. For example, if you teach algebra 1, what do students absolutely need to know in order to be successful in geometry and algebra 2? You can also determine need-to-knows by considering the enduring ideas of your discipline. What ideas are at the heart of your discipline? It is also helpful to collaborate with other teachers in your discipline. You can decide as a department what students will learn at each grade level or in each course in the continuum of courses in your subject area.

Once you have determined the need-to-knows, make these the foundation of your curriculum and lesson planning. Plan your units and lessons to address these first. Once you're done, look for spaces to add the nice-to-knows. The nice-to-knows become enrichment activities and should enhance students' understanding of the need-to-knows.

 Yes, but... the nice-to-knows are what make my curriculum interesting! Why should I deprive my students and myself of the fun parts of my subject?

Those of us who have accrued a number of fun activities over the years may have a hard time letting them go. The good news is that you do not have to give up all of your nice-to-knows, but you will have to look at those activities differently. They cannot take precedence over the need-to-knows. Instead, they should supplement and enrich the crucial material.

Unfortunately, there are no twelve-step programs to help us let go of our nice-to-knows. But, there are steps you can take to give the nice-to-knows their proper place in the curriculum.

First, use the nice-to-knows to generate interest or engagement in the need-to-knows. Second, use nice-to-knows to enrich or deepen students' understanding of the need-to-knows. Finally, use nice-to-knows as a way of differentiating the material for students who have already mastered the need-to-knows.

Try This

• Specify what students must know, subtract what they know already, and teach students the rest.

• Work with other teachers in your department or on your grade level to determine the need-to-knows for your subject or grade. Spend some time examining the curriculum together and comparing it to the state or district-level assessments and standards. Then decide as a group what the need-to-knows will be.

- Make a list of all of the need-to-knows of your curriculum. Use the following criteria to distinguish the need-to-knows from the nice-to-knows:

1. Will it be tested on the state-mandated or end-of-the-year test?
2. Will students need the knowledge or skill in order to be successful in the next grade level?
3. What knowledge and skills are essential to understanding your subject?

Determine How Well Students Need to Know the Need-to-Knows

Once you have determined what students absolutely need to know, the next step is to decide how well students need to know it. Some need-to-knows need to be introduced and refined while others require mastery. This distinction is important because it clarifies the need for quality over quantity. As Grant Wiggins and Jay McTighe (1998) point out, "Not everything we ask students to learn must be thoroughly understood" (p. 22). Some knowledge and skills only require a surface understanding. Students need to be aware of them, but understanding them deeply is not crucial for students to be successful at one level or to move on to the next level. There are other knowledge and skills that students will need to thoroughly understand because this understanding is foundational to the subject area or grade level. Students will need to be able to access this knowledge automatically.

Understanding the difference helps you determine to what level students need to know something. In both cases, students will need practice, but the degree and amount of practice students need to become aware of or extend their knowledge of important content is significantly less than the amount of practice and exposure students will need to reach mastery.

Max Thompson (2008) suggests that teachers prioritize their curriculum based on how well students need to know the need-to-knows. Based on his analysis of the research and of state testing procedures, he suggests that 50 percent of most curricula is critical and needs to be learned to the level of mastery. Another 30 percent of a curriculum is important and needs to be introduced to students and refined. The last 20 percent of most curricula is usually nice-to-knows and information that should be maintained or compacted. In his prioritized lesson plan model, he argues that teachers should spend between 70-75 percent of their time helping students master essential content, 20 percent of their time introducing or extending students' knowledge of essential content, and only 5-10 percent of their time helping students maintain their understanding of a few key nice-to-knows.

Determining how well students need to understand what you are about to teach helps you allocate the time you spend on each learning objective and activity. Prioritizing your curriculum gives you more time to focus on the essentials and make sure that students master these rather than simply covering a wide array of material without mastering any of it.

Try This

• Prioritize your curriculum. Identify the 80 percent of your curriculum that should be need-to-knows and the 20 percent that should be nice-to-knows. Break down the need-to-knows even further by determining which content needs to be learned to the level of master (approximately 50 percent of your overall curriculum or 60 percent of your need-to-knows) and which need to be introduced and extended (approximately 30 percent of your overall curriculum or 40 percent of your need-to-knows). Focus first on the part of your curriculum students need to master, then on those things students need to be aware of or extend their understanding of but do not need to master, and finally on the nice-to-knows.

• One way to determine whether something needs to be understood to the level of mastery is to figure out whether that knowledge or skill is really a subset of another knowledge or skill. If the skill or knowledge in question is a subset of other important knowledge and skills and not knowing it to the level of automaticity will slow down students' ability to perform, then students need to master it. If not, then students can be introduced to the knowledge but may not need to master it.

Focus on Distributed Practice Versus Full-length Performance Every Time

Another way to stay focused on quality versus quantity is to allow students distributed practice opportunities. For example, if I am teaching students how to write hypotheses, do I really need them to conduct an entire experiment based on the hypothesis? Can't they just write an effective hypothesis? If I am trying to teach students how to write an effective thesis statement, do they

really need to write the rest of the essay? Can't I just have them write the introduction and outline the rest of the essay so that they can see the connection
between a well crafted introduction and the structure of the rest of the essay?
Do I really need full-length performance every single time?

Distributed practice means that you divide a learning experience into
smaller parts so that students can learn one part at a time. Research has
shown that distributed practice leads to better learning than full-length performance because it focuses students on the key understanding or skill rather
than bogging them down in several related but not key skills (Snowman &
Biehler, 2000). Short practice sessions distributed over several weeks will
work better than one or two long practice sessions at the end.

Try This

• Rather than have students practice a skill over and over, teach students
how to use mental visualization as a form of practice. Having students imagine themselves performing a task or practicing a skill for a few minutes each
day can be just as effective as taking the time to actually practice.

• As you are planning a unit, schedule opportunities for students to
practice skills or knowledge that they have learned from prior units as a way
of reinforcing information and helping students to retain and transfer skills
learned in one unit to other units of study.

The Principal in Action

Sylvia taught AP literature, a college-level class that emphasized close reading
of texts—mostly plays, novels, and poems—and a thorough understanding
of the conventions of literature. Students were required to take a rigorous
three-hour national exam at the end of the year, which, if they passed, would
earn them college credit for the course.

Sylvia's students were not what you would consider college-bound. They
attended an impoverished public school in the Bronx. Many of them had
not read more than a few books in their entire lives. Not only that, but their
writing skills were very weak. Many of them had never written more than a
five-paragraph essay.

Worried that her students were so far behind, Sylvia developed a syllabus
designed to help them catch up on all of the skills and knowledge they had

missed since grade 9. Her syllabus required students to read 28 novels during the year and write a paper per week. They would read a total of 62 poems, 40 short stories, and 5 plays. Sylvia crammed into one year, the curriculum she felt the students should have had for the last three years. Essentially, Sylvia attempted to teach four years of high school English in one.

Clearly, Sylvia was doomed to failure. Her intentions were noble, but her strategies undermined her intent.

When I visited Sylvia's classroom one fall, she was very frustrated. Her students weren't keeping up with the reading schedule, they were barely turning in their homework, and many of them were giving up and dropping the course. She had heard me talk about quality versus quantity and knew that her syllabus was too dense, but she couldn't understand how to pare it down without sacrificing the rigor or her course After listening to Sylvia's frustration, I suggested that we take a look at her syllabus and see how we could make it more manageable.

We started with the AP test itself and looked at what skills and knowledge the test asked of students. The tests changed each year, so we looked at the past three released tests. When we analyzed the first test, we found that the test used excerpts from *Hamlet, Cry the Beloved Country, Pride and Prejudice, Beloved,* and *The Scarlet Letter*. The next test examined *The Adventures of Huckleberry Finn, A Lesson Before Dying, Wuthering Heights, Othello*, and *The Stranger*. The last test we looked at contained excerpts from *Faust, The Great Gatsby, Native Son, Death of a Salesman*, and *The House of Spirits*.

"You see?" Sylvia pointed to the tests. "That's why I have to give them so much to read. They haven't read any of these works. How will they pass the test?"

"Sylvia, there is no way that you will be able to ever have them read all the books that might be on the test. The test changes each year. You'd have to have them read every book that was ever written."

Sylvia nodded. "That's the problem. The kids who pass this test read all the time. They have been readers for years. My kids haven't read more than four or five books in their lives. They will never catch up."

"Maybe they don't have to," I said, as I picked up the test and looked at it thoughtfully. "Let's look at the test again."

This time, we looked at what students were being asked to do with the works of literature excerpted on the test. We wanted to know what skills would be required of students in order to pass the test. We soon realized that while exposure to multiple works was helpful, it was not a necessary condition for passing the test. We made a list of skills that students would need and found that these skills were consistent across all three tests. What the test demanded was that students were able to thoughtfully analyze literature and effectively convey their analysis in writing.

"Sylvia. Can you teach these skills to your students with fewer readings?"

Sylvia looked down at the list we'd made. "You know, I just might be able to."

Together, Sylvia and I pared down her reading list to 8 novels, 3 plays, and 20 short stories. We focused on the skills she would need to develop in her students and figured out how to use the works of literature to teach the skills. We focused on teaching the skills in a way that would allow students to transfer the skills to other works and other activities. By the time we were finished, we had a manageable plan for both Sylvia and her students.

What Sylvia learned is something that we all must learn at one time or another. It is easy to get so overwhelmed by what our students have to learn that we begin to focus on quantity versus quality. But it is not how much we cover that counts; it is how strategic we are about what we cover that will ultimately determine how well our students master the goals of our curriculum.

Getting Started

1. Examine your curriculum for overlap and for unnecessary activities. Eliminate these in order to buy yourself more time to backfill important skills.

2. Distinguish between what items in your curriculum are the need-to-knows versus the nice-to-knows.

3. For the need-to-knows, distinguish between what needs to be learned to the level of automaticity and what needs to be learned to the level of controlled processing.

4. Spend the majority of your time on the need-to-knows automatic processes. Use distributed practice, reviewing, error analysis, and revision to provide more focused practice on these areas.

5. For controlled processing, provide students with more opportunities for full-length performance.

7

Never Work Harder
Than Your Students

How to tell students what to look for without telling them what to
see is the dilemma of teaching.

Lascelles Abercrombie

I was working with a middle school doing some job-embedded coaching for
the 8th grade teachers. Audrey asked me to observe her class and give her
some help with her students who didn't seem to be motivated to do the work.
When class started, Audrey put up an overhead of the day's agenda and asked
students to copy it down. A few did. Most did not. Then Audrey projected a
PowerPoint presentation on the screen. The first few slides reviewed salient
points from the assigned reading the night before. The next few slides posed
discussion questions about the reading.

"Okay class," Audrey began. "What was significant about the red apple
in the story?"

The students sat in their seats and looked at Audrey. "Come on guys, you
know this." Still no hands. "Remember? Jonas couldn't see the color red before
and now suddenly he could see color?" A few students nodded. Next slide.

"Okay. Why did Jonas stop telling his dreams to his family?" She asked.
This time, a student raised her hand.

"Because he didn't want to?" the student replied.

"Good, Theresa," Audrey praised. "Why didn't he want to?"

Theresa shrugged. "I don't know."

"Come on Theresa. You know this. His dreams were. . . ." Audrey trailed off and looked at Theresa meaningfully. Theresa looked back blankly. "His dreams were not the same, they were. . . " Audrey prompted.

"Different?" Theresa answered.

"That's right. Jonas's dreams were different from his family's dreams and his family could not understand them. In fact, Jonas couldn't even understand them at first. It was like seeing color. How do you explain to someone who has never seen color what color is? It just became easier for Jonas to say that he did not dream so he didn't have to try to explain to his family what his dreams were."

After a few more minutes of this type of questioning, Audrey switched off the LCD projector and went over to the tape player. "Take out your books, everyone, and turn to page 25." Most of the students took out their books. Audrey switched the tape player on and a voice on tape began to read the chapter. Some of the students followed along. Others put their heads on their desks.

When the tape finished, Audrey switched off the tape player. "We are going to play a review game to help us remember what we just read. You are already seated in groups of four. These will be your groups for this assignment." With that, she handed out envelopes to each group. Inside the envelopes were strips of paper, each with a sentence describing an event from the story. "Take these strips and put them in order based on what happened in the chapter we read today." Audrey explained.

The students began to put the strips in order. Audrey looked at one table of students who weren't working.

"Hey, guys, how come you aren't working?" she asked.

The students shrugged. "Come on. You can do this," Audrey encouraged as she picked up the first strip. "Now where does this one go?"

The students looked up at her silently. "You remember in the story when Jonas saw that the apple was red," she prompted. The students waited for her to finish. "Remember? That was after he started his training so it would go. . . ." Audrey waited for the students to respond.

"Second?" one student volunteered.

"No, not second," Audrey responded.

"Third?" another student guessed.

"That's right. It goes third," Audrey beamed. "Now what goes second?" she asked.

"I dunno," a student shrugged.

"Well if this strip goes third and it happened *after* Jonas began his training, what do you think goes before that?" Audrey asked.

The students waited.

"Come on guys," Audrey encouraged as she pointed to the next strip.

"Oh, that one goes before it," the students guessed as they picked up the strip to which Audrey had pointed.

"Right," Audrey nodded. So if this happened second and this happened third then this," Audrey picked up a strip "must have happened first. Which means that this," Audrey picked up the last strip and placed it at the bottom, "must have happened last."

The students sat and watched as Audrey completed the exercise for them.

I think every teacher has that moment when, at the end of the day, they look up exhausted from a long day of teaching to see the students running, skipping, and jumping out of the classroom and think, "this isn't fair." And it isn't. Not to the teacher and more importantly, not to the kids. Learning takes work. If the teacher is doing all of the work, the kids cannot learn as well as they should be learning. That's why master teachers never work harder than their students.

When I teach *Master Teacher Mindset* workshops, many teachers read the handouts and cannot wait to get to this step. I don't blame them. They are working awfully hard and are eager to learn how to give the work back to the students. But giving the work back to the students isn't just about how to make the students work; it's about how to give the right work to the students. It's about getting clarity on what is your work and what is their work, and making sure that you do your work and they do theirs.

Common Practice

Traditionally, most of the work in the classroom is done by the teacher. Teachers plan the lessons, deliver the lessons, and assess the lessons. Sure, students passively listen to the lecture or watch the demonstration, take notes, complete the worksheet, and take the test, but the real work is done by the teacher. Many of us see our jobs as making students learn—by any means necessary. Rather than facilitate students' learning, we orchestrate every aspect of it.

Some teachers dictate learning because they truly believe that it is their role to do so. They think that their students cannot or will not do the work if they did not control every aspect of the classroom experience. They think that by imposing a linear and orderly process onto the classroom, they can protect their students and sometimes themselves from the messiness of learning. Other teachers dominate the classroom not with structure, but with their highly charismatic and passionate personalities. They are on stage and are rarely willing the share the spotlight. While this kind of teaching is entertaining and even inspiring, it requires very little from the student in terms of actual thinking. In the end, we take over the learning process, often quite unintentionally, and our students rarely complain. They are content to allow us to do the lions' share of the work.

We say that we want students to take more responsibility for their own learning, yet we continue to control every aspect of their learning. We dictate what is taught, what are acceptable responses, how students will learn the material, when students will learn, and how students will demonstrate what they have learned. It's not that students are incapable of doing more in the classroom, it's just that they have rarely been asked to do so. How will students learn to take more responsibility unless we first relinquish some of the control?

We can also fall into the trap of compensating for students' lack of responsibility by doing their work for them. But in doing so, we prevent them from ever learning how to take responsibility for their own learning. Or, we go to the other extreme and foist upon students responsibilities that are developmentally inappropriate. Then, we blame them when they fail to execute these responsibilities effectively.

Swinging back and forth between a totally teacher-centered classroom and a classroom that is completely student-centered—or even trying to find a balance between the two—misses the point entirely. No one person, not the teacher nor the students, is at the center of the classroom. The classroom is a community of learners. In this community there are roles that students must play and roles that teachers must play. Rather than jockey for control of the community, why not create classroom structures where everyone can be more effective in their particular role?

The Principle

Most problems in the classroom occur because the work of the classroom is improperly distributed. Either the teacher is doing the students' work or is asking the students to do work that really belongs to the teacher.

We underestimate our students' abilities and overestimate the value of our own contributions. When students are faced with a problem, our first impulse is to quickly solve the problem and move on. But doing so transfers the work of learning from the student to us. Instead, we should pose questions that help them think through the problem, model problem-solving strategies, and point them to the resources they need. Rather than solve the problem for them, we show them how to solve the problem for themselves.

Many of us do not realize that much of what we are currently doing is actually impeding students' mastery. By doing the work for the students, we are preventing them from reaching the learning targets on their own. There is a thin line between helping students and enabling them. Helping students means providing them with the minimum amount of assistance they need to learn to do something on their own. Enabling students means doing it for them.

Constructivist theory argues that meaningful learning happens when students try to make sense out of the world by filtering new information through their own existing knowledge and schemas. Meaningful learning occurs when students create their own knowledge, concepts, rules, hypotheses, and associations from personal experiences. Our job is to help our students find their own voices and develop their own understanding of the subject matter. If we really want students to assume more responsibility in the classroom then we have to help them understand what their role is and build in supports to help them assume their roles effectively.

We also need to make sure that we are not giving them too much work. Often students struggle because we are asking them to do something that is really our job. The teacher who asks students to figure out how to read the textbook chapter on their own, or expects students to make sense of a complex worksheet or project at home because there was no time to cover it in class is asking the students to do the teacher's work on top of their own work.

The key is to make sure that you and your students are fulfilling your proper roles in the classroom. That means that you are doing your work and they are doing their work and, together, you are ensuring that students are meeting and exceeding the learning goals of your course or grade level.

Practicing the Principle

Master teachers clearly delineate their role and their students' roles. They make sure that they do not ask their students to do the teacher's work and they are careful not to do work that really belongs to their students. Master teachers don't just hand students their work however. They make sure to show students how to do their jobs, put structures in place to help students be more effective at their jobs, and hold students accountable for doing their jobs.

Clarify What Is Your Work

The first six principles of this book outline in detail what is your work. This last principle is really about the work that belongs to the students. Yet, even here, you still have a part to play.

Students are more likely to accept their responsibilities for appropriate classroom behavior when it is clear to them that you are fulfilling your responsibilities. In fact, you must first make sure that you are showing students that you are doing what you are supposed to do before you can expect students to do what they are supposed to do in the classroom.

Your responsibilities include

1. Being well-prepared to teach.

2. Determining what will be taught and to what degree, what behaviors you expect students to demonstrate as they are learning it, what procedures you and the students will use to learn it, what products students will produce, and at what point the lesson will close.

3. Providing clear directions and explanations of the material and ensuring that students understand the criteria.

4. Clearly communicating, modeling, and enforcing behavior expectations.

5. Demonstrating enthusiasm and encouragement for both the subject area and for student success.

6. Establishing structures and supports so that students can access the material.

7. Assessing student progress, adjusting your instruction based on this feedback, and sharing the feedback with students.

Just as it is important to understand what your role is, it is also important to understand what your job is not. Your job is not to solve problems for your students. Your job is to provide them with just enough guidance so that they can solve problems on their own.

Another area teachers work too hard in is classroom management. We cannot control how students behave. We can only influence it. Your job is not to manage student behavior; your job is to teach students how to manage their own behavior.

Your responsibility is not to solve students' underlying issues such as their difficult home life or their mental and emotional problems. Indeed, in many cases, you cannot solve these problems anyway. Your job is to help students do well in class in spite of their constraints outside of the classroom.

And your job is not to do the thinking for students. We often make the mistake of seeing students struggle with finding the correct answer and swooping in to deliver them from their discomfort by providing them with the right answer. We don't want to see students struggle. But intervening too soon is one of the most common ways we prevent students from doing their work. It isn't easy to watch students struggle, but doing so will help them to do their own thinking and ultimately their own learning.

I saw a great although painful example of this one morning when I was observing Rebekah's classroom. They had just finished completing a warm up and were moving to a discussion of the Declaration of Independence. "The first line of the Declaration of Independence says that 'We hold these truths to be self-evident.' What does that mean?"

The students silently stared back at Rebekah. She crossed her arms over her chest, leaned back on her desk and waited.

And waited.

And waited.

Two minutes passed in silence. Two painful minutes where the students sat and stared at Rebekah and she stood and smiled at them. Two minutes of excruciating silence where I shifted uncomfortably in my seat and thought seriously about raising my hand or passing the answer to the student who sat next to me so that he could raise his hand and the class could move on.

Finally, a few students took out their textbooks and began turning pages. "That's a good idea Shaine," Rebekah said, as a student reread the text. "Rereading the text is an excellent strategy." And then she waited.

And waited.

And waited.

A few more students opened their books and began to read. Even they were beginning to look a little uncomfortable. Rebekah stood there at the front of the room smiling expectantly. I was beginning to think she was a little crazy.

Then one hand came up. Hallelujah! I thought and silently thanked the student who raised her hand to answer. Now we can end this torture. But Rebekah didn't call on that student right away. She waited. And waited. After what seemed like an eternity, a few more students raised their hands. When five hands were up, Rebekah called on one of the students to answer the question. Then she called on another student to extend the first students' answer. Then she called on a third student. Each student's answer delved more deeply into the document than the last. By the time the third student answered, the rest of the class was drawn into the discussion. For the next twenty minutes, the students engaged in one of the most thoughtful discussions of the Declaration of Independence I have ever heard.

I met with Rebekah afterwards and asked about her use of "wait time." I confessed that I was very uncomfortable during that long two or three minutes of silence. "So was I," she laughed and leaned back in her chair. "But, I didn't want students to just give me a pat answer. I wanted them to really think about it."

"But why wait? Why not ask a follow up question or give them hints?" I asked, curious about her choice of strategies.

"We teachers talk too much. We don't give students time to think. Sometimes, I think kids just need time to process, so I give that to them. I had to teach myself how to just shut up and give them space and time to think. When I do, we have much better discussions."

I think Rebekah is right. Learning is a messy process and we cannot control it. Sometimes we have to let it get messy, let students struggle a bit, get out of the way and let learning happen. It's a delicate balance, of course. You can't leave students twisting in the wind forever. But we can step back and allow students to grapple with material, encouraging them from the sidelines and managing their discomfort so that they don't become too frustrated, but ultimately letting them figure it out for themselves. That is really what learning is all about.

Yes, but…does this mean that I never use direct instruction?

Although direct instruction has earned a bad reputation over the years, there is nothing wrong with direct instruction in and of itself. It is the overreliance on direct instruction that inhibits learning. The key is to match your instructional approach to the subject matter and the teaching needs of your students. Direct instruction is an efficient means of helping students learn and can be very effective with helping students acquire certain types of knowledge. Grant Wiggins and Jay McTighe (1998) recommend that teachers use direct instruction to teach discrete, unproblematic, and enabling knowledge and skills and use more constructivist approaches—coaching, facilitating, discussions, guided inquiry, Socratic seminars, and problem-based learning—to help students understand those ideas that are more subtle, require personal inquiry, or are prone to misunderstanding.

Try This

• Look at the list (in figure 7.1) of your work and their work. What work are you currently doing that really belongs to the students and what work are you asking your students to do that really belongs to you?

• Resist the temptation to give students all the information they need at once or up front. Let students engage in discovery for themselves and provide them only with the information they need to facilitate their discovery.

• Ask students more open-ended questions and answer fewer questions yourself. Only provide answers to questions that will enable students to answer other, larger questions.

7.1   Dividing the Classroom Work

Your Work	Students' Work
Provide the necessary supplies.	Come to class prepared.
Provide clear directions and explicitly stated expectations.	Follow directions and ask questions when directions seem unclear.
Structure the physical environment to increase the likelihood that students will remain engaged and will learn.	Respect the physical environment and take care of it.
Determine learning outcomes and evidence of mastery.	Use learning outcomes to set personal learning goals and demonstrate mastery.
Break the curriculum into manageable learning units.	Engage in curriculum units and complete work on time.
Decide on timing and pacing and make adjustments as necessary.	Provide feedback on timing and pacing, letting teachers know when things are going too fast or too slowly.
Help students relate the content to their own lives.	Look for ways to relate the content to their own lives.
Facilitate learning.	Actively make meaning by examining what they are learning, connecting ideas, asking clarifying questions, and problem-solving.
Check for understanding and adjust instruction accordingly.	Let the teacher know when they don't get it.
Provide support when students don't get it.	Ask for help, try, and persevere.
Provide direct instruction in facts, discrete knowledge, skills, and techniques.	Observe, listen, take notes, ask clarifying questions, and practice.
Coach students toward better performance.	Listen, reflect, retry, and refine performance.
Provide growth-oriented feedback.	Use feedback to improve learning.
Create a respectful learning environment.	Respect themselves and other students.

Clarify What Is Your Students' Work and Give Their Work Back to Them

Your students also have a role to play in the classroom. Their primary job is to come to an understanding of the learning standards of your grade or course. Constructivist theory argues that students must come to this understanding by creating meaning for themselves. They cannot be mere passive recipients of someone else's explanation.

Giving the work of learning to your students means letting go of some of the control in the classroom. It is often difficult to find opportunities to share the work with your students because there are things that only a teacher can do. Only you can unpack the standards and plan units. Only you can continually assess students' mastery and adjust your instructional strategies to help students reach mastery. Only you can assign grades.

But the list of things only a teacher can do is fairly short. Much that takes place in the classroom can be done by someone other than you. A student can maintain many of the bulletin boards and posted items such as calendars, homework boards, or the make-up assignment folder for students who have been absent. A student can be in charge of putting up the warm-up each day or moderating classroom discussions. A student can pass back papers or hand out textbooks. The students can track their own performance and set their own achievement goals. So the first step toward giving back to students their work is to recognize that, with the right supports, students are capable of doing more than you think they can.

My colleague Traci learned that there were tutorials and simulations available online that could serve as supplemental material for her biology students. Normally, Traci would have spent hours researching these sites and compiling a list of appropriate tutorials. I encouraged Traci to think about ways she could give some of the work to her students. After some thought, Traci decided to pass out a list of the topics she would be covering for the year and offer a few extra points to students who found an appropriate simulation or tutorial. The students had one week and, at the end of that week, submitted almost 100 potential sites. She spent about two hours visiting the sites the students suggested and created a master list which she had another student post on the electronic class discussion board. For the rest of the year, when students struggled with a particular concept, Traci could point them to one of the sites for extra help without having to provide the extra help herself. And she could use the list again and again. Soon students started rating how help-ful the various simulations and tutorials were. Traci monitored the process but the work remained with the students.

Traci recognized that her job was not to find the material. Her students were perfectly capable of finding the material on their own with the right guidance. Traci focused instead on setting her students up to be successful by providing them with a list of topics and parameters and showing them how to find the tutorials and simulations through a basic Web search. She monitored their process along the way, but she allowed them to do most of the work. As a result, Traci not only had a great resource she could use to help her stu-dents, she showed her students how to use the internet to find resources and supports they could use to increase their understanding of complex concepts. They learned how to learn and developed a skill they could use for the rest of their academic careers.

> Yes, but... giving work back to the students still requires that I do more work myself.
>
> When I do workshops with teachers, especially on differentiated instruction, the ques-tion that will inevitably come up is this: What about the students? When are we going to ask them to take responsibility for their own work? It's a legitimate question. The problem is that the teacher wants to ask students to take responsibility without first laying the groundwork for students to do so.
>
> Before we can ask students to take responsibility for their work in the classroom, we have to be clear what their job actually is. What can we reasonably ask children and adolescents to do and what supports and structures do we need to put in place to make sure that they are successful?
>
> It is unreasonable to expect children and adolescents to automatically act like adults. We have to teach them how to be responsible. You can't just simply hand students their work. You also have to structure the work in a way that will make it more likely that they will do it. We have to set up our classrooms in such a way that they learn how to take responsibility for their learning and their behavior and put supports in place to help them do so.

Another step toward giving the work back to the students is to set up systems so that they are able to do more on their own. These routines will clarify for students what their jobs are and give them clear expectations for how they should perform their jobs in the classroom. Because students are not accustomed to doing the work themselves they will need a structure that helps them figure out the right way or at least a more efficient way of fulfilling their responsibilities. For example, if you want students to keep organized copies of their notes, then you need to have a routine for note taking and a routine for how notebooks should be organized. If you want students to find out for themselves what they missed when they were absent, you need to establish a routine for how students will find out about their missed assignments. If you want students to track their own performance, you need to give them a routine for finding out and recording their grades.

For instance, at my former middle school, the teachers decided to create a system that would help their students take on more responsibility for being organized, keeping track of their homework assignments, and taking effective notes. They designed an entire organizational routine for students that required them all to keep their notebook organized the same way. There was a section for each subject and a system for how papers were organized. At the front of the notebook was a student agenda book. The teachers paused during the last three minutes of class to check to see if students had written down their assignments. During their advisory period, teachers checked students' notebooks and worked with students to keep their notebooks organized. By helping students stay organized, the teachers were able to hold students accountable for doing their homework, studying their notes, and completing long-term assignments on time. The teachers did not do the organizing for students; they put a system in place so that students could stay organized themselves.

If you structure the environment so that students can more easily do their work, you will go a long way toward helping students assume more responsibility for their behavior and their learning.

Try This

• Give students meaningful responsibilities in the classroom. Place students in charge of maintaining the classroom space or give them the responsibility for implementing classroom routines. For instance, students can take turns taking notes for the absentee folder, which is available as a resource for absent students, or students can decide how best to arrange the classroom to facilitate their learning.

- Use cooperative learning activities or reciprocal teaching as a way of helping students act as resources for each other.
- Give students checklists for how an assignment should be turned in. Require that students apply the checklist to each assignment to identify missing pieces before they turn it in. Place the onus of making sure assignments are ready on the students.
- Create contracts for each unit outlining what students must do in order to complete the unit. Give students options within the contract but hold all students responsible for demonstrating mastery of the unit objectives. Have students sign the contract and hold them accountable for fulfilling it.
- Use the following guidelines when giving work back to the students.
    1. Clarify the parameters of the assignment.
    2. Define potential pitfalls. Show students how to avoid these.
    3. Establish and communicate how the work will be evaluated and by what standards.
    4. Identify and make available the resources students will need to complete the work effectively.
    5. Establish consequences for not doing the work.

- Use a four-step process suggested by Strong, Silver, and Perini (2001) to help student do their own intellectual work and refine and deepen their own thinking about a topic:
    1. Introduce the concept.
    2. Pose a problem that requires students to apply the concept or skill in some way.
    3. Have students solve the problem. Students may work alone or in small groups to experiment with how they can apply the concept to solve the problem. As they work, you circulate, coaching students on concepts reexplaining if necessary or clarifying any confusion the students may be experiencing. Also push students to not only come up with solutions or strategies but to explain why their solutions or strategies work.
    4. Finally, bring students together for a whole class discussion in which students discuss their strategies and explanations. As students explore what worked and what didn't work, ask probing questions to help them elaborate

on their explanations, draw conclusions, and develop alternative explanations or approaches.

• Ask students the following questions:

1. How would I know that you are being responsible for your own learning? What behaviors would I see?

2. How would I know that you are being responsible to the success of the class? What behaviors would I see that would show me that you are able to respond to the needs of the class and therefore contribute to the success of the class?

Chart their responses on a poster and discuss with them their responsibilities in the classroom. Post the chart in the classroom and refer to it throughout the year as a reminder to students about their role in the classroom.

• Make a list of all of the tasks in the classroom (i.e., posting assignments, leading class discussions, reviewing homework, etc.). For each classroom task, list all of the skills and knowledge it would take to do each job effectively. Then consider which skills and knowledge your students have already and what they can easily acquire with a small amount of instruction or support from you. Make these the students' responsibility. You assume responsibility for those things only you can do.

• Work with students to establish classroom routines in order to clarify how students are to carry out their responsibilities in the classroom. At the bare minimum, work with your students to establish routines for the following:

  ○ Homework (how will it be collected, how will students find out the assignment)

  ○ Late work (how students turn it in and what consequences they will face for turning in work late)

  ○ Absences (how students will find out what work they missed, when will they need to turn it in, and how they will turn it in)

  ○ Grade Updates (how often will you post grades, where will you post grades, how will students track their performance)

  ○ Beginning of class (what will signal the beginning of class, how will class begin, where should students be, what counts as tardy)

  ○ Ending of class (what will signal the end of class, how will students be dismissed, how should students leave the classroom)

○ Attendance (how will you track, what consequences will be in place for tardies and unexcused absences)

○ Note taking (what format should students use, how will they store their notes, and how will they use their notes)

○ Tests (how will the classroom be arranged, what kind of student interaction will be allowed—talking or complete silence, how to ask questions, how to turn in tests)

○ Discussions (how will students participate, what type of participation is appropriate, who will facilitate, how will discussions be facilitated)

○ Transitions (how will papers be passed back, how will students move from one activity to the next)

Hold Students Accountable for Doing Their Job

It isn't enough to just give the work back to students, you must also hold them accountable for doing their work. That means that if students do not do their work, you need to apply logical consequences. Logical consequences help students see the connection between their behavior and its consequences.

> ### Yes, but... what if the logical consequences do not work?
>
> Just because a student chooses to experience a logical consequence rather than changing his behavior does not mean that the logical consequence did not work. Students always have a choice and there will always be times when students choose to face a consequence rather than do their jobs. But, by applying consistent, logical consequences, you can help students see the relationship between their choices and the consequences of their choices so that they will be able to make better choices in the future. You can increase the likelihood that students will eventually make better choices by a) making sure that your consequences are logically and directly related to the behavior, b) being consistent in implementing the logical consequences, and c) not becoming engaged in power struggles with students. Instead, calmly and firmly apply the consequence and refuse to argue with students. Keep the conversation about the student's behavior and choices rather than the student himself.

There is a difference between a logical consequence and punishment. Logical consequences are directly and rationally related to the student's behavior. They are designed to help students take responsibility for their own behavior and choices. Logical consequences communicate to students that they are capable of controlling their own behavior. Punishment, on the other hand, is a contrived consequence that puts the responsibility on the teacher by removing the choices from the student. Because the power of punishment lies in the teacher's authority rather than in the students' developing awareness of their own power to make appropriate choices, punishment communicates that the teacher must control the student's behavior. Punishment may temporarily suppress inappropriate behavior, but rarely does it point students toward more acceptable behavior and choices in the future.

Many of the consequences we have in the classroom may seem logical, but in essence, they allow students to get off the hook for not doing their work. We think that we are holding students responsible by letting them face certain consequences, but these consequences often teach students to be more irresponsible.

For example, if students come to class without the supplies they need— pencils, calculators, or textbooks, for example—most of us do one of three things. Either we admonish the students for not bringing their supplies and allow them to sit in class while the rest of the students do the work. Or, we send them to the office. Or, we give the students what they need to do the work. In all three cases, we are working harder than the students.

A better option is to look for a logical consequence that puts the responsibility firmly back on the students to solve their own problems. You could, as Robert J. MacKenzie (2003) suggests, set up a classroom rental center where students who do not bring their supplies can rent them from you during the class period. You could take one of the student's shoes as collateral and return the shoe at the end of the period once the student has worked off the debt by staying after class and quickly cleaning off the desks or washing the boards. In this way, you make the students responsible for solving their own problem.

The same is true for when students do not turn in their homework or complete their in-class assignments. Typically, the only consequence they face is to earn a zero. While a zero may seem like a logical consequence for not doing their work, a zero does not hold students responsible for learning the material. If the students' job was to learn the material, and they do not demonstrate that they have learned the material, then it is important to hold them responsible for doing their jobs.

> ### 👉 Yes, but…what about rewards?
>
> One of the most subtle but powerful ways of helping students take ownership over their own work lies in how we treat students' success. In the old model, when students did what they were supposed to do, we rewarded them. Rewards, we were taught, helped motivate students to do the right thing. The problem with this approach is that it puts the onus on the teacher, not the student. It assumes that the teacher must do something to motivate students, must watch to see that students are doing what they are supposed to do, must identify the reward, and must deliver the reward. Soon, students are doing what they were supposed to do anyway not because it is their job, but because they will get a reward.
>
> Rather than rewarding students for doing their job, we should help them celebrate a job well done. It's a subtle shift but an important one. Celebrating their success leaves the onus where it should be, with the student.

A more logical consequence, therefore, would be that if students do not learn the material during the time you have allotted, they have to learn the material on their own time. Rather than give the student a zero, give the student an incomplete and set up a time after school or during lunch and recess for the student to complete the work. The goal is not to punish the student. The goal is to have the students fulfill their responsibility and complete the work. Be careful too that in holding the student responsible, you do not punish yourself in the process. For instance, if a student needs to come in at lunch to complete an assignment, that does not mean that you give up your lunch in the process. You can have the student work in the media center during lunch and turn in the assignment at the end of the period. Find ways to hold the student responsible without punishing yourself in the process.

Try This

- Check to see if the consequences currently in place in your classroom are logical consequences or punishment.

• Think about what logical consequences you can implement for students who do not do their job. Look at the list of student jobs you have developed. Then, develop one or two logical consequences for each student job on your list. Use the following questions (adapted from Levin & Nolan, 1996) to help you:

• What would be the logical result if the student continues the behavior?

• What is the direct effect of the student's behavior on the teacher, other students, and the student?

• What can be done to minimize these effects?

• Give students a choice of changing their behavior or experiencing a logical consequence. In this way, you put the responsibility for taking appropriate action on the student. If the student chooses to continue with the inappropriate behavior or continues to fail to do his or her job, then calmly apply the consequence. If the student chooses to behave more appropriately or do his or her job, congratulate the student on making a good choice and move on.

The Principle in Action

"Our kids just don't care," sighed Janice, a high school literacy teacher who was attending one of my workshops.

"Why do you think they don't care?" I probed.

"They just don't. No matter what I do to get them engaged they just don't care. They don't do their homework. They don't pay attention in class. They just don't care."

I sat down next to her. "Can you give me an example?"

"Well, I work with students who are reading below grade level and so I team teach a double period of reading and social studies. The other teacher and I gave the students a reading test last week. Then, we spent hours scoring each student's test and interpreting the results. When we gave them their results, they barely looked at them. I even found one student's results in the trash at the end of the period. Here we were giving them something that could actually help them, not just in social studies, but in life, and they don't even care!"

"I see your frustration, Janice. Why don't we take a look at the principles and see if any of them apply to your situation?"

"After hearing your talk this morning, that was the first thing I asked myself. But, I looked over your principles and I don't see where I've violated any of them."

"Okay, but let's take another look at them anyway. You never know."

Reluctantly, Janice agreed but I could tell that she was convinced that the problem was her students and not her. I sympathize with Janice and with the thousands of teachers like her. She sincerely wanted to see her students do well and she worked very hard to make sure that they did. How frustrating it was to see that her hard work was met with apathy.

I asked Janice how she introduced the assessment to the students.

"I told them that they were going to take a test that would show them what their reading strengths and weaknesses are."

"Good." I encouraged. "It sounds like you helped them see the relevance of what they were doing. You demystified the academic process. Tell me about the test itself."

"It's a great test," she said enthusiastically. "It doesn't just give them random multiple choice questions. It actually asks them to do activities that mimic real reading behaviors. That's why I thought that they would love the test."

"Okay, so It sounds like you honored principles five and six and only measured whether the students could apply what they learned."

"I told you that I didn't violate any of the principles. My students just don't care," she insisted.

"Hmm," I thought for a moment. "Okay. Tell me about the process you used to give them their results."

Janice described the process. "Well, first we gave them the test. That took two days. Then, my coteacher and I scored the tests and used the testing guide to interpret the results. Then we spent hours typing up an explanation for each student of what the scores meant. Finally, we gave students copies of their tests, their scores, and their interpretations. Then we spent several class periods meeting with students individually to explain to them what their scores meant and help them to set goals for their reading."

"What did your students do?" I asked.

"What do you mean?

"I mean, you told me all the things that your coteacher and you did. I am just wondering what your students did."

"Well, they had to take the test." She said.

"Okay, what else?"

"And, they had to read the test results and the interpretation."

"Okay, what else?"

"They had to meet with us individually to set goals."

"Is that it?" I asked.

Janice looked at me quizzically. "Yeah, that's pretty much it. Why?"

"Let's see. You and your coteacher gave the tests, interpreted the results, wrote an explanation for each student, and met with each student. Is that right?"

"Yes," she nodded. "That's right."

"And your students took the test and then met with you."

"Yes."

I looked at her, "Who did most of the work, Janice?"

Janice looked at me for a long moment. Then she smiled widely and shook her head. "We did," she said. "We violated principle seven—we worked harder than our students. Okay, okay. I admit it," she laughed. "But Robyn, I don't see what that has to do with my problem. My students don't care enough to do more of the work."

"Have you tried?"

"They don't do the work I give them. Why would I give them more?"

"Look at the work that you're giving them. What are they really being asked to do? They take tests that you give them. They receive the results. They are told to set goals. It's all pretty passive. What if they were given the chance to take a more active role in their learning?"

"What do you mean?"

"Well, what if instead of being given their results, they were taught to interpret their own results. What if when they met with you, they were asked to explain their test results to you and then tell you what they thought they needed in order to become better readers?"

"Hmm," Janice thought for a moment. "I guess I could let them tell me what their goals are for themselves rather than give them reading goals."

"I bet you could find several ways to give the work back to the students."

The rest of the day, Janice worked on a plan. She examined her upcoming lessons and looked for ways that she could let the students do the work. By the end of the day, she had a plan.

I talked with Janice about it a year later. "It wasn't a magic bullet," she said. "They were still apathetic sometimes. But I got more work out of them than I had gotten before and there were days when my students were actually excited about what they were learning. It was hard for me to let go of doing some of the work and there were days when I gave them too much of the work and had to take some of it back. But, when I got the balance right, I felt like my students were taking more ownership over what they were learning."

Getting Started

1. In order to prevent working harder than your students, clearly decide what is your work and what is your students' work.

2. Take back your work from the students by taking responsibility for teaching and supporting. Learn to tolerate the messiness of learning.

3. Give back their work to the students by shifting the responsibility for learning to the students. Do not solve their problems; help them acquire the tools they need to solve their problems on their own.

4. Hold students accountable for doing their work by applying logical consequences.

8

Putting It All Together

The problem is not that we do not know enough—it is that we
do not do what we already know. We do not act on or refine or
apply those principles and practices that virtually every teacher
already knows.

Mike Schmoker

I walked over to a group of math teachers at one of my differentiation work-shops. They were working on creating a differentiated unit plan.

"Wait a minute," said one teacher. "Although this standard is basically a content standard, students still need to know how to solve word problems in order to be successful on the assessment we have picked."

The other teachers paused for a second and thought this over. "You're right, Mike," another said. "That means we have to back up and figure out how we can make sure that the kids understand how to do word problems. That way, if they fail the test, we will know for sure it's because they haven't mastered the objectives."

I smiled to myself as I walked to the next group. *They're getting it*, I thought. They are getting the gift.

*

I visited Lisa's 2nd grade class to check her progress in completing her mastery action plan. Lisa had decided to focus on principle 4 ("master teachers use feedback to help them and their students get better") and wanted me to see the progress she'd made. I slipped into one of the tiny seats in the back of the class just as she began. "Okay 2nd graders," Lisa said, clapping her hands for attention. "I am going to pass back your latest vocabulary tests. Take out your data notebooks so that you can record your grades on the graphs just like we practiced. If you got 10 out of 10 answers right, where do you draw your dot?"

"At the 10!" the students shouted in unison.

"Good," Lisa smiled as she began passing back papers. "Now, if you got three or more wrong on this quiz, then during learning time today you are going to do some work at the vocabulary station so that you can be ready to retake the quiz on Friday. If you got more than five wrong, you will also need to sign up for an appointment with me." I smiled as the students graphed their latest grades on their "learning growth charts" and excitedly exclaimed, "I'm getting better!" and "Look, my line is going up!"

She's got it all right, I mused. She's got the gift.

*

"I just wish I could get there faster," Shaine sighed. Shaine was a novice teacher attending one of my Master Teacher Mindset workshops, and we were working together to develop her action plan.

"Shaine, focus on the journey, not the destination," I reminded her.

"I know. It's just that I see my students suffering because I am not getting better fast enough. I wish I could just take a pill and poof! I'm a master teacher!"

I laughed and glanced down at her action plan. She had outlined several important steps that would take her to the next level and beyond. If she sticks with her plan she'll have it, I thought to myself. She'll get the gift.

*

At the beginning of this book, I made a radical proposal—ANY teacher can become a master teacher. It is a radical statement because of the persistent myth in education that master teachers are born, not made.

Although some people seem to arrive at mastery naturally, they didn't. It comes only with the disciplined and consistent application of mastery principles. Those who seem to come by it naturally are just better at applying the mastery principles. And they have done so for so long that it just seems natural.

Jim Collins (2001) and his team of researchers spent years studying how successful organizations make the shift from "good to great." One of his most surprising findings was that

> no matter how dramatic the end result, the good-to-great transformations never happened in one fell swoop. There was no single defining action, no grand program, no one killer innovation, no solitary lucky break, no wrenching revolution. Good to great comes by a cumulative process— step by step, action by action, decision by decision, turn upon turn of the flywheel—that adds up to sustained and spectacular results. (p.165)

That is the hard work of becoming a master teacher. It doesn't happen overnight. You cannot just read this book and suddenly become a master teacher. There is work you must do, and that work is pretty hard. It will take time. It will not be easy, or comfortable, or random. Becoming a master teacher requires consistent, focused effort over time.

There will be times when it will seem from the outside that no change is taking place at all. It will seem as if you are not making any progress and that you are stuck at one level or another. It is at these times it is most important that you keep at it, because it is at these times that the real work of becoming a master teacher takes place. The process is like the experience of growing flowers. You plant bulbs in the fall, and it doesn't seem like anything is happening all winter long. But, when the spring comes, almost overnight, tulips and daffodils sprout out of nowhere. What we know about bulbs is also true of becoming a master teacher. During that period of dormancy, all winter long, it seemed as if nothing was happening. There were no green shoots pushing through the earth, no signs of life at all. But inside that tiny bulb, things were happening. It was preparing to bloom. If I had dug up those bulbs before the spring, I would never have seen the gorgeous flowers.

You may be thinking that you don't have time to engage in such a long process. You want a breakthrough right away. You are facing outside pressures that demand that you improve now. If you ever want to become a master teacher, however, you are going to have to resist the pressure and apply the mastery principles consistently. This will allow you to experience continuous, incremental growth that will propel you toward becoming a master teacher.

Although growth may be slow at first, over time you will build up momentum. Because the principles are interconnected, as you improve in one area, you will naturally begin to improve in other areas. For instance, if you focus on starting where your students are, as you begin to recognize your students' currencies, you will naturally begin to practice principle 4 by finding ways to anticipate and unscramble students' confusion and create support systems; principle 5 by paying attention to feedback and using this feedback to adjust your instructional approach; and principle 3 by confronting the brutal facts of your current reality in terms of what students can and cannot do already. You will find the unwavering faith to persist by looking at the surprising things students can do that you may have never noticed before. So, by getting better at practicing one principle, you will naturally get better at practicing the other principles, and, over time, you will build momentum as you improve until you reach a point of breakthrough.

Some of you will be tempted to skip the stages and move from novice to master teacher in one fell swoop. I understand the temptation. You want to become a master teacher right away. You may be facing outside pressures or your own internal time line and feel as if you needn't bother with the intervening stages. You don't have time to waste, and besides, incremental change is kind of boring. There is nothing sexy about slow, incremental growth.

But moving toward mastery is an organic and cumulative process. You cannot make the jump overnight. Sustained momentum rather than lurching back and forth between reform efforts and quick fixes is the only thing that will produce the breakthrough you are looking for. You cannot expect lasting change if you skip the work that makes it possible.

The Master Teacher Trajectory

I'll say it again. There is really no secret to becoming a master teacher. It is simply a matter of applying the mastery principles consistently over time.

Although it is possible to move through the trajectory very quickly, becoming a master teacher does not happen instantly. Mastery takes time and practice and the path to mastery will look different for every teacher.

Rather than trying to become a master teacher overnight, just focus on moving to the next step. If you scored in the novice range, focus on moving from novice to apprentice rather than trying to jump straight to master teacher. Taking your time and moving deliberately through the trajectory will ensure that in time, you will become a master teacher. If you move too quickly through the trajectory and skip steps along the way, you will never achieve mastery. Mastery only comes through the disciplined and consistent practice of the mastery principles. Thus, even though the path toward mastery is highly individual in terms of pacing, it is fairly predictable in terms of the steps involved.

Moving from Novice to Apprentice (Acquire)

At the novice stage, your goal is to simply acquire the skills and dispositions you need in order to begin applying the principles to your practice. Notice that I said focus on applying the *principles*. I did not suggest that you learn a specific strategy such as differentiated instruction or backwards design. A strategy is about what you do. A principle is about *how* you do something. It's a subtle distinction but an important one. Rather than focus on learning new teaching strategies, focus on learning the principles and thinking about how they apply to your own teaching. You might end up doing many of the same things you have always done, but when you begin to practice the principles, how you do those things will be very different.

You will know when you have made the move from being a novice to being an apprentice when you begin to break some of the rigid rules you have about teaching. Novice teachers tend to have only one way of doing things, either because they lack the experience to know that there are alternate approaches, or because they have been doing things one way for so long that they just don't consider other alternatives. In either case, novices operate by a set of rigid rules, either those that were given to them or those that they have developed over the years. When you begin to notice that you can take a different approach, when you begin to experiment with your teaching, that is when you begin to move from being a novice to being an apprentice.

In order to facilitate that move, select a principle with which you would like to experiment. Try some of the suggestions about applying the principle in your classroom and see what happens. Take note not only of how your students react, but how you react as well. It is okay to be a little uncomfortable trying a new principle. In fact, it is to be expected. But, try it anyway and pay attention to the difference it makes in your teaching. One good place to start is with Principle 2: Know Where Your Students Are Going. Once you begin to plan more effectively, unpack the learning standards, and really understand the teaching task before you, you will naturally start to see how the other principles apply to your teaching task. From there, you can begin to experiment with other principles as you implement your teaching plans.

It is also a good idea to find a practitioner or a master teacher to serve as a mentor or coach as you go through this process.

Moving from Apprentice to Practitioner (Apply)

Moving from apprentice to practitioner means that you have begun to apply the different strategies to your teaching practice. You have already acquired an understanding of the mastery principles and you recognize areas in your own teaching that would benefit from applying the mastery principles. You may have even started experimenting with some of the principles in your own teaching, but you are still not sure how to consistently apply them.

Don't try to apply them all at once. This will become too overwhelming and your practice will be much too disjointed. Instead, select one or two principles at a time to work on and begin to apply them to your teaching. Once you have become more comfortable practicing those principles, begin to add others to your practice.

To apply the principles you have selected to your teaching, begin by working through all of the "getting started" steps. Take each step one at a time and systematically begin applying it to your teaching. You can use the action planning template on page 216 to help you plan how you will apply the principle to your teaching. At this stage, it is also helpful to enlist an accountability partner to help you stay on track.

Moving from Practitioner to Master Teacher (Assimilate)

When you reach the practitioner stage, you have successfully acquired a range of teaching strategies and skills. However, you have not yet learned how to integrate them seamlessly into your teaching practice. That is the final step to becoming a master teacher—assimilation. The way that you learn to assimilate the skills you have learned is to purposefully practice them. But it isn't just that you practice these principles; to move from practitioner to master teacher, you are going to adjust how you practice these principles. So far, you have been practicing them in isolation of one another. Now you are going to begin integrating them.

The first step to integrating the principles into your practice is to look to see how all of the other principles will help you better practice an individual principle or how all the principles connect. Spend some time thinking through how each principle connects to the other principles and how practicing one principle involves practicing other principles.

The next step is to shift your thinking. Don't think so much about the fact that at any one time you are practicing a particular principle. Instead, think about the fact that you are applying a set of principles to your teaching.

Third, begin to use the mastery principles in different ways. For instance, rather than just practice the principles, you can also start to use the mastery principles as a way to help you think through any instructional challenge you may be facing. The problem-solving sheet in Tool 6 will help you use the mastery principles to solve an instructional challenge.

Becoming a Better Master Teacher (Reflect and Refine)

The challenge for the master teacher is no longer how to become better at practicing the mastery principles, but how to maintain this practice over the long term. The strength of master teachers is that they practice the mastery principles seamlessly and automatically. But, if they are not careful, this strength can also be their curse. If their practice becomes too automatic, then it also becomes mindless. Thus, master teachers need to be deliberately mindful about how they practice their teaching craft or they are in danger of stagnating.

One way to remain mindful is to select a principle that you want to refine, and work to hone your practice of that principle in your teaching. If you would like to develop a formal plan to help you, use Tool 2 to create a formal action plan.

You can also take time periodically to reflect on your teaching practice either through a formal reflection sheet (such as Tool 4) or informally with another colleague. By deliberately reflecting on your practice, you can analyze the effect of your teaching behavior on students, evaluate the appropriateness of teaching strategies, discover alternate strategies, become more open to new ideas and approaches, analyze your own decision making, weigh competing points of view, examine your own personal goals, and unearth commonalities, patterns, differences, and interrelations in your teaching attitudes and behaviors.

Another way to remain mindful is to identify one novice or apprentice teacher for whom you can serve as an informal mentor. Explaining how you apply the principles to your own craft will further refine your understanding of the principles and help you be more reflective about how you apply the principles in your own practice.

Sticking With It

The road to mastery isn't easy. There will be missteps and struggles along the way. The following suggestions will help you manage the challenges you will inevitably face and ensure that you stay the course.

Find an Accountability Partner

An accountability partner is a colleague with whom you meet once a week to review your progress in your action plan. Just having someone to whom you must report your progress will help you remain more accountable to your plan. Try to pick someone who will not let you off the hook. Pick someone who will commit to meeting with you, and schedule a regular time to meet. Your partner's role is not to mentor you, although your partner may make suggestions when you get stuck. Your partner's primary role is to ask probing questions such as "Why do you think you are not making as much progress as you thought?" or "You seem to have had a successful week. What did you do differently this week or to what can you attribute the change?" These questions will help you be reflective about your progress and challenge you to move forward with your plan. Your accountability partner can also help you collect evidence that you are indeed improving in your practice of the principle by conducting a peer observation of your class and looking for the specific evidence you identified in your action plan.

Find a Mentor

A mentor is someone who can coach you toward mastery. When selecting a mentor, you can do one of two things. You can either select someone who has scored at the Practitioner or Master Teacher level to provide you with general coaching. Or you can find someone who is particularly adept at the principle on which you are currently working to provide you with specific coaching. Either way, your mentor's role is to coach you toward better performance. In order to facilitate this coaching, meet with your mentor and ask for feedback as you and your mentor develop an action plan together. Then, as you work toward your plan, set aside a time to meet with your mentor to go over your progress, to make adjustments to your plan or your approach, and to ask for help or support on those parts of the plan that seem challenging. Then at the end of the six weeks, meet with your mentor to evaluate your progress and to decide on the next steps.

Work Through This Book with Colleagues

There is something to the cliché that there is strength in numbers. Meeting with other colleagues can help you remain focused, consider other perspectives on the principles and how they can be applied in the classroom, brainstorm ideas about how to apply the principles or solutions to challenges you are facing, and create a study group around a shared purpose and work. Tool 8 will help you organize such a group.

Stay True to Yourself

In order for you to fully incorporate these principles into your classroom, you will need to find a way to apply the principle using your own teaching style. The beautiful thing about a principle is that while it is universal in its application, it is also highly individual. There are many ways to apply a principle. For instance, take the principle of feedback. One teacher may decide to write highly detailed coaching feedback on each student's paper. Another teacher may write minimal feedback but meet with each student after a major assessment to set learning goals for the next unit based on students' performance. A third teacher may use a rubric to give students feedback on an assignment. Another teacher may choose to use a standardized test but spend the first 20 minutes of class explaining in detail what students' test scores mean and what they indicate about student progress. From there, the teacher may ask students to meet in small groups based on their scores to make corrections and determine future learning targets. All of these teachers are practicing the principle in the way that fits best with who they are and what they teach.

The way to figure how to apply the principle in a style that fits you is to think about your own classroom practice. You will need to make changes, certainly, but many of those changes are really small tweaks and adjustments rather than radical overhauls of what you are currently doing. Over time, as you continue to make adjustments, your practice will look very different from when you first started but will still be consistent with who you are as a teacher.

Now I know what some of you are thinking. You are thinking that some teaching is so ineffective that it requires radical changes. Or, you came to this book because you are looking to make a radical change in your own teaching practice. But, I am here to tell you that radical changes right away do not work. Every January people vow to make radical changes in their lives and by February, most of them have gone right back to living the way that they always have. Trying to make a radical change right away not only dooms you to failure, it creates a cynicism about change in general.

Take It One Step at a Time

Trying to change everything at once can be overwhelming. You are creating new teaching habits and doing so, like developing any new habit, takes time. Rather than make big changes all at once, I am suggesting that you make changes gradually. It's not that I don't want you to aim high; it's just that I want you to only do what you are capable of doing right now. That way, you are more likely to stick with the changes you make and make those changes a real part of your practice. Work through the stages of incorporating each principle into your practice one at a time. As you get comfortable with one step, you will be more likely to take on the next step.

Look to See What You Need to *Stop* Doing

Practicing the principles implies that there is something that you should start doing. But equally important are the things that you should stop doing. The simple answer is that you should stop doing anything that does not align with one of the mastery principles.

I'll give you a moment to take that in. Yes, that means that you are going to have to stop doing all those assignments that have been a lot of fun but do little to help students achieve your learning goals. It means that you are going to have to stop assuming that students are lazy just because they do not do their work. It means that you have to stop doing all of the work of learning and let your kids take on most of that work for themselves. It means, in short, that you are going to have to stop wasting time on anything that does not fit with these principles so that you have more time to do the things that actually make a difference.

Remember That Real Change Takes Time

If you are looking for a quick fix, I am sorry to tell you that there isn't one. I don't care what anyone promises you, lasting change does not happen in a day, or even a month. It takes time to make these changes an integral part of your practice and for the adjustments you make to your teaching to feel natural. But, applying the mastery principles to your teaching step-by-step over time will furnish you with a series of ongoing victories as you become more adept in making these principles a permanent part of your teaching practice. As these victories add up, you will be amazed at the changes that you will see in your teaching. Becoming a master teacher is a process in the same way that all learning is a process. Even if you scored in the master teacher range, there are still things you can do to improve your practice. As teachers, we are to never stop learning, for the moment we do, we also stop being effective teachers. How can we expect to inspire life-long learning in our students if we do not practice it ourselves? The key is to focus on the process rather than fixate on the final result.

Reassess After Six Weeks

At the end of six weeks, take some time to evaluate how well you have implemented your action plan and whether or not doing so has made a positive difference in your teaching. In order to evaluate your plan, first look at your goals. What were you trying to accomplish? What principle were you trying to put into practice in your classroom? Next, take a look at the individual steps you planned to take. Did you take all of the steps? If not, why? For the steps you did take, how did you do? Look at the evidence you identified for each step and evaluate how effective it was. Did taking the step make your job easier or help your students be more successful on a particular assignment or task? Finally, spend some time reflecting on how practicing the principle fit into your own teaching style. You can use Tool 4 to help guide your reflection.

Final Thoughts

I have made much of the idea that becoming a master teacher takes hard work, and it does. But, I believe that it doesn't take any more work than it does to remain a mediocre teacher and never improve. In fact, I think that staying where you are takes even more work.

Here is what we typically do. We go to a workshop or read a book and then try to apply the strategies we've learned to our own teaching. After a few days or weeks of hard work, we don't get the results we thought we would so we are on to the next new fad or quick fix. Or, we decide that there is nothing that can be done and we continue to deal with the same frustrations, become overwhelmed by the same challenges, and beat our heads against the same brick walls year after year. Both approaches sound like a lot of work with little or no reward.

But what if instead of working hard and not getting better, we found a way to simplify and focus our efforts? What if we figured out that much of what we are already doing is a waste of our time because it yields little or no results, and we decided to do something different and much more effective instead?

If we stopped doing all the things that are not working and focused our efforts on practicing these simple principles instead, our work would not only be much simpler, but much more fruitful and rewarding. We'd still be working hard, but we would see our efforts pay off.

What's more, when we see our efforts pay off, we find that we are even more motivated to work harder. Conversely, when we see that our efforts are mostly in vain, as is the case with staying the way that we are, we only grow more unmotivated, apathetic, or cynical.

All of us have been told countless times that our work is meaningful, perhaps one of the most meaningful things we can do with our lives. But sometimes, it just doesn't feel that way. When we are working day in and day out, facing impossible constraints with very little progress, our work can feel meaningless and downright futile.

You have to believe enough in the importance of your role as a teacher to make becoming a better teacher more important to you. You have to care enough about the work that you are doing to become more careful at it. You have to love your students enough to want to give them the best education possible. You have to be passionate about what you do in order to want to do it better.

Ultimately, becoming a master teacher is more about this passion than it is about anything else. It is this passion that will compel you to persist with practicing the principles even when they don't seem to make a difference. It is this passion that will make you commit to getting better even when doing so seems like an awful amount of work. It is this passion that will make you suffer seemingly slow, microscopic increments of growth when you long to just skip all of the stages and look for an instant solution. It is this passion that will help you stay the course in spite of overwhelming constraints even when it feels easier or saner to just give up.

Why did you become a teacher? I bet it was because you wanted to make a positive difference in the lives of young people. If that is still your goal, then the only way that you will make that kind of difference is to become a master teacher. I began this book by talking about "the gift." At the time, I debunked the idea that mastery teaching is a gift with which you are endowed. It is not. Mastery teaching is indeed a gift, but it is a gift you become and it is a gift you give. When you consistently apply the mastery principles to your own teaching, you *will* become a better teacher and as a result, your students will become better learners. They will feel more valued and accepted in your classroom. They will be motivated to try their best and feel ownership over their own learning and their own work. They will learn from their success and their failures and use both to consistently improve their performance. In the end, you give your students the gift of your best teaching self and they will be all the better for having been in your class.

I wish you joy in your own journey toward becoming a master teacher. May you too find your gift along the way.

Appendix

Tool 1

The Master Teacher Trajectory

Principle	Novice	Apprentice	Practitioner	Master Teacher
1. Start where your students are	Has a superficial understanding of who students are based on stereotypes and generalizations. Does not recognize that students have different currencies or does not value those currencies.	Recognizes that students have different values and attempts to get students to exchange their own currencies for those that are accepted in the classroom. Attempts to change students' values to those of the dominant culture.	Recognizes and appreciates students' currencies but focuses on helping students acquire new currencies rather than also showing them how to use the currencies they bring with them to acquire the capital of the classroom.	Understands students in terms of the currencies they value. Sets up the classroom so that these currencies are fairly negotiated and traded. Capitalizes on students' currencies and helps them use these to acquire the capital of the classroom.
2. Know where your students are going	Uses objectives provided by the state or district without a real understanding of what they mean.	Takes time to understand what the objectives mean and attempts to move students toward these objectives.	Unpacks objectives but does not align all learning activities to these objectives or break them down into steps toward mastery.	Sees course objectives as the floor rather than the ceiling. Clearly communicates objectives to students and breaks objectives down into steps toward mastery.
3. Expect to get your students to their goal	Bases expectations on his or her perceptions of who the students are and what they believe the students can do.	Confronts the brutal facts but loses faith in the process.	Maintains unwavering faith without addressing the brutal facts. Looks for outside solutions rather than focusing on own actions.	Bases expectations on his or her own efficacy rather than on his or her perception of students. Maintains unwavering faith while confronting the brutal facts of their reality.

4. Support your students along the way	Has a limited number of explanatory devices. Uses remediation as the sole source for helping struggling students. One-size-fits-all approach to instruction.	Differentiates instructional strategies for students at different levels. Focus is still on remediation but does begin to institute some supports within instruction.	Creates an intervention plan with red flag mechanisms along the way but waits until these red flag mechanisms are tripped before providing support.	Proactively plans support to catch students before they fail. Spends time anticipating and unpacking confusion as a normal part of the instructional process.
5. Use feedback to help you and your students get better	Uses assessment only to evaluate performance. Creates tests after the unit has been taught.	Uses assessments to inform instructional planning (backwards design) but does not use the feedback to inform or adjust instruction.	Uses assessment to inform instruction but does not use it to provide growth-oriented feedback to students.	Uses assessment to adjust his or her own instructional practice as well as to provide growth-oriented feedback to students.
6. Focus on quality rather than quantity	Focuses on coverage and task completion versus true understanding. Just trying to get through the curriculum.	Gets through the curriculum by jettisoning some activities that do not explicitly move students toward mastery.	Focuses on quality rather than quantity by making conscious decisions about what students need to know, but attempts to teach all need to knows to the level of automaticity.	Focuses on quality rather than quantity by making conscious decisions about what students need to know and how well they need to know it.
7. Never work harder than your students	Does the lion's share of the work in the classroom and sets up activities and assignments so that students learn passively.	Requires that students do most of the work, including some of the work of the teacher.	Attempts to balance the workload but still rescues students when things get too uncomfortable.	Appropriately distributes the work between the teacher and the students. Allows student discomfort as part of the messiness of learning.

Tool 2
Developing an Action Plan

It isn't enough to simply say that you want to become better at teaching. Sometimes you need to develop a plan that will help you get there. In the same way that we must set goals, develop a plan to achieve those goals, collect feedback and make adjustments, and monitor progress for our students, we must do the same things for our own professional development. This action plan will help you do just that.

Your action plan is only as good as your commitment to see it through. You could create an action plan today and then file it away and never use it. Six weeks later, you are likely to be in the same place you are now. There is no magic in the action plan.

The action plan merely helps you be more intentional as you progress toward your goals.

Where you are in the mastery trajectory will determine how you go about developing your action plan. What follows are guidelines for each stage of your journey. Then there are specific directions for completing your action plan, along with an Action Planning Template, and a sample Action Plan Questionnaire.

Novice

In order to move from being a novice to an apprentice, the first step is to review your scoring sheet and look at the principles in which you scored a two or higher. (See Scoring Sheet exemplar, p. 217.) Those are the principles in which you are already practicing as an apprentice. Now, look at the principles where you scored lower than a two. Those are the principles on which you need to work first. Select the principle where you scored closest to a two and develop an action plan for that principle. Identify a mentor (preferably someone who is either a practitioner or a master teacher) who is adept at the principle you are planning to practice. Share your action plan with your mentor and ask for input and suggestions. Invite your mentor into your classroom toward the end of the six-week period to provide you with feedback on your progress.

If you have not scored a two within six weeks, sit down with your mentor teacher to adjust your plan. Reread the chapter to see how you can better practice the principle, including trying some of the "try this" suggestions and consulting some of the recommended resources for a more in-depth discussion of the principle and its practices. Once you have scored a two or higher in your selected principle, move to the next principle on which you were closest to a two, and so on.

Apprentice

To move from apprentice to practitioner, separate those principles in which you scored a three or higher and those principles in which you scored below a three. Of those principles where you scored below a three, select the one whose score is closest to a three and develop an action plan for that principle first. Identify a mentor who is a practitioner to help you remain accountable to the plan and to provide you with feedback. Also, observe at least one master teacher, paying close attention to how you see the principle on which you are working play out in that teacher's classroom (Use Tool 5 to record your thoughts).

Check your progress in six weeks to see how you are doing, keeping in mind that you want to score at least a three in that principle on the reassessment. If you have not scored a three within six weeks, sit down with your mentor teacher to adjust your plan. Reread the chapter to see how you can better practice the principle, including trying some of the "try this" suggestions and consulting some of the recommended resources for a more in-depth discussion of the principle and its practices. Once you have scored a three or higher in your selected principle, select the next principle in which you scored below a two that is the next closest to a three and begin to practice that principle.

Moving from Practitioner to Master Teacher

To move from a practitioner to a master teacher, first separate those principles in which you scored a four from those principles below a four. Of those principles in which you scored less than a four, select the principle with the highest score and develop an action plan for that principle. Check your progress in six weeks. If you have not moved to four in that time, complete the reflection sheet (see Tool 4) and use it to revise your action plan. If you have moved to a four in that principle within six weeks, select the next principle closest to a four and develop an action plan to begin practicing it.

Master Teacher

To develop an action plan that helps you become an even better master teacher, select the principle in which you received the lowest score. Then, complete the action plan for this principle. At the end of six weeks, check your progress. If you have not made progress, complete the reflection sheet (see Tool 4) and use it to refine your action plan.

Creating the Plan

In developing your action plan, you will start working on the principle in which you are closest to achieving the next step. The reason you will start here instead of the principle in which you need the most improvement is twofold. First, when you are first beginning to practice the principles, it is important to go for the quick win. You will need to see some improvement right away to stay motivated. The other reason we start from where you are strongest is that in improving your practice in this principle, you will also improve your ability to make improvements in the other principles. Because all of the principles are connected, by getting better at practicing one principle, you will improve your ability to get better at practicing the others.

The actual action plan is divided into eight parts. The first part asks you to identify the *Principle* you will work to develop and conduct an analysis of how you have been applying the principle to your practice thus far. This part of the plan is designed to help you be reflective about what the principle means in general and what it means to your individual practice. Although you may want to get to your action planning right away, do not skip this step. It is crucial that you first analyze where you are currently and have a good understanding of where you are headed before you begin to identify specific actions.

The second section concerns the *Getting Started* steps. Each principle is broken down into specific steps to help you get started. As you work to develop your practice of a specific principle, you do not have to develop the steps on your own. Use the *Getting Started* steps to help you figure out what specific steps you will need to take in order to improve your own practice of the principle.

Keep in mind that you do not have to apply all of the steps right away. This is another example of how practicing the principle is highly individual. You may choose to develop an action plan where you just work on developing your proficiency with one or two steps instead of the entire set of steps. Then, after you have developed your ability to apply one step, you can move to one or more of the other steps. Or, you can choose to develop a plan where you work step-by-step through an entire principle at one time. It is entirely up to you. Just keep in mind that you want to develop an action plan that you can reasonably achieve in about six week's time.

The next part of the action plan is the *Specific Actions*. Here you will detail what specific actions you will take in order to apply each Getting Started step to your own teaching. Again, this is highly individual to you. You can look back over the chapter's *Practicing the Principle* or *Try This* sections for ideas of specific steps. Or, you can decide on other specific actions. The key is to make sure that the actions you choose actually help you apply the principle to your own teaching practice.

The fourth part of the plan is *Evidence*. In this section, you will decide what feedback you will collect to tell whether or not you are making progress. How will you know that you have indeed accomplished the goals of your action plan? The type of evidence you choose to include could range from examining student work, peer observation, videotaping your class yourself and evaluating the tape, student surveys, etc. (See Tool 3 for a list of evidence for each principle.) Determining your evidence is important for two reasons. One, it will help you monitor your progress toward incorporating the principle into your practice. And, it will also help you remain objective about your progress. It will keep you from being either overly optimistic or overly pessimistic.

The next part of the action plan asks you to identify any *Resources* you will need to implement the action steps. These resources may include physical resources such as student survey instruments, curriculum documents, pre- or post-tests, supplementary texts, etc., or they may include more less tangible resources such as time to unpack the standards, professional leave to attend a one-day workshop on differentiated instructional strategies, or support from a mentor teacher. Figure out what resources you will need to implement your plan and how you will acquire these resources. Sometimes this will mean asking for support from your administration, which may be difficult for many of you. However, showing that the resources you are requesting are tied to a viable action plan designed to improve your teaching may make it easier to convince your administrators to supply the needed resources.

The plan also asks you to identify a *Due Date* for when you will implement each step. This is to help you think realistically and remain accountable to the plan. You don't want to say that you will start applying the principle at some point in the future. Give yourself a deadline so that you can hold yourself accountable.

The next part of the plan asks you to anticipate any *obstacles* you may face along the way. These obstacles may be external, such as a lack of support or a lack of resources you need, or these obstacles may be internal, such as a lack of motivation or an attempt to do too many things at once. Either way, you need to be brutally honest about what may stand in your way and plan for how you will deal with these obstacles before you implement your plan. That way, you can discover ways to mitigate barriers before they prevent you from implementing your plan. In thinking through these obstacles, you may find that you need to adjust your plan. That's OK. The goal is to create a plan that you can actually implement given your particular situation and its constraints.

The final part of the plan asks you to think about how you will *Monitor* your progress and when your *Completion Date* will be. This is important because you don't want to implement your plan indefinitely. You need to see whether your plan is working and if it is not, then you can make adjustments to your plan rather than continue to work at something that is not producing the results you want to see in your teaching and in your students' learning. Giving yourself a due date is another way to hold yourself accountable to your plan by forcing you to revisit your plan at some point and evaluate your progress. I typically recommend due dates of around six weeks. That time-frame gives you enough time to practice your principle in multiple situations and to begin seeing results. It also gives you time to make mistakes along the way and to adjust. And, it is not too long in the future that you will have abandoned your plan before you have had a chance to evaluate it.

Action Plan Questionnaire

Principle: Based on your assessment, what principle will you work on next?

Write the principle in your own words. Explain what it means and how it relates to your individual practice. In what ways are you already practicing the principle and in what ways do you need to practice it more?

Turn to the chapter where this principle is discussed and list the Getting Started steps below:

Now, develop a plan for applying these steps to your own teaching. Use the Practicing the Principle sections to help you figure out how to apply the Getting Started steps. And, look at the Try This suggestions at the end of each section for concrete ways that you can begin practicing the principle in your own classroom.

What obstacles may be in your way and how will you mitigate these obstacles?

How will you monitor your plan?

Completion date:

Action Planning Template

Getting Started Steps	Specific Actions	Evidence of Mastery	Resources	Due Date

Sample Scoring Sheet

Principle 1		Principle 2		Principle 3		Principle 4		Principle 5		Principle 6		Principle 7		Row Totals
1	2	2	2	3	2	4	4	5	3	6	2	7	1	16
8	4	9	2	10	2	11	2	12	2	13	2	14	2	16
15	3	16	3	17	1	18	2	19	2	20	2	21	2	15
22	3	23	3	24	3	25	2	26	2	27	2	28	2	17
29	2	30	2	31	2	32	3	33	1	34	2	35	2	14
36	2	37	1	38	2	39	2	40	2	41	3	42	2	14
43	2	44	2	45	2	46	2	47	2	48	1	49	2	13
Principle Total	18	Principle Total	15	Principle Total	14	Principle Total	17	Principle Total	14	Principle Total	14	Principle Total	13	Overall Total
Principle Average	2.6	Principle Average	2.1	Principle Average	2	Principle Average	2.4	Principle Average	2	Principle Average	2.0	Principle Average	1.9	105

Sample Action Plan Questionnaire

Principle: Based on your assessment, what principle will you work on next?

Principle 1—Start where your students are.

Write the principle in your own words. Explain what it means and how it relates to your individual practice. In what ways are you already practicing the principle and in what ways do you need to practice it more?

Starting where your students are means that I pay attention to what my students already bring to the classroom and start with what they already know. I need to think about what I value in terms of students' behavior. I also need to think about the ways my students may be presenting behaviors that are different from those I value.

Turn to the chapter where this principle is discussed and list the Getting Started steps below:

1. Examine your own currencies. Look to see what currencies you value in the classroom.
2. Pay attention to your students to discover what currencies they value and what currencies they are spending.
3. Look for any disconnection between the currencies you are accepting in the classroom and those the students are spending. Also look for ways that you may be spending currencies that the students do not value.
4. If the disconnection is because the students do not have classroom currency, help students use the currency they have to acquire classroom currency by showing them how their currencies are valuable, helping them acquire additional currencies, and learning how to code switch.
5. If students have classroom currency but refuse to spend it, create a shared classroom economy and reward them in currency they value.

Now, develop a plan for applying these steps to your own teaching. Use the Practicing the Principle sections to help you figure out how to apply the Getting Started steps. And, look at the Try This suggestions at the end of each section for concrete ways that you can begin practicing the principle in your own classroom:

Sample Action Planning Template

Getting Started Steps	Specific Actions	Evidence of Mastery	Resources	Due Date
Examine your own currencies. Look to see what currencies you value in the classroom.	Use the reflection sheet to figure out what currencies I value. Make a list of those things I think are important.	List	None	1/23/09
Pay attention to your students to discover what currencies they value and what currencies they are spending.	-Give students a survey to see how they want to be rewarded.	Student survey results	Create or find student survey	2/04/09
	-Spend a week observing students to see what currencies they are spending. Keep a record in my teaching notebook.	Observation notebook	Time to write in notebook	2/14/09
	-Make a list of students' currencies based on the survey and the observation.	List	None	2/16/09
Look for any disconnection between the currencies you are accepting in the classroom and those the students are spending. Also look for ways that you may be spending currencies that the students do not value.	-Compare the two lists to see where there is a disconnection.	Annotated lists	Need someone to look over list to see if I missed anything	2/17/09
	-Based on comparison, set up a new reward system that is a compromise between what I value and what the students value.	New reward system	None	2/28/09
	-Try to spend a least one currency that is on the students' list but not on mine.	Reflection sheet	Reflection Sheet	3/30/09

What obstacles may be in your way and how will you mitigate these obstacles?

1.   I may not be able to recognize all of my own currencies or my students. So, maybe I should get Sam, who teaches next door, to help me by coming in one day and observing.

2.   I may not have time to get all of this done. Finding time for reflection is really hard. So, I guess I should schedule some time now and maybe have Pat, my staff development teacher, sit down and reflect with me so that I will be sure to do it.

3.   I am not sure how to create the survey. Maybe I can find something online, or if I can't, I wonder if I can do a class discussion or journal writing assignment instead?

How will you monitor your plan?

I will put the plan in my grade book so that when I go to record grades, I can check to see how I am doing. I also will put the dates on my calendar so that I have things scheduled. And, I am going to ask Sam to be my accountability partner so that I can make sure that I get it done.

Completion date:

March 30, 2009

Tool 3
Sample Action Plan Evidence

Principle	Getting Started Step	Sample Evidence
1. Start where your students are.	Examine your own currencies	Journal reflection Student feedback (survey)
	Determine students' currencies	Student surveys Student journal reflections Teacher observations Pre-assessment results
	Help students use the currencies they have	Specific lessons to this end (observed or videotaped and analyzed)
	Help students acquire currencies they do not have	Specific lessons to this end (observed or videotaped and analyzed)
	Help students choose to use the currencies they already have	Class observation for climate Examination of rewards system Statement of the unspoken rules of engagement
2. Know where your students are going.	Unpack the standards	Written analysis of the standards for the next unit
	Look for implied content or process	Written analysis of the standards for the next unit
	Break goal down into smaller learning segments	Unit plan Lesson plans
	Match learning activities to learning goals	Lesson plan Classroom observation
	Set goals in terms of minimal rather than maximum performance	Differentiation plan
	Communicate goals effectively to parents and students	Student communications Parent communications Classroom observation Unit handouts or syllabi

Principle	Getting Started Step	Sample Evidence
3. Expect to get your students to their goal.	Remember that expectations say more about what you think you can do than what you think your students can do.	Reflective conversation Journal reflection
	Confront the brutal facts (beliefs)	Situation analysis Journal reflection Reflection conversation Unit plans
	Maintain unwavering faith (values)	Journal reflection Reflective conversation Values analysis
	Use the entire equation	Classroom observation Reflective conversation Journal reflection
4. Support your students along the way.	Anticipate confusion	Unit plan Lesson plan Classroom observation Reflective conversation or journal
	Unearth misconceptions	Classroom observation Videotape analysis Error analysis of student work
	Set up an intervention plan	Intervention plan
	Demystify the academic process	Unit plan Lesson plans Classroom observation Videotape analysis Classroom handouts
	Gradually remove supports	Unit plan Lesson plan Intervention plan
5. Use feedback to help you and your students get better.	Use feedback to inform your instructional choices	Feedback from a variety of sources Revised lesson plans Student surveys Revised lesson plans based on feedback
	Use feedback to help students make better learning choices	Explanations of what students' grades really mean Evidence of coaching feedback on students' papers Retake or resubmission opportunities and plans Student data notebooks

6. Focus on quality rather than quantity.	Decide the need-to-knows	Unit plan Need-to-know worksheet
	Decide whether students need to know the need-to-knows to the level of automaticity or controlled processing	Need-to-know analysis Unit plan
	Use distributed practice for those things students need to know to the level of automaticity	Lesson plans Classroom observations
	Require full-length performance for those things students need to know to the level of controlled processing	Lesson plans Classroom observations Student work samples
7. Never work harder than your students.	Determine what is your work	Journal reflection Reflective conversation Your work/Our work chart
	Determine students' work and give their work back to them	Your work/Our work chart Student journal reflections Student survey Data notebooks Classroom observation Classroom procedures and routines
	Hold students accountable for doing their work	Classroom rules list List of logical consequences Classroom observation

Tool 4
Reflection Sheet

The purpose of reflection is to help you think intentionally about your instructional practice. During reflection you can identify any instructional challenges, develop a plan of action, and decide what supports you will need. Look for commonalities, patterns, differences, and interrelations in your teaching attitudes and behaviors so that you can make connections between your behavior or attitudes and student achievement.

Think about your instructional practice and the impact that it has on students. Look at your self assessment results and identify any areas where you need to improve. Then, ask the following reflection questions:

Principle One: Start where your students are.
• What currencies do you value? Do you carry these currencies yourself?
• How do you convey what currencies are accepted in your classroom? What currencies are not valued in your classroom?
• What currencies do your students value? How can you tell?
• What currencies do your students regularly spend in your classroom? How do you react to these currencies?
• In what ways do you help students acquire other currencies?
• How do your react when students spend currencies you do not value? How do you react when students refuse to spend the accepted currencies of the classroom?
• In what ways do you code switch?
• How can you teach your students to code switch?

Principle Two: Know where your students are going.
• What is mastery? What does mastery look like for your course?
• How do you communicate what is mastery in your classroom?

- How do you determine when students have reached mastery? Is this matched to how you have asked students to demonstrate mastery?
- What are the steps to mastery? How do you convey these steps to your students?
- What role do you see parents playing in students' reaching mastery? How can you help parents fulfill this role more effectively?
- What is the minimum level of acceptable performance for your students?
- Should all students reach the minimal level of performance or are there some times when it is acceptable for students to not reach this level?

Principle Three: Expect to get your students there.
- What are the brutal facts of your reality?
- What is the current state of your faith? Do you believe that you can help any student reach mastery? Why or why not?
- What impacts your faith?
- What constraints did you face? How did you see these constraints? Did they seem insurmountable?
- Are your current teaching skills able to help all your students reach mastery?

Principle Four: Support students along the way.
- What explanatory devices do you currently use? Are they effective with all of your students?
- What support systems do you currently have in place? How did you select them? How effective are they with your students?
- When do you first notice that students are not succeeding? What mechanisms do you have in place to help you notice?
- Are you systematic in both identifying struggling students and providing support?
- What strategies do you use to uncover confusion?
- What are the most common misconceptions about your subject or subjects? What strategies do you use to clear up these misconceptions?
- How many students are currently not meeting the standards of your course? What explanations can you give for their lack of success?
- What do you do to provide more challenge to students who have exceeded the standards?

Principle Five: Track progress and use effective feedback.
• How do you know when students are learning?
• What feedback do you currently collect on students' progress and how do you use this feedback to improve your own instruction?
• What other feedback could you collect?
• How do you currently provide feedback to students? How do students use this feedback?
• What feedback would help coach students towards better performance? How can you give students this kind of feedback?

Principle Six: Focus on quality rather than quantity.
• What are the most important assignments you give to students? What are the least important assignments you give to students?
• What are the need-to-knows of your course, grade level, or discipline?
• What concepts or processes do your students need to learn to the level of automaticity? What concepts or processes do your students need to learn to the level of controlled processing? How do you make this decision?
• What things could you stop doing right now without a discernable difference in student success?

Principle Seven: Never work harder than your students.
• What is your work in your classroom?
• What is your students' work in your classroom?
• How comfortable are you with releasing some of the control in the classroom? What makes you most uncomfortable and why?
• What work could your students be doing in the classroom that they are not doing already?
• How do you determine what work is yours and what work in your students?

Although you can reflect in general about your instructional practice, it is often more helpful to think about a specific teaching situation that illustrates how you typically apply one or more of the principles, and then ask yourself the following questions:

> • Why did you make a particular instructional decision?
> • What was the impact of that decision on the students?

- Which students were most impacted by that decision and how?
- How did the lesson connect to other lessons in this unit?
- How will you know that students have mastered the objectives?
- How do you make decisions about what you will and will not teach?
- How could you improve the lesson next time?
- How did your last formative assessment measure affect this lesson?
- Who is the primary audience for this lesson?
- What was the single most important concept and skill you wanted every child to know at the end of this lesson? How successful were you?
- Generally, how prepared were your students to receive this lesson prior to the start of class? What do you believe they already knew? What do you believe they did not know?
- What teaching skill or skills did you use to deliver this lesson? Was there a match between the skills you used and the needs of your students?

Tool 5
Master Teacher Observation Form

Principle One: Start where your students are.	
Principle Two: Know where they are going.	
Principle Three: Expect to get them there.	
Principle Four: Support students along the way.	
Principle Five: Use feedback to help you and your students get better.	
Principle Six: Focus on quality rather than quantity.	
Principle Seven: Never work harder than your students.	
Additional Comments	

Tool 6

Using the Mastery Principles to Solve Instructional Challenges

In addition to practicing the principles as a way of moving toward increased mastery in your own teaching practice, you can also use the principles as a way of diagnosing your instructional challenges.

Here is the way it works. The next time you are facing a challenge in your classroom, first describe the challenge as clearly as possible. Then, use the problem-solving sheet on the next page to figure out which principle is most relevant to your current challenge. Once you have identified the principle or principles that address your challenge, revisit the chapter that discusses the principle for ideas on how to use the principle to resolve your current challenge. Tool 7 will also help you figure out which principle may apply to your problem.

When you use the principle to fix the challenge, you will often find that you need to make adjustments in other principles as well. For instance, if you find that you need to give the work back to the students, you might also find that in order to do so, you will also have to provide them with more careful scaffolding, adjust the quantity of the work, provide more accurate assessments of what students are able to do so you can figure out what work you can give to the students, and demystify the academic process so that students are able to do the work you give them. Because the principles work in concert with each other, you may find it difficult to pinpoint only one principle that will apply to your problem. That's OK. If you find that there are several principles that apply, select the one that seems most relevant or that seems easiest for you to practice, and start there.

Problem-Solving Sheet

Step One: Describe your current challenge. Write down what is happening and who is involved.	
Step Two: What do you think is causing this challenge? List the possible causes.	
Step Three: How do you solve the problem? Which principle applies?	
Step Four: Based on the principle you identified, what steps should you take?	
Step Five: What resources do you need?	
Step Six: How will you know when you have solved the problem?	

Sample Problem-Solving Sheet

Step One: Describe your current challenge. Write down what is happening, and who is involved.

My students don't seem to be motivated. They don't turn in their homework, they don't do the reading in the textbook at night so I cannot have class discussions in class. I spend the majority of my time lecturing about what they should have read at home. So, I am behind in my curriculum. Even when I lecture about the information, they don't take good notes and many of them are failing the tests. I would say about 60 percent of my students are failing right now.

Step Two: What do you think is causing this challenge? List the possible causes below.

I am not sure why they aren't doing the homework. My first instinct is that they are lazy but I know that isn't fair. They just don't seem to be interested in doing the reading. Many of them complain that the chapters are too long and boring. Some of my students work after school so they say they don't have time to do the reading. Many of my students take horrible notes or no notes at all. They fail the reading quizzes even though they say they read the chapter, so maybe the problem is that they don't really know how to take good notes.

Step Three: How do I solve the problem? Which principle applies?

When I look back over the principles I think a couple of principles apply. Principle 7—"Give the work back to the students" seems to make sense. When they don't read the chapter, I end up rescuing them by lecturing about the information they should have learned the night before. So I need to give the work back to my students, but when I try to do that by requiring them to read the chapter on their own, they won't. I guess I can fix that by applying principle 4. I could show my students how to take notes and how to identify what in the chapter is the most important for them to know.

Step Four: Based on the principle I identified, what steps should I take?

I think I need to start with principle 4 first because before I can give more work to my students I first have to show them how to read the chapter more effectively. I can give them a graphic organizer of the chapter and have them fill it in as they read. Then, I can start by allowing them to use their notes on the reading quizzes each day to encourage them to take good notes. Once they have had some practice in taking effective notes, I can stop letting them use their notes on the quizzes. I can also use Socratic seminars for the discussion of the materials so that students can generate their own questions about the chapter.

Step Five: What resources do I need?

I will need a graphic organizer for the chapter, which I can make pretty quickly using the new software program the reading specialist showed us at the last staff meeting. I'll ask her to help me do the first one. I will also need to bone up on how to run Socratic seminars. I think I can find something on the Web that may help me.

Step Six: How will I know when I have solved the problem?

My students will do the reading for homework each night, take effective notes that they will have organized in their notebooks, and use their notes to participate in lively discussions of the topic.

Tool 7
Classroom Problems by Principle

Principle One: Start where your students are
Sample problems:
- Students are disengaged.
- Students feel marginalized in the classroom.
- Students refuse to participate in class.
- Students act out in class.
- You experience interpersonal conflicts with students or their families.
- Students seem unmotivated.
- Students claim that they feel insignificant, powerless, or slighted.

Principle Two: Know where your students are going
Sample problems:
- Instruction seems disconnected.
- Students do well in class but do poorly on state or standardized tests.
- Students have little sense of what they are learning or why they are learning it.
- Students seem unmotivated. They are merely complying.
- Students cannot transfer what they have learned to other activities.
- Students cannot tell what is important.
- You are not sure which activities to include in your next unit.

Principle Three: Expect to get your students to their goal
Sample problems:
- You have lost your love for teaching.
- You are overwhelmed by the many demands being made on you.
- You are facing many outside constraints that interfere with your ability to teach.
- You feel frustrated that your students can't seem to do the work.

Principle Four: Support students along the way
Sample problems:
- Students are failing.
- Students fail a particular test and quiz.
- Students do not understand the material.
- Students lack the background knowledge they need to do well in your course.
- By the time you realize students are failing, it is really too late to help them.
- Students are regularly lost.
- Students don't retain concepts.

Principle Five: Use feedback to help you and your students get better
Sample problems:
- You have no idea how your students are doing.
- Students fail the same type of assignment again and again.
- Students do not know how to improve their own performance.
- Students turn in assignments that are unacceptable time and time again.
- Students reach the point of frustration and give up.

Principle Six: Focus on quality rather than quantity
Sample problems:
- There is more work to do than time to do it.
- Students are overwhelmed by the amount of work they have to complete.
- There is little to no improvement between one assignment and the next.
- Students are so far behind that you fear they will never catch up.
- Students are not prepared for the upcoming standardized test.
- You don't know what activity to select.

Principle Seven: Never work harder than your students
Sample problems:
- Students are disengaged.
- Students are not doing their work.
- Students are not turning in their homework.
- Students are disruptive.

- Students are disorganized.
- Students are not paying attention in class.
- Students take a long time getting to work once class begins.
- You are working harder than your students.

Tool 8
Guidelines for Forming
a Study Group

The purpose of forming a study group around the principles in this book is so that you can create a support network where you all work together to analyze and improve your current classroom practice and ultimately make a rich and rigorous curriculum accessible to all students. By engaging in ongoing cycles of questions about your own teaching practices and the impact that these practices have on student performance, you will refine your own teaching practice and make better decisions about what you teach, how you teach it, how you determine whether students have learned it, and how you will respond as a teacher and as a team of teachers when students experience difficulty learning it.

When you are creating your study group, in addition to working through the study group questions found on the companion Web site (www.mindstepsinc. com), it is important to consider the following questions:

1. What do we want to learn?
2. How will we know when we have learned it?
3. How will we respond as a group when one of us is experiencing difficulty?

Your answers to these questions will form the foundation of your study group and allow you to work together more effectively.

Here are a few other guidelines that will help you:

• Develop group norms and protocols to clarify your groups' expectations regarding roles, responsibilities, and relationships. What role will each group member play? What is each group member expected to contribute? What guidelines will you use to govern your interactions with each other? Clarifying these up front will make your work together go much more smoothly.

• Begin by reading the introduction and then taking the assessment together and discussing your results. From there determine areas of expertise and areas where you will need support. Tap into the shared expertise in the room and support each other.

• Decide on how often you will meet and stick to your schedule.

• Assign specific topics, chapters to read, discussion questions to consider, and data to examine for each meeting. Establish an agenda with goals and time limits to make sure that each meeting will be worth your time.

• Choose a leader for each meeting. Rotating the leadership helps all members to take ownership of the group. Be flexible. If a leader has to miss class for any reason, choose another leader for that meeting.

• Share the workload. The most important factor is a willingness to work, not a particular level of knowledge.

• Set general goals. Determine what the group wants to accomplish over the course of the time you will spend together.

• Help each other learn. One of the best ways to solidify your knowledge of something is to teach it to someone else. In addition to working through the study questions, take turns sharing strategies, resources, anecdotes about successful lessons, and lessons that fell flat, being sure to discuss what you learned in the process.

• In addition to working through the study questions, share your own questions, opinions, comments, and reactions.

• Encourage members to reveal their weaknesses so that they can strengthen them. This will only happen if you agree as a group to treat all discussions as confidential and if members refrain from critical comments about one another.

Tool 9
Developing a Student Intervention Cycle

When developing an intervention cycle to help struggling students, there are four things you must consider:

1. What is mastery?
2. What are your "red flags"?
3. What interventions will you put in place once a student's progress has raised a red flag?
4. How will you share this information with students?

Example:

Red Flag	Intervention
Grade point average of 79% or below at first two-week checkpoint	Conference with teacher to develop a plan to get back on track. Assigned online simulation or tutorial.
Grade point average of 79% or below two consecutive times	Mandatory attendance at acceleration/remediation sessions; call home.
Grade point average of 79% or below three consecutive times	Conference with teacher, student, guidance counselor, and parent. Mandatory after-school tutoring.
Test grade of 79% or below	Mandatory make up session.
Missing two homework assignments	Mandatory after-school session to make up homework.
Missing five or more problems on a quiz	Mandatory retake.
Missing two or more consecutive classes	Call home; mandatory Saturday make up session; assigned online tutorial.

Intervention Cycle Do's and Don'ts

- Do establish escalating red flags and interventions.
- Do establish regular intervals at which you examine student progress.
- Do clearly communicate the intervention cycle to students and parents. It may even be helpful to treat it like a contract and have all parties sign.
- Do establish interventions that are designed to help students master the material rather than provide busy work.
- Don't make interventions punitive. All interventions should be designed to help students get back on track as early as possible.
- Don't randomly enforce the cycle. The cycle works best when it is consistently applied.
- Don't use the intervention cycle to address behavior concerns. The cycle should only be used to address academic concerns.

REFERENCES

Bruner, J. (1983). *In search of mind: Essays in autobiography.* New York: Harper and Row.

Collins, J. (2001). *Good to great: Why some companies make the leap...and others don't.* New York: HarperCollins.

Dufour, R., Eaker, R., & DuFour, R. (2005). *On Common Ground: The Power of Professional Learning Communities.* Bloomington, IN: National Education Service.

Dweck, C. (2006). *Mindset: The new psychology of success.* New York: Random House.

Harris, J. R. (1998). *The nurture assumption: Why children turn out the way they do.* New York: Simon and Schuster.

Levin, J., & Nolan, J. F. (1996). *Principles of classroom management: A professional decision-making model* (2nd ed.). Boston: Allyn and Bacon.

MacKenzie, R. (2003). *Setting limits in the classroom: How to move beyond the dance of discipline in today's classrooms* (Rev. ed.). New York: Three Rivers Press.

Marzano, R. (2003). *What works in schools: Translating research into action.* Alexandria, VA: Association for Supervision and Curriculum Development.

Marzano, R. (2007). *The art and science of teaching: A comprehensive framework for effective instruction.* Alexandria, VA: Association for Curriculum Development.

O'Conner, K. (2002). *How to grade for learning: Linking grades to standards.* Glenview, IL: Pearson Professional Development.

Palmer, P. J. (2007). *The courage to teach: exploring the inner landscape of a teacher's life.* San Francisco, CA: Jossey-Bass.

Polanyi, M. (1958/1974). *Personal knowledge: Towards a post-critical philosophy.* Chicago: University of Chicago Press.

Saphier, J., & Gower, R. (1997). *The skillful teacher: Building your teaching skills* (5th ed.). Acton, MA: Research for Better Teaching.

Saphier, J., & Haley, M. A. (1993). *Summarizers*. Action, MA: Research for Better Teaching.

Sedlaceck, W. (2004*). Beyond the big test: Noncognitive assessment in higher education*. San Francisco, CA: John Wiley & Sons.

Senge, P. (2000). *Schools that learn: A fifth discipline fieldbook for educators, parents, and everyone who cares about education*. New York: Doubleday.

Snowman, J., & Biehler, R. (2000). *Psychology applied to teaching* (9th ed.). Boston: Houghton Mifflin Company.

Sternberg, R. J., Forsythe, G. B., Hedlund, J., Horvath, J. A., Wagner, R. K., Williams, W. M., et al. (2000). *Practical intelligence in everyday life*. Cambridge: Cambridge University Press.

Strong, R., Silver, H., & Perini, M. (2001) *Teaching what matters most: Standards and strategies for raising student achievement*. Alexandria, VA: Association for Supervision and Curriculum Development.

Thompson, M. (2008). *Leadership, Balanced Achievement, and Accountability: Benchmarking to Exemplary Practice*. Boone, NC: Learning Focused.

Wiggins, G., & McTighe, J. (1998). *Understanding by design*. Alexandria, VA: Association for Supervision and Curriculum Development.

Yelon, S. L. (1996). *Powerful principles of instruction*. White Plains, NY: Longman Publishers.

Yero, J. L. (2002). *Teaching in mind: How teacher thinking shapes education*. Hamilton, MT: MindFlight Publications.

INDEX

The letter *f* following a page number denotes a figure.

ABOUT THE AUTHOR

 Robyn R. Jackson, PhD, has been an educator for more than a decade. As a National Board Certified English teacher, she increased the enrollment of minority and nontraditional students in her AP Language and Composition classes and tripled her overall course enrollment within one year without a decrease in her students' test scores. As a middle school administrator in Montgomery County, Maryland, she has worked to revise the district's Gifted and Talented policy to be more inclusive of all students and helped craft the district's critical Middle School Reform Plan. She also helped lead the largest middle school in the district to state and national Blue Ribbon status. As an educator, she has served as an adjunct professor and presents her own research at several national conferences.

Because of her practical approach to instruction, Dr. Jackson has become a nationally recognized presenter and consultant who has been featured in *The Washington Post*, a PBS/Annenberg television series, and Lifetime Television's *Lifetime Live*. She works regularly with schools throughout the United States, helping them build their capacity to meet the diverse needs of their students and to remove the institutional barriers to student success. Most recently, she has worked with schools and school districts in the District of Columbia, Delaware, Florida, Georgia, Illinois, Maryland, Massachusetts, Ohio, Texas, Virginia, and Wisconsin, as well as several nonprofits on everything from improving the planning and delivery of instruction to developing the leadership capacity of school leadership teams. Recently, Dr. Jackson was named a senior fellow with the Phelps Stokes Fund to research ways to improve teacher preparation.

Dr. Jackson is also the author of *The Differentiation Workbook: A Step-by-Step Guide to Creating Lessons That Appropriately Challenge All Students* and *The Instructional Leader's Guide to Strategic Conversations with Teachers.* You can reach Dr. Jackson at robyn@mindstepsinc.com.

Want more?

For additional resources, strategies, and ideas, visit
www.mindstepsinc.com and
- Download copies of the tools found in this book
- Find free resources
- Get even more *Try This* suggestions
- Link to other great resources
- Read bonus chapters
- Download podcasts of Robyn
- Post your own comments and hear what other readers are saying
- Receive a free monthly e-newsletter
- Explore much more reader-only content

Click on the registration tab and type in keyword *Master Teacher* to get started
today!

Related Resources

At the time of publication, the following ASCD resources were available; for the most up-to-date information about ASCD resources, go to www.ascd.org. ASCD stock numbers are noted in parentheses.

Networks

Visit the ASCD Web site (www.ascd.org) and click on About ASCD and then on Networks for information about professional educators who have formed groups around topics, including "Quality Education." Look in the "Network Directory" for current facilitators' addresses and phone numbers.

Print Products

ASCD Infobrief 22 (August 2000): Ensuring Teacher Quality by Carol Tell (#100297)

Better Learning Through Structured Teaching: A Framework for the Gradual Release of Responsibility by Douglas Fisher and Nancy Frey (#108010)

Educational Leadership, March 2006: Improving Professional Practice (Entire Issue #106041)

Handbook for Qualities of Effective Teachers by James H. Stronge, Pamela D. Tucker, and Jennifer L. Hindman (#104135)

How to Give Effective Feedback to Your Students by Susan M. Brookhart (#108019)

Improving Student Learning One Teacher at a Time by Jane E. Pollock (#107005)

Teacher Evaluation/Teacher Portfolios (ASCD Topic Pack) (#197202)

Videos and DVDs

Qualities of Effective Teachers (three video programs on one DVD, plus a facilitator's guide) (#604423)

A Visit to Classrooms of Effective Teachers (one 45-minute DVD with a comprehensive viewer's guide) (DVD #605026; Video #405026)

For additional resources, visit us on the World Wide Web (http://www.ascd.org), send an e-mail message to member@ascd.org, call the ASCD Service Center (1-800-933-ASCD or 703-578-9600, then press 2), send a fax to 703-575-5400, or write to Information Services, ASCD, 1703 N. Beauregard St., Alexandria, VA 22311-1714 USA.